RACE
RULES

RACE RULES

WHAT YOUR BLACK FRIEND WON'T TELL YOU

FATIMAH GILLIAM

BK

Berrett–Koehler Publishers, Inc.

Berrett-Koehler Publishers, Inc.
1333 Broadway, Suite 1000
Oakland, CA 94612-1921
Tel: (510) 817-2277
Fax: (510) 817-2278
www.bkconnection.com

Rat Race (written by Bob Marley)
© 1976 Fifty-Six Hope Road Music Ltd & Primary Wave/Blue Mountain Music.
Copyright Renewed. All Rights Reserved. Used By Permission.
All rights administered by Primary Wave/Blue Mountain Music.

Troublesome '96
Words and Music by Tupac Shakur, Johnny Lee Jackson, Jalil Hutchins, and Lawrence Smith.
Copyright © 1996 UNIVERSAL MUSIC CORP., AMARU PUBLISHING, UNIVERSAL MUSIC—MGB SONGS, UNIVERSAL MUSIC—Z TUNES LLC, IMAGEM LONDON LTD., and FUNK GROOVE MUSIC PUBLISHING CO.
All Rights for AMARU PUBLISHING Administered by UNIVERSAL MUSIC CORP.
All Rights for IMAGEM LONDON LTD. and FUNK GROOVE MUSIC PUBLISHING CO. Administered by UNIVERSAL MUSIC—Z TUNES LLC.
All Rights Reserved Used by Permission.
Reprinted by Permission of Hal Leonard LLC.

ORDERING INFORMATION
Quantity sales. Special discounts are available on quantity purchases by corporations, associations, and others. For details, contact the "Special Sales Department" at the Berrett-Koehler address above.
Individual sales. Berrett-Koehler publications are available through most bookstores. They can also be ordered directly from Berrett-Koehler: Tel: (800) 929-2929; Fax: (802) 864-7626; www.bkconnection.com.
Orders for college textbook / course adoption use. Please contact Berrett-Koehler: Tel: (800) 929-2929; Fax: (802) 864-7626.

Distributed to the U.S. trade and internationally by Penguin Random House Publisher Services.

Berrett-Koehler and the BK logo are registered trademarks of Berrett-Koehler Publishers, Inc.

Printed in Canada

Berrett-Koehler books are printed on long-lasting acid-free paper. When it is available, we choose paper that has been manufactured by environmentally responsible processes. These may include using trees grown in sustainable forests, incorporating recycled paper, minimizing chlorine in bleaching, or recycling the energy produced at the paper mill.

Library of Congress Cataloging-in-Publication Data is available. ISBN: 978-1-5230-0448-5

First Edition
31 30 29 28 27 26 25 24   10 9 8 7 6 5 4 3 2 1

Cover illustration and design by Ilse Torres Harrison
Interior illustrations by Ilse Torres Harrison, copyright Fatimah Gilliam

Just because I fight for my people
doesn't mean I'm an enemy of yours.

—Fatimah Gilliam

For my mother, grandpa, father, siblings, and ancestors who play a role in shaping how I see my country and relationship to its peoples.

You instill pride and respect for myself, people, and nation that I willingly share through this book to improve life and freedom for everyone.

Contents

PART 6: IMPROVE DAILY INTERACTIONS—COMMUNICATING, SELF-EDUCATING, AND REPAIRING RELATIONSHIPS   233

PART 7: TAKE ACTION—MOVE BEYOND COMPLICITY AND GRADUATE TO RACISM DISRUPTOR   295

Preface

I wrote this book in response to seeing and advising countless white people floundering in cross-racial interactions and slipping when sharing views on people of color. They struggle, not knowing what's acceptable or assuming their actions, behaviors, and perspectives aren't racially offensive.

White people need a "race etiquette" manual—a practical handbook on how to not offend, what's racist, and how to improve behaviors, choices, and interactions in a racially diverse country. You need someone sharing unvarnished truths "your Black friend" won't say to your face (but quietly thinks after racist encounters or says once you leave the room). In saying the quiet part out loud, I'm providing rare access to educate and help you.

You may not always understand or agree with what I say. You may feel uncomfortable and challenged. This book may contradict your beliefs, sense of self, traditions, and what you believe to be true. You may even feel attacked or offended. But there's value in looking at race, white supremacy, and racial harm through the lens of what many people of color privately feel and believe. Even those who become defensive will benefit from seeing a different perspective. I can't illuminate a better path for you unless I shine a light on dark truths about racism and white people's choices. Approach this book with an open outlook and a growth mindset—accepting bluntness as a sincere, positive, and unique gift.

On your self-discovery voyage, you'll expand understandings about yourself, your neighbors, the country, your family, and your workplace. This book is a tool to help break the cycle of racism. I seek to provoke behavioral change, disrupt white perspectives, curtail intergenerational racism, and help whites remove blinders. I want to help whites evolve past denialism, complicity, and individual racism to minimize the overwhelming daily volume of racial trauma inflicted on people of color.

By educating and truth-telling, I'm fighting not for what society is but what it could be.

ROLE OF BRUTAL HONESTY

I will be transparent throughout this book in ways I can't when sitting down with clients, who are often allergic to looking in the mirror and receptive to only pats on the back. Not everyone wants to take themselves on as a project.[1] In picking up this book, you've taken a critical first step in accepting you have room to grow. Candor is my starting, middle, and end point.

If you expect a road with diplomatic sugarcoating, that's unrealistic and undermines progress. I'm not glossing over racism's root causes. Disrupting white supremacy is a painful, difficult topic. But the point isn't to make you squirm or feel attacked for sport. There's a strategy behind boldly lifting the veil on Black and brown perspectives on everyday offensive white conduct and ideologies.

My book is designed to foster stronger connections with people of color. It's a tool to move communities away from harmful anger, contempt, and ignorance one person at a time. But to get there, you have to do the work and know the assignment.

TARGET AUDIENCE AND REPRESENTED VOICES

This book is written predominantly to white people—the *you* in my chapters. It's helpful for *every* white person, regardless of how evolved or anti-racist you believe you are. *Every* white person engages in offensive behavior. I seek to expand your understanding of your role in racial trauma, no matter where you are along a "wokeness" spectrum.

If a person of color gives you this book, don't be offended. Look at it as a sign they care enough to help you grow in a way that gives them some peace. This book provides people of color an opportunity to aid you while allowing them emotional distance from being directly involved in your education. This approach can safeguard personal and working relationships.

Primarily, I focus on Black experiences to illustrate points, drawing on years of practical experience in corporate America and my lived experiences as a Black woman. I'm not excluding fellow people of color, but I can't speak for them. You can extrapolate to other racial groups. But we're not mono-lithic, nor do I represent every Black voice since we have diverse opinions.

HOW TO APPROACH THIS BOOK

Except for chapter 7, which is foundational and explains White Welfare, the rest of the chapters don't inherently depend on each other—allowing you to choose your own race-knowledge adventure. You can read from cover to cover following topic groupings to build your knowledge. Or you can bounce around and explore subjects as issues arise or when you want to understand something specific. This book provides real-world advice on how to react when stuck in a racial "what-do-I-do" quandary that can be implemented immediately. Use it as a reference book to educate yourself.

Periodically, hashtags are used in this book to punctuate key points raised, draw attention to racially offensive and toxic behaviors, or under-score the consequences of highly problematic choices and white suprema-cist ideologies. When you see hashtags calling out behaviors and mindsets, reflect on (1) the impact of these actions and attitudes on societal trends and racial harm and (2) your personal role in mainstreaming collateral damage or participating in similar conduct that hurts people of color.

HOW TO MAKE THE BEST USE OF THIS BOOK

This book has many dimensions, uses, and purposes. It's flexible, written for both individuals and organizations—for personalized work and collective transformation.

For individuals, you can read this book on your own. You can spend time absorbing the material on a tour of self-discovery and personal evolu-tion. You can also read it as a family, with friends, in a book club, with your congregation or classmates, or in other cohorts you belong to or form.

For companies, institutions, and groups, you can use this book in trainings and to facilitate group discussions. In particular, the Bedrock Race Rule is a universally applicable three-step guide to cross-racial interactions with colleagues, clients, and key stakeholders. Coupled with the topic-specific Race Rules, this book can move organizations forward and encourage better choices.

ADVICE ON MANAGING EMOTIONS AND GETTING DEFENSIVE

As you begin reading, start by taking down defensive walls to let the information penetrate. Keep an open mind. Prepare yourself for discomfort. Manage your feelings.

Resist shutting down and rejecting truths. Maintain self-awareness. Learn to navigate your triggers when activated if your goal is a more equitable society.

If you feel too angry, overwhelmed, or paralyzed by emotions; find yourself continually debating what's written; or keep thinking of excuses, counterarguments, or comparisons shifting away from specifically exploring racism, take a short break. It's okay to pause.

Don't fully walk, away but decompress and regroup. Return recharged to trust the process.

Thank you for pursuing your self-discovery journey with me. If you follow this book's Race Rules, you can help disrupt racism and become a better person and citizen.

Becoming a Racism Disruptor

I've had a lifetime of toxic encounters. I've been exposed to whites who've gotten too comfortable when they don't realize who I am *and* when they do. Sometimes they're lulled into my white-looking skin's false sense of racial license and comfort. Other times they relax, identifying with me since I went to Wellesley, Harvard, and Columbia. Some think I'm "one of the good ones" because I'm not some trifling, downtrodden person of color that's a stereotypical caricature of what they presume Blacks are, look like, and achieve.

My lived experiences unmask a consistent, daily pattern and understanding of white transgressions. I see you, you don't see me, and in not seeing me, you don't see yourselves but reveal yourselves to me, and I see you even more. I know more about you than you know about me, and I know more about you than you'll admit to yourselves. And by "you," I mean white people.

Years ago, when I was a graduate student visiting a college classmate, we went to a party at her friend's apartment. The energy was joyful—people were laughing and joking.

Then, one of the guys told a story about an encounter with a stranger. As it unfolded, he did what I've witnessed many whites do. He puffed up his feathers to feel more important, summoning racism to center stage. He referred to this other man as a "nigger."

My ears perked up and body language changed. I went from being relaxed to intensely alert.

"Don't use that language in my presence! Don't say that racist bull-shit. You shouldn't say it no matter who's around." Suddenly, everyone was laser-focused on our tense exchange. The room's vibe took a hard right turn. The boisterous, cheerful atmosphere dissipated. The chatter abruptly died. All eyes were glued on us.

He retorted, "There's no need to get serious." I leaned forward, raised my eyebrow, and said, "Don't *make me* get serious." It's not like I was going to tussle with this buffoon. But I said he was a white supremacist and had problems if the only way he could feel good about himself were to belittle Blacks.

Several of his friends embraced the familiar comfort of "protecting their own." They defended him. He "didn't mean anything by it" and "was joking," and there was no need to make a "big deal" over it. I should "let it go."

But it was a big deal. *Nigger* is the ultimate insult sitting on centuries of violent oppression—weaponizing words to support a caste system. It's an intimidation tool of white supremacy to keep Blacks "in their place" and maintain America's social order with whites on top and Blacks at the bottom.

The general sentiment spread, with hostility increasingly directed toward me. I could feel people's resentment and antipathy. Most sided with the bigot, while others were conveniently silent. Complicit. I was the supposed killjoy ruining their night—the party pooper blocking the fun by refusing to ignore the "N-word incident." Any pseudo-allies acknowledging the N-word is bad just wanted my pacification. No one had my back. Someone even said I shouldn't blow things up since "it isn't like you're Black."

News flash—I *am* Black, which shouldn't even matter. Yet again, I was with a coterie too comfortable in their whiteness who assumed they were among their own given my white-looking skin and blondish hair. My college classmate knew I'm Black. Her friends didn't. The instant the N-word was uttered, she knew things would get heated. She tried to mediate, feeling torn between her friends and guest. Her problematic excuses only confirmed my suspicions. She exposed her own racism *and* inflicted bigots on me. Given how naturally hate speech rolled off the tongue and no one flinched, undoubtedly it wasn't the first time her crew used racial slurs.

After calling them out for defending him and focusing blame on me, I saw no need to remain. They were *all* white supremacists—collectively upholding white supremacy—*including* the silent collaborators who left me hanging on a ledge alone without support. It's hard to come back from dropping N-word bombs. It wasn't my job to drive relationship repair nor solutions. I hadn't signed up for that emotional labor. I left and haven't seen that classmate since.

Let's juxtapose this racist incident with one from my adolescence. I was a high school student walking alone to water polo practice on a beautiful day. My skin was sun-kissed tanned, hair blonder than today, and frizzy curls on full display. Given how I dressed back then, there's a good chance I wore clothing expressing my Black pride—a T-shirt with Malcolm X or a map of Africa on it. Maybe even a dashiki. It was Berkeley, California, after all. My parents raised me to be proud of my culture, bolstered by a public high school with the nation's first Black studies department and only one of its kind.

As I happily walked to practice, excited to dive into the pool, I reached an intersection. I entered the crosswalk just as a car with two white guys pulled up. Annoyed by my presence, the driver screamed, "Nigger, hurry up!"

I was flabbergasted. I'd never been called this derogatory insult before. My light-skinned, Stanford-educated father had been called it by a teenager with Down syndrome pointing in his face. My fair-skinned mother deemed this as a sign of how whites indoctrinate racism far and wide, including to the neurodivergent. But it's typically directed at darker Blacks. Not that I'm immune from personally experiencing racism's uglier sides or inheriting traumatic intergenerational discrimination. It permeated my family—like how in 1930 my grandfather didn't accept the University of Southern California athletic scholarship he won as a state track champion because USC's coach made "nigger jokes" as a warning. This negatively impacted his earning potential, his dreams of becoming a surgeon, and my family's wealth and opportunities.

Still, I was shocked to hear the N-word, and even more surprised the slur was aimed at me. I was just a kid minding my own business living my young-person life.

Experiencing racism stopped me in my tracks, sucking the air out of me. I could feel blood rushing to my face and neck. My cheeks were getting hot as I felt an intense wave of anxiety sucker punch me. I felt hurt, attacked, violated, and abused. I was angry and filled with rage. They wanted me to feel worthless, inferior, and unwelcome. Undoubtedly, they wanted me to feel consumed by terror.

My heart pounding, fearing violence on the menu, I confidently looked at them. They wore smug facial expressions, smirking for logging a pathetic win on the White Man's racial-oppression scorecard. I don't fully remember what happened afterward. I recall they sped off, and I crossed the street physically unharmed. Knowing my younger self, I probably flipped them the bird once getting to the curb. But I remember watching their car drive away and feeling the gut-wrenching sting of a racist epithet. Blatant racism was in my face. I felt disgusted by the personification of America's byproduct. It left a lasting impression.

I was called *nigger* in Berkeley—not Baton Rouge, Louisiana, where I have relatives. Not in the Jim Crow 1950s but 1990s. This was hippie-ville "progressive" Berkeley—bastion of the white liberal. Back then, I remember Berkeley had skinheads. But the men in the car weren't dressed like neo-Nazis, looking instead like "ordinary white people." What I knew then and know today remains unchanged—that average whites, even liberals and wannabe wokes, aren't immune to bigotry, are routinely offensive, and fervently protect white privilege.

Whites habitually do racist things, often without realizing it. This is why I'm telling it like I see it in this book—the quiet part out loud. I'm disclosing what your Black friends won't tell you but may secretly think about you, how you behave, and your choices.

I know that even whites with an evolved understanding of race dynamics need rudimentary help with basic concepts to minimize the racist behaviors they engage in daily, including subconsciously. No matter how racially aware you think you are, if you're white, you still need this book. It's necessary medicine for you to look within to understand the personal role you play in bigotry and racial trauma.

There's a constant stream of white supremacy in every Black life. No matter the actual color or shade, *all* Blacks must endure a normalized pattern of racist behaviors, including from "nice white people." We're living with the incessant burden of wearing psychological armor and leveraging lifesaving street smarts to survive. It's an assaulting continuum of offensive and exhausting experiences repeating over and over.

I've been experiencing, befriending, going to school with, and working among you all my life. Without fail, you keep unveiling your true selves.

You do it whether you're a Republican or Democrat. You do it when you're a liberal, including when trying to prove you're my anti-racist "ally," professing "Black Lives Matter," or volunteering to advance diversity initiatives. And you do it voting for the status quo in elections or clinging to NIMBY (not-in-my-backyard) mindsets in your community. I've heard you talk about years-old community organizing and humanitarian work like it's a badge of honor absolving you from resolving what's happening today while simultaneously being microaggressive.

Whites often don't feel threatened when looking at me—either walking down the street or working beside me. Well, that's *until* they experience my intelligence. Then some employ predictable strategies to thwart my success—feeling compelled to realign with a white-centered social order to avoid accepting their personal mediocrity or working harder to fairly compete to earn their spot.

This is my life. I move in your circles and see how racist many of you are—how average whites are bigots without realizing it and even when thinking you're a good person.

Being a light-skinned woman of color provides a unique, unconventional lens into white behaviors, mindsets, and perspectives on privilege, racism, opportunity hoarding, and complicity. I have firsthand experience seeing whites float through life wearing blinders—living in an alternate reality where their perceived world isn't the real world as experienced by people of color. I have insight into how drastically whites' perceptions are grossly misaligned and detached from accurate history and what many people of color actually think about interactions with whites. This includes when you think you're likable and we're "friends" but we'd never "invite you to the cookout."

This is why I'm taking the gloves off to tell you what you *need* to hear. You need someone who looks like you but isn't like you to say the unvarnished truth—unfiltered and ripping off the band-aid. As a society, we can dance around white feelings for only so long. Keeping whites in the dark about harms inflicted on people of color isn't helping the country improve.

You won't grow if my book is just another exercise in tiptoeing around white feelings, tears, and fragility—dysfunctionally coddling white denial and discomfort. If that strategy worked, we'd have less racism by now. While this book may be a tough pill to swallow, it's time to digest some harsh realities. Contrary to what you might feel is a personal attack on your character or a battering for the sake of it, I actually want you to evolve and be your best self.

I've written this book mostly for whites, but my core motivation is to help people of color. We deserve better treatment. I want oppressive and toxic behaviors to change. And I seek a world where people of color don't have to experience as much daily trauma and racist psychological warfare. This book will help you get your knee off our necks.

THE BIRTH OF RACE RULES—
A HANDBOOK FOR WHITES

Having lived through a lifelong loop of dehumanizing misconduct by clueless, insensitive, ill-informed whites and extreme self-actualizing bigots, one evening I had a lightbulb moment. I was watching the evening news. Like clockwork, another racist "Karen" was going viral for falsely calling the police on an innocent Black person. I reflected on my lived experiences and background as a diversity expert. I ruminated on those who sit in silence as privileged spectators, choosing to cosign on white supremacy yet falsely believing their complicit inaction isn't racist action when that's exactly what it is.

I thought, "White people need a manual"—a how-to guide to be less offensive—an innovative guidebook of Race Rules that candidly spells out the guardrails of acceptable cross-racial behavior. Practical, actionable advice could minimize the outward expression of white prejudices while educating whites to shift their detrimental behaviors.

I found myself acknowledging how whites habitually choose racism by supporting the status quo. Wanting to explain that the *only* state of being that matters is proactively choosing to stand against racism *each day* since action defies the comfortable laziness of society's current situation. As the newscast continued, I contemplated how it's whites' job to dismantle racism since they invented, uphold, and benefit from it to protect what I describe as White Welfare.*

---

* White Welfare is America's and the Western world's ultimate entitlement program for whites leveraging past oppression and present-day discrimination for contemporary power-and-wealth windfalls of white privilege and supremacy built on unjust wealth transfers and theft. See Race Rule #7 and glossary.

HOW TO UNLEARN RACISM AND
BECOME A RACISM DISRUPTOR

To jump-start change, I developed my Bedrock Race Rule as a foundational principle. It's this book's overarching Race Rule: Choose to Disrupt Racism Every Day. Whether you have a question, knowledge gap, general topic you want to better understand, or specific challenge where you don't know how to act, proceed, interact, respond, or think, use my Bedrock Race Rule as your guiding North Star. You can approach your quandary by running it through the Bedrock Race Rule's three-step process to expand your thinking and get direction on what to do and how to evolve your mindset.

Implementing this rule is the pathway to transforming into a Racism Disruptor (i.e., a proactive, action-oriented, anti-racism advocate). Being a Racism Disruptor is a position above ally. Allies can be bystanders. Their role requires no real action steps, often drifting into complicity and relying on hearts-and-minds ideologies. Erroneously, allies are prone to believing that merely disagreeing with racist behaviors or empathizing with people of color is enough—granting themselves a pass from taking action, speaking up, or moving beyond performative steps. Racism Disruptors outwardly express their support for anti-racism through deeds and choices that *positively impact* people and communities of color. They seek to align internal thoughts with helpful external action.

BEDROCK RACE RULE:
CHOOSE TO DISRUPT RACISM EVERY DAY

Complacency supports racism, and the best way to unlearn and disrupt racism is through action and behavioral change, starting today:

Step 1—Learn to unlearn (external education)
Step 2—Reflect to repair (internal evaluation)
Step 3—Act to address (positive action)

This three-step process is a learning-and-action model that prompts you to learn by educating yourself and by acting. It encompasses various themes: avoiding complacency, edifying through a continuous improvement cycle, prioritizing impact over intent, breaking patterns of intergenerational racism, and developing empathy to humanize people of color. These concepts are baked into the change model.

Skills develop through experience, habit, and ongoing exposure. This allows you to adapt to changing circumstances and maintain a baseline competency. Unlearning racism is a lifelong routine of perpetual learning through the ongoing ritual of doing and not choosing inaction. When you take stock of what worked and failed, this helps create a continual improvement cycle of learning, unlearning, and growing. Eventually, a perpetual learning loop becomes second nature. Over time, you develop into a more culturally aware, empathetic person making better choices that cause less harm to people of color.

Here is more detail on the three steps:

Step 1. You *learn to unlearn* by challenging assumptions about what you perceive to be true, educating yourself where you have knowledge gaps, and seeking to deprogram misinformation. You proactively absorb external educational sources to create space to change your mindset. This is how you can begin to align what you perceive to be true about yourself, society, people of color, and what they think about your behavior and choices with what's actually true.

Step 2. You *reflect to repair* by conducting an internal evaluation into how you've behaved in the past, your thinking, and whether your decisions and actions have harmed others. This is where you take an honest look at how your beliefs and behaviors are anchored in racist ideologies. It requires admitting hard self-truths as a necessary step in becoming a Racism Disruptor. Without looking within, it's difficult to evolve and move toward proactive action.

Step 3. You *act to address* by taking affirmative steps to *choose* to disrupt racism. This goes beyond just thinking something is wrong and instead involves stepping into action to correct what is wrong. Without positive action, you'll have marginal impact—limiting your ability to humanize people of color and validate their experiences as demonstrated not just by what you think but what you do. This is a process of transforming not just mental outlooks but also behaviors. Disrupting racism through acts and deeds is your desired destination.

Collectively, all three steps are critical to a cyclical lifelong process of continually learning to unlearn racism, reflecting to repair, and acting to address. As a unified process and with repetition, you build foundational momentum for continual improvements. This Bedrock Race Rule helps you understand people of color. It enables you to develop genuine relationships as a byproduct of shifting behaviors. This happens by curtailing the amount of daily racism experienced as a result of your choices.

To help your journey with specificity, the various Race Rules in this book provide guidance to stimulate learning and create this foundation. The book's situational Race Rules are the conduits to activate, implement, and kick-start learning to unlearn. They enable you to transform your routine behaviors from those of an ally into those of a Racism Disruptor.

RACE RULES ARE BINARY CHOICES TO DISRUPT RACISM

Let's be clear about what the Race Rules are and aren't and how they can help you and people of color. They're binary dos and don'ts, often with little gray area. The alternative to not following and trusting them is selecting the racist path and engaging in white supremacy. Opting not to embrace them is *choosing* racism. This is why they're called *rules*. I'm offering you unequivocal, unambiguous guidance on what offends and harms many people of color. And what's "offensive" is code for unmistakably subjecting us to racism.

Follow the Race Rules and adjust your behavior *even before* your mind has caught up. While I'd prefer that you understand how you're offending and why certain decisions are racist, treating us better as a starting point is far superior to paralyzed inaction or sticking with bad habits. Behavioral change prior to mindset shifts is still an improvement over no change at all. Take a leap of faith.

If you trust these rules and their tenets, you're less likely to cause traumatic collateral damage to marginalized groups as a consequence of your choices and them having encountered you. This means people of color are less likely to have a tarnished view and think poorly of you.

BENEFITS OF LEARNING
THIS BOOK'S RACE RULES

By reading this book, you clearly want to do and be better. You're open to learning and absorbing different perspectives. This book provides many benefits for you, people of color, and society.

This book's Race Rules will help you do the following:

- Behave more like the good person you want to be.
- Foster a sense of control over your educational journey.
- Make better choices and move from passive ally or bystander to proactive advocate (i.e., Racism Disruptor).
- Become better at understanding racism and people of color.
- Develop authentic relationships and form strong connections with people of color.
- Contribute toward moving the country past racial divisions and positively participate in the nation's racial reckoning.
- Model good behaviors for those around you and the next generation.

Go forth and learn my situation-specific Race Rules to begin your journey of becoming a Racism Disruptor. The next time you hear someone say the N-word or something like "People of color need to 'move on' from and 'get over' over the past," you'll be less anxious and afraid in responding because you have tools at your disposal. You'll be better equipped in knowing what to do and how to act to not complicitly endorse white supremacy through your choices and behaviors.

I have been gravely disappointed with the white moderate . . . [reaching] the regrettable conclusion that the . . . great stumbling block . . . toward freedom is not . . . the Ku Klux Klanner, but the white moderate who is more devoted to "order" than to justice; . . . who constantly says, "I agree with you in the goal you seek, but I can't agree with your methods of direct action"; who paternalistically feels that he can set the timetable for another man's freedom; . . . and who constantly advises [Blacks] to wait until a "more convenient season."

—Dr. Martin Luther King, Jr., civil rights activist

Bedrock Race Rule: Choose to Disrupt Racism Every Day

This overarching Race Rule, Choose to Disrupt Racism Every Day, will help you make better decisions in your life, understand people of color, and improve relationships across race. This universal Race Rule can be applied to a broad range of daily cross-racial encounters and lead to less harmful decisions impacting people of color.

When faced with knowledge gaps and uncertainty in how to proceed, interact, or behave in navigating across race or struggling with what to think or say, use this Bedrock Race Rule's three-step process as your guide. This learning-and-action tool helps you change behaviors, shift mindsets, and know what to do.

This book's other Race Rules are situation specific. This rule helps no matter the topic.

If you are neutral in situations of injustice,
you have chosen the side of the oppressor.

—*Rev. Desmond Tutu, anti-apartheid activist*

RULE SUMMARY

CHOOSE TO DISRUPT RACISM EVERY DAY

Complacency supports racism, and the best way to unlearn and *disrupt racism is through action and behavioral change starting today:*

Step 1—Learn to unlearn (external education)
Step 2—Reflect to repair (internal evaluation)
Step 3—Act to address (positive action)

Anti-racism is about making choices supported through proactive action. Upholding white supremacy and privilege is a choice. Disrupting racism is also a choice. You cannot become a Racism Disruptor (i.e., a proactive, action-oriented, anti-racism advocate) by merely focusing on your internal mindset, misbelieving that disagreeing with racist societal wrongs is the desired destination or all that's required of you as a beneficiary of White Welfare. Dismantling racism requires not just choosing to act but also immediately implementing choices in real time. Thoughts without deeds don't lead to adequate progress. Choices with delayed timelines prioritize the status quo. Self-education without behavioral change is half stepping—and often morphs into lip service requiring people of color to wait for justice, equality, and humanizing treatment.

KEY TAKEAWAYS FROM THE THREE-STEP PROCESS

Unlearning racism is a lifelong process. Not only does this three-step model adapt to changing circumstances to pivot with your needs and situational realities, but it also encourages a normalized routine of perpetual self-education and reeducation. It involves a cycle of learning from mistakes and growing as society evolves:

- **Lifelong learner**—Every white person needs continuous learning to counter systemic racism and deprogram prejudices ingrained since childhood.

- **Daily proactive action**—You must act each day to diminish racist beliefs and behavioral choices, including society's level of racism.
- **Joint learning and action**—Learning and doing must happen together and not in isolation to evolve and positively affect others.
- **Impact over intent**—What's important is how marginalized groups experience you and what's happening to them as a byproduct of your choices, inaction, and interacting with you and *not* what you intend or believe.
- **Inaction equals choosing complacency**—There are no neutral positions with white supremacy. Supporting status quo power structures elevates whites at the expense of people of color.
- **Transformation from ally to Racism Disruptor**—The role of Racism Disruptor is above ally, which is passive, requires no action steps, and enables lazy bystanders. Racism Disruptors are action-oriented advocates whose behaviors positively support and uplift people of color, aligning the intent of choices with the impact of actions.
- **Goal is disrupting racism**—Unlearning racism provokes internal and external disruption to your perceived world, prompting behavioral change, reshaping white perspectives, and breaking cycles of intergenerational racism.

Nothing will change and you won't evolve if you don't take the first step. Everything hard in life is actually just a series of easy steps, with the first step being to act. You need to commit to action.

THREE STEPS TO TRANSFORMATIONAL MINDSET AND BEHAVIORAL CHANGE

The three-step process helps you achieve this Race Rule's mandate of continually choosing to disrupt racism every day. It encourages ritualizing doing and avoiding inaction. Each step has a series of questions with universal applicability to any scenario, enabling you to tackle race-related questions and navigate racism in real time as issues arise in your daily life.

By incorporating these steps into everyday decision-making and learning incrementally from successes and failures, you create a continual improvement cycle. Increasingly assess and benchmark your cross-racial interactions, workplace practices and challenges, and community issues through the lens of the multipart model (i.e., learn to unlearn, reflect to repair, and act to address). This normalizes integrating cultural intelligence into how you act and modulate behaviors. This is how unlearning and disrupting racism become second nature. Cumulatively, this process builds a transformational foundation with a lasting positive impact on how you treat people of color and encourages taking bigger steps to disrupt racism in your life and society.

Figure 1.1 shows a snapshot of the three-step process and how each step fuels a lifelong learning loop and improvement cycle to unlearn racism.

Each step of the three-step change model process has five reflective questions to ask yourself to guide your behavior and decision-making toward fewer racist behavioral choices.

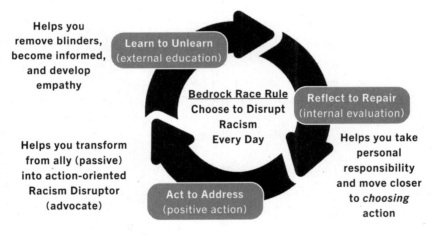

FIGURE 1.1. Lifelong learning loop to unlearn racism. There is no final destination or free pass but a continual momentum cycle of daily improvements. Racism Disruptors commit to action.

STEP 1—LEARN TO UNLEARN (EXTERNAL EDUCATION)

Step 1 focuses on external education about history, systems, and structures and how they impact people of color. This enables you to learn new information, unlearn previous beliefs, challenge what you believed was true, and stress test whether your perceived world is the real world as experienced and seen by people of color.

Here are five self-reflective questions to ask yourself:

1. What information will help you better understand the situation, people of color, and possible options to pursue in deciding how to proceed? What should you learn to add context?
2. What options and choices do most white people consider and take? Have you questioned why these responses are so common?
3. Who has historically benefited from these common actions?
4. How will each of the various options available to you impact people of color?
5. Which option is the least racist, causes the least harm to people of color, and results in protecting the dominant culture's power in lieu of distributing power the least?

STEP 2—REFLECT TO REPAIR (INTERNAL EVALUATION)

Step 2 focuses on an internal evaluation to force you to reflect on how your thoughts and behaviors may be offensive and causing harm. It pushes you past a perpetual state of denial about your personal role in harming people of color. It nudges you to accept that your past actions may be racist and your insights into racism are inaccurate and instead helps drive personal accountability and behavioral change. Looking in the mirror is necessary to becoming a Racism Disruptor. This step also helps move you closer to choosing to act.

Here are five self-reflective questions to ask yourself:

1. What does the information learned in educating yourself teach you about your values and your understanding of society?
2. What did you learn about your past actions, choices, behaviors, and inaction? Could they be viewed as racist, and did they cause people of color harm? How have your past racialized actions and choices also harmed you?
3. How does it feel to actively or passively ignore or deprioritize the feelings and rights of others? Does this behavior support a sense of

superiority, bolster your self-esteem, or elevate a "white identity" at the expense of people of color?

4. If you wait any longer to act, will you ever truly act? If you were the one waiting for racism disruption, how quickly would you want to see action? By doing nothing or remaining silent, what message are you conveying?

5. What are you protecting or gaining from your choice? How does your choice help or harm people of color? If your choice hurts people of color, is it worth it?

STEP 3—ACT TO ADDRESS (POSITIVE ACTION)

Step 3 moves you past complicity by requiring positive action. It forces both action and a continual learning cycle by asking you to take stock of your chosen action steps. It encourages you to address racism and racialized issues in yourself and in society. As you move past complacency (i.e., inaction) to proactive action to unlearn racism, you're able to transform into a Racism Disruptor.

Here are five self-reflective questions to ask yourself:

1. When deciding to act, did you listen to people directly impacted by this action or decision?

    Listening doesn't mean reaching out and speaking to a person of color. Self-education should be achieved through books, articles, podcasts, documentaries, films, and other resources to limit transferring emotional labor to people of color and burdening them with carrying your knowledge gaps for you. Their job isn't to relive racial trauma or become your Race Professor Nominee curating curricula to make your learning easy. If people of color are present during real-time incidents, listen when they speak. Watch their body language. Take in nonverbal cues. Don't pepper them with questions or draw them into sharing their opinions if they're not raising their hands.

2. How did your actions empower someone other than yourself? Whom did you share your power with through this action?

3. Whom else did you include who looks like you and needs to learn?

4. Did your actions positively impact people of color and disrupt status quo power structures? Did your actions protect and help minimize harms experienced by them? Did you focus more on your impact instead of the intent of your actions?

5. Now that you've acted, what did you learn? What should you replicate, avoid repeating, and learn for next time? What do you need to learn now and share with other white people?

MAINTAINING THE IMPROVEMENT CYCLE

Since learning continues for a lifetime, once you get to Step 3, keep the cycle going. Take stock of what worked well to duplicate it and what went over like a lead balloon to avoid in the future. When reaching a milestone or breakthrough, keep your foot on the gas. People of color don't get a vacation from racism, thus you don't get any free passes, and there is no final destination.

If the learning stops, then you've proactively demoted yourself and stepped down from Racism Disruptor status. Racism Disruptor status disappears when you elect to take a break since you've halted your unlearning racism learning loop. It's replaced by complicity and supporting status quo racism, which is why disrupting racism is a lifelong obligation and journey requiring consistency.

If you're resting on laurels from yesteryear, ask yourself, "What have I done for people of color lately?" That's your Racism Disruptor tagline to perpetually unlearn racism and sustain anti-racist engagement. Each day you choose *actions* against racism, you're choosing to disrupt racism.

APPLYING THE BEDROCK RACE RULE'S THREE-STEP PROCESS— RESPONDING TO HEARING THE N-WORD

Let's walk through an example using this model, revisiting the N-word incident described in this book's introduction from the perspective of hearing hate speech (see table 1.1). Most people know the N-word is a deplorable racial slur and don't use it. Upon hearing it, many emotionally distance themselves from the racist act since *they* didn't say it—it was someone else who was inappropriate, offensive, or straight-up racist.

While many whites don't step into the hate-speech-spewing-perpetrator category, plenty float in the deep end of the silent-and-complicit cesspool. This wallflower-witness scenario plays out daily. Countless white spectators watch trauma and pain inflicted on people of color yet sit back—leaving marginalized groups with less power to fend for themselves. Typically, very few whites openly stand in solidarity alongside people of color and proactively choose to minimize the impact of toxic harms. But whites need to disrupt racism as windfall beneficiaries of White Welfare. It's their obligation.

TABLE 1.1 Problem situation—the N-word

Racial Quandary and Decision Crossroad: "My friend just said the N-word. I know this word is taboo racist. What should I do? Remain silent? Let it blow over? Say or do something?"

BEDROCK RACE RULE:

CHOOSE TO DISRUPT RACISM EVERY DAY

THREE STEPS TO DECIDING HOW TO REACT (ANALYSIS AND APPROACH)

This rule's three-step process, along with each step's accompanying five questions, guide you in choosing fewer racist behaviors. For each step, ask yourself that step's related questions.

Step 1—Learn to unlearn (external education)

- Educate yourself to fill knowledge gaps beyond solely relying on knowing that this word is universally racist. The historical background of how the N-word was leveraged as a tool against Blacks helps you understand the reach of its negative impact on the Black community and its linkage to broader strategies of oppression.
- Research can help challenge assumptions about the Black American experience and prevalence of current N-word uses. Explore your past and current views about the term and Black people (i.e., learning to unlearn).
- Think about the impact of choosing to do nothing on those in the room and Blacks in general, and consider whether inaction moves you toward being a Racism Disruptor.

TABLE 1.1 (*continued*)

Step 2—Reflect to repair (internal evaluation)

- After self-educating and challenging your thinking, look within and explore your past mindset and actions—either in choosing inaction, remaining silent when witnessing racism, or consuming racist entertainment that uses the N-word.
- Honestly analyze why and when you've been silent in the past and what this says about you and your commitment to disrupting or upholding white supremacy—be open to making hard admissions about yourself and whether past choices make you complicit, immune to hate speech or racist behaviors, lazier, or more inclined toward inaction.
- Consider the impact of immediate action on people of color—and then value impact over intent (i.e., avoid hearts-and-minds outlooks, which are actually false rubber-stamp support for anti-racism that deprioritizes the effect of inaction on the lives, feelings, pain, and condition of people of color).

Step 3—Act to address (positive action)

- Now it's time to act and speak up. Positive action supporting people of color is how you move *away* from racist complicity or being a passive ally who just mentally disagrees with racist behaviors (i.e., intellectual performative practice) and *toward* being an action-oriented Racism Disruptor with an actual, meaningful impact.
- You must be less focused on your desire to feel comfortable and align with what's right and wrong. Racism has no neutral positions.
- Consider if your impact is aligned with your intent. Think about what worked well and what didn't to encourage a cyclical learning loop of improving by choosing to act and do. Research improved talking points and ask yourself what additional information would be helpful and could be shared with others. Then, implement your ongoing learning process of being a proactive and vocal disruptor—not a wallflower.

(*continued*)

TABLE 1.1 Problem situation—the N-word (*continued*)

- Reflect on future actions you can take to protect and support people of color. Brainstorm additional ways to reduce the harmful impact of racist behaviors on them. Disrupting racism is a daily choice.

ADDITIONAL CONSIDERATIONS

Here are several other points to consider:

- **Quick real-time decisions**—Sometimes things are unfolding quickly with little time to self-educate and you need to make an immediate decision to act. As a real-time guide when faced with limited decision time, think about how you'd feel if this happened to you. Then, circle back and learn more later.
- **Flexible three-step model**—The steps aren't rigid. Depending on the circumstance, they can happen simultaneously and start out of order—especially when facing a time-sensitive issue. What's important is you engage in the core steps: learn to unlearn, reflect to repair, and act to address. Your goal is to advance toward learning and doing.
- **Bedrock Race Rule**—Your guiding North Star is whether your decisions align with the Bedrock Race Rule that underlies this three-step process. Are you choosing to disrupt racism every day? If not, you need to make different choices and adjust your behavior accordingly.
- **Race Rules as your guide**—Use this book's various topic-specific Race Rules to help remove your blinders, kick-start your unlearning racism process, and make better choices to ultimately cause less harm. They're great starting points for tackling areas where whites repeatedly fumble and offend.

If you watch someone called or use the N-Word and you do nothing, you are actively engaging in a racist act. While witnessing bigotry or discrimination, you become an approving accomplice. You don't have to be the person engaging in the overt racist act. If you're a bystander and member of the dominant culture (i.e., white) who's doing nothing to curtail racist behavior, then whether you meant to or not, you've used your power to join their racism and support it. This is what upholding oppression looks like—through seemingly small, individual choices with cumulative impact. It's how white supremacy perpetually continues. You can't be silent and claim you're behaving like a good or nice person.

While the act of inaction may be easier and more comfortable, let's not pretend it's not a choice. The neutral position stands with the status quo, aligned with society's racist power structures. It advances white supremacy and oppression since it does nothing to disrupt it. The only time sitting on the sidelines is acceptable is when your physical safety is legitimately in danger (e.g., not due to general *perceived* fears of Black and brown people, which is not reasonable fear but fear rooted in bigotry). But deciding on inaction to protect relationships or because you're averse to uncomfortable conversations safeguards racism rather than disrupts it. It leaves people of color exposed and standing alone to protect themselves from structures they didn't create and don't control.

Although your decision may be understandable, don't fool yourself. With eyes wide open, you chose the racist path. Instead of rationalizing it, admit you made a trade-off.

> In the end, we will remember not the words of our enemies, but the silence of our friends.
>
> —Dr. Martin Luther King, Jr., civil rights activist

PART 1

Stop Othering Who's Racist— Start with Yourself

PART 1 focuses on expanding your definition of what's racist and who's racist to include family, friends, colleagues, and yourself. The goal is for whites to stop "othering" who's a racist. This shouldn't be confused with how people of color are "othered" (i.e., made to feel excluded, outside the mainstream, or like visitors in their homeland). Othering who's racist is about shifting away from white exceptionalism or seeing racism in extreme forms (e.g., Klansmen and hate crime perpetrators) where racism manifests elsewhere and never at home.

Look within to see your role in offending, upholding the status quo, and supporting white supremacy. Individual behaviors fuel a larger framework perpetuating racism. Collective microdecisions have macroimpacts that feed into developing systemic racism. Your seemingly small, insignificant choices aren't minor. They're amplified through a multiplier effect.

Approach this work with a growth mindset. Exploring racism and self-analysis is inherently uncomfortable. It's unrealistic to assume this process is easy. You'll feel challenged, called out, and defensive. The objective is to evolve so you can develop stronger, sincere relationships with people of color. You can't become a Racism Disruptor if you're coddled and fail to do the work. In exposing unspoken truths, advice and explanations are brutally honest and hard to swallow.

This book's ethos genuinely wants you to be better. When feeling defeated, hopeless, or emotionally spent, revisit why you're on this journey. Remind yourself you've chosen a path of self-discovery and reeducation as an anti-racist act toward disrupting racism.

Race Is a Social Construct, and Racism Is Real

Black people don't care about race. They care about justice.

—*Elie Mystal, author and political commentator*

RULE SUMMARY

Race is a social construct. It's something human beings collectively built—a social creation we've all shared and influenced, passing it along generation after generation. It's a human invention that's socially constructed and not biologically grounded. Racial categories aren't rooted in science, genetics, or nature, nor are they anchored in an objective reality about the world and humanity. This is why what's considered "Black" in America could be "Coloured" in South Africa or "white" in other countries, making racial categories arbitrary.

Race was invented centuries ago by European whites to morally justify slavery, colonization, imperialism, genocide, land theft, and Christian evangelism—assigning positive and negative characteristics to races, intentionally elevating whites, and strategically oppressing people of color for white domination, control, power, and wealth. This created profound impacts on inequality, opportunity, social status, and upward and downward mobility (i.e., white supremacy).

The word *race* first emerged in the English language in the late 1500s—timed with white supremacy going on a world tour.

While race is a social construct, *racism is real*.
The new racism is to deny that racism exists.

Rejecting that something is racist or someone experienced racism is racist. It invalidates lived experiences while aiding whites in wearing blinders.

Contrary to what some believe, we aren't in some post-racial world. The country isn't free from discrimination, prejudice, or racial preferences. Just because some people of color aren't downtrodden doesn't mean we solved society's white supremacy problem. Racism and racists are alive and thriving—wreaking havoc at work, in politics, on local school boards, and at your family gatherings.

Even when recognizing racism exists conceptually, you may unconsciously block yourself from seeing its presence in your direct orbit or it being caused by your personal choices, including that while you see it in society, somehow it's magically not thriving at your workplace or in your home. This denialism encourages gaslighting. Part of the process of unlearning racism includes expanding your concept of what racism is, how it shows up in everyday life, and when you're personally perpetuating it.

Take a look at these examples of the race-social-construct versus racism-being-real dichotomy:

- There's no biological nor genetic difference between how whites and Blacks feel pain, yet there's racial bias in how physicians treat pain management (many believing Blacks feel less pain), with a significant number of doctors holding false beliefs about biological differences between Blacks and whites (e.g., 25 percent of medical residents believing Blacks have thicker skin). Medical racism impacts treatment and physicians' decisions across all areas and specialties of medicine and healthcare, including how seriously they listen to Black patients' legitimate concerns about ailments and symptoms.[1]
- Whites are more likely to consume marijuana in their lifetime than Blacks (53.6 percent versus 45.3 percent), yet Blacks are 3.64 times more likely to be arrested for possessing weed. Fabricated, negative, racist perceptions of Blacks' drug use play a role in arrests and incarceration.[2]

Today's racism is often more subtle and covert. This strengthens misconceptions that racism was eradicated once overt segregation ended or through the implementation of diversity programs and affirmative action. Everyday racism's cunning nature can shield you from seeing that encounters you witness or are involved in are sometimes racist—wrongfully interpreting incidents as misunderstandings instead of discrimination. Post-racial fallacies are further emboldened when coupled with thinking racism only comes in the embodiment of rabid racists frothing at the mouth vomiting obvious hatred, joining domestic terrorist groups, and gunning down defenseless shoppers because they're not white.

But that's an illusion. Racism is less about being evil or having a rotten heart and more about complicity, behavioral change, and daily actions and choices. We need to unlearn constrained misconceptions that promote emotional detachment from white supremacy and evade personal responsibility for bigotry. Racism has been normalized for centuries, making it easier to reject its presence and escape looking in the mirror to get a glimpse of what typical racists look like—which could include you, your family, your workplace, films you watch, news outlets you follow, social media influencers you admire, and political campaigns you support.

The longer you swim in a culture, the more invisible it becomes. This makes many whites blind to seeing how racism is everywhere. It clouds recognizing how individual behaviors contribute to systemic racism.

One reason it's so hard to acknowledge racism's presence is because it threatens your self-image and whether you think of yourself as a good, nice, moral, and just person. This instinctively triggers defensiveness, being hardwired psychologically to defend your position. A lack of self-awareness can prevent recognizing racism is real and exists where you live and work or that you might be racist or prejudiced. If you're unable to empathize or sympathize, then you'll probably struggle in identifying racism and seeing it in your own actions, thoughts, and choices and how your workplace operates.

SUFFERING FROM "NOT-HERE SYNDROME"

In 2021, South Carolina senator Lindsey Graham denied the existence of systemic racism in the United States, going on to say, "America's not a racist country."[3] The proof he cited was the election of a Black president and Black vice president (i.e., leveraging tokenism as evidence).

Saying racism exists broadly as a concept but not in your company, community, or family plays out daily. This mentality is the same "not-here" gaslighting espoused by Graham. Racism is always somewhere else in a distant land, like how it's supposedly concentrated in the South but not the North, East, and West.

NIMBYing the presence of racism undermines progress. It threatens the physical and emotional safety of marginalized groups.

Denying racism is linked to anti-Black prejudice. This mindset allows for victim-blaming to explain away discrimination and inequity, which makes it harder to address and take responsibility for the ongoing effects of systemic racism.

You can overcome this and deprogram falsehoods by embracing an expanded definition of racism. Instead of othering whom you see as racist or where racism is festering, look around you. More importantly, look within to remove your blinders.

Broadening your understanding of who and what's racist will empower you to see and accept the existence of proximate racism, including in your daily life and actions. This step is foundational for becoming a Racism Disruptor. You can't disrupt what you can't see. And you can't reinforce a perpetual lifelong cycle of learning to unlearn and choosing proactive disruption when racism is viewed in extreme or faraway rather than quotidian, local, and personal terms.

SELF-REFLECTIVE QUESTIONS

These questions can help broaden your understanding of how racism shows up in daily life:

1. Do you think racism exists in society? Our country? Your community? Your workplace?
2. When you think of a racist person, what do they look like? How do they behave? What do they think, say, or do? Describe them.
3. Name five examples of where you see racism in your home (including through media)?
4. Do you think you've had racist thoughts? If so, what are or were they?
5. Think of when you've participated or engaged in racially offensive behavior or thinking. What did you say, do, or think? How did your actions or thoughts impact people of color? Impact you? Do you consider this advancing racism? If not, why?
6. Can you think of any examples of a person of color whom you personally know who's never experienced racism and had it negatively affect their life? If so, how is that possible? Thinking about how racism operates, how did you reach that conclusion?
7. Does recognizing the presence of racism in your inner thoughts, home, community, or workplace make you feel guilty? If so, what strategies do you use to navigate these feelings?

8. How can you and society disrupt racism without first admitting how you personally engage in, uphold, and benefit from it?

9. If you believe you're a good person, can you still be racist? If racism is ideologically against your values, can you still be racist? Are goodness (or beliefs that racism is wrong) and racism mutually exclusive?

10. How does thinking about racism in your inner thoughts, home, and workplace impact your future decisions?

To effectively understand anything we have to understand its history and what necessitated its existence. . . . But we can't do that without critically interrogating who made these constructs and who benefited from them.

—Michael Harriot, self-proclaimed "wypipologist"

Everyone Is Prejudiced, but Not Everyone Is Racist

A white identity is a trust fund, and its currency
is grievance that is stolen from others.
—*Nesrine Malik, author*

RULE SUMMARY

No one is immune from having prejudicial beliefs or thoughts based on another's race or ethnicity, including people of color. But while *everyone* is prejudiced, not everyone is racist. There's a critical difference between prejudice and racism.

Racism = Prejudice + Institutional or Societal Power
Prejudice ≠ Racism

Prejudice—Preconceived negative views, feelings, opinions, and stereotypes based on someone's perceived group membership that disregard facts.

Racism—Marginalization and oppression of people of color based on a socially constructed racial hierarchy that predominantly privileges whites, supporting the superiority of the powerful caste and inferiority of the less powerful (i.e., white supremacy).

Racism combines discrimination (an act of oppression) with racial prejudice (a preconceived opinion not based on reason or actual experience).

Racial oppression involves impacts on *groups*—exercising power to support the dominant group's sustained societal position or power.

Just because a person of color is prejudiced doesn't mean they're racist.

For example, a prejudiced person of color needs privilege or power *over* white people—political, economic, or social leverage to discriminate against whites and affect their life chances. Evaluating racism can't take place in a bubble negating the existence of structural, systemic, and institutional racism. Racism sits in an unignorable, integral context that's fundamentally linked to oppressive policies, laws, and practices. There's no historic or systemic support for any racial prejudices people of color may have. They don't systemically benefit from their racial prejudices, nor do they have racial dominance from birth. There's no *system* of anti-white racism, which is a needed ingredient to transform prejudice into racism or racial supremacy.

This is why reverse discrimination or reverse racism doesn't actually exist—because racism is both racial prejudice and racial oppression, and whites are *not* oppressed as a group.

Thinking *everyone* is racist omits the critical role played by power and systemic impacts on groups. It means every unfavorable thought about whites by people of color is "racism." Equating prejudice with racism can morph into assuming that all forms of race-based preferential treatment are bad and bigoted. This makes it difficult to advance anti-racism and implement solutions seeking remediation, restorative justice, and equitable access to opportunity. This undermines implementing policies like affirmative action that try to level the playing field as they're perceived as racism against whites. Affirmative action serves as a corrective measure to curtail the effects of racism.

Failing to see the instrumental role of historic oppression and collective power facilitates operating in a false alternate reality. It helps you wear blinders negating truths. Blurred vision blocks you from seeing how your daily choices and behaviors can perpetuate white supremacy, where individual acts feed into cumulative white decisions that uphold structural and institutional racism. At its core is an underlying belief in racist colorblind ideologies, as if race doesn't impact life's outcomes—except we don't live in a race-neutral society.

If it's impossible to consider race or we see every prejudicial thought or race-based policy as *racist*, then disrupting racism is unattainable. And it's corrosive since it emboldens a white victimhood mentality.

HIJACKING ANTI-RACIST TERMINOLOGY TO DENY PERSONAL BIGOTRY

Being opposed to racism and promoting racial tolerance (i.e., engaged in anti-racist actions) doesn't mean you're not racist. For many, this means you're a work in progress who's moving in the right direction. People love to throw around the phrase *anti-racism*. But something doesn't become not racist merely by attaching terminology often used just to make whites feel good and think they're anti-racists. This also applies to cavalier usages of *Racism Dsruptor*, *ally*, or *woke*.

HOW RACISM SHOWS UP IN DAILY LIFE

Racism shows up in many ways in your daily life:

- Clutching your purse or crossing the street when a Black man approaches.
- Routinely calling on the white kids in class or assigning plum work projects to white staff (including inviting white team members to the client dinner or meeting and excluding or overlooking employees of color).
- Feeling threatened when a Black or Latino person expresses anger or is upset—especially when their feelings are justified.
- Talking about how job candidates of color aren't the right culture fit.
- Complaining about a talent pipeline problem and not having enough qualified candidates of color to hire when doing nothing to diversify candidate pools and failing to mention qualifications when referencing white candidates or staff, many who are probably mediocre and nothing special.
- Referring to good schools or good neighborhoods versus bad ones— because we can guess what races come to mind at these good or bad places.
- Being up in arms when policymakers try to desegregate your local school, adjust property tax appropriations to equalize school funding, or teach more accurate American history in classrooms, moving away from whitewashed stories of American exceptionalism centered on white greatness.
- Objecting to low-income housing, power plants, correctional facilities, waste dumpsites, and other forms of NIMBYism in your town while being totally fine with them in communities of color.
- Blocking zoning law changes and housing developments, complaining they bring more crime.
- Complaining about critical race theory and calling it racist.
- Believing whites as a group are victims under attack, are targets of discrimination, or have less access to opportunities than people of color.
- Assuming Black Lives Matter protests are all violent or bringing up All Lives Matter as if valuing white lives isn't a given.

- Wanting to have a White History Month in response to Black History Month.
- Randomly asking an Asian work colleague questions like they're all in tech support or mathletes.
- Ignoring how films about people of color typically include a *white savior*—often making the white person the main character or otherwise supporting *white exceptionalism* since it's nearly impossible to have stories about people of color without simultaneously making whites feel better about themselves and their role in racism. This becomes doubly racist if, when pointing out to friends of color why they too must see the film, you use it as an opportunity to highlight societal racism to them as if they don't live it daily or don't have innate racism radars (i.e., culturesplaining, which is the race, culture, and ethnic heritage and background version of mansplaining).

If you've done any of these, you should stop doing them immediately. Develop avoidance strategies for the future.

If you're confused or wonder why any of these examples are racist, research why people of color may view these as bigotry. This will help you self-educate and use external sources to fuel your learning.

If you disagree, rejecting they're racist, or if classifying some examples as racist makes you angry—after doing the research and trying to walk in their shoes—ask yourself *why* this is your emotional reaction. Explore the underlying motivations, fears, and assumptions beneath your instinctive response, including how your perspective could be linked to racism and your perceived definitions of *white supremacy* and *racism*. Continue to research how these terms are defined and what constitutes racist white behavior, turning to sources supported by *most* people of color and *not* outliers in communities of color (e.g., don't rely on Clarence Thomas, Candace Owens, Condoleezza Rice, Tim Scott, Ben Carson, Kanye West, or conservative news commentators as broadly representational Black voices). Then reevaluate how your views may have changed and how your evolving outlook will impact your behaviors today and moving forward.

SELF-REFLECTIVE QUESTIONS

These questions can help you see that prejudice is not the same as racism:

1. What's the definition of *prejudice? Racism?* How are these two terms different?
2. Can whites be victims of racism? If yes, how? Revisit the definition of *racism* in this chapter along with the description of the levels and examples of racism terminology in the glossary (table G.1).
3. Does reverse discrimination (i.e., people of color discriminating against white people) exist? What informs your decision? Are white people oppressed as a group?
4. What's the difference between *diversity, inclusion, equity,* and *equality?* After defining these words based on your own understanding, look them up in the glossary.
5. Name five ways believing in reverse discrimination undermines racial progress. How does believing in it hinder your, someone else's, or society's ability to develop stronger connections with the people of color in your or their life or with people of color in general?

> Prejudice is a burden which confuses the past, threatens the future, and renders the present inaccessible.
>
> —Maya Angelou, poet and civil rights advocate

PORTRAIT OF A RACIST

Most Racists Look like You

"Political correctness" is a label the privileged often use to distract from their privilege and hate.

—*DaShanne Stokes, author and social justice advocate*

RULE SUMMARY

Mental reframing alert! Real racism ain't about Grand Dragons and neo-Nazis. Real racism involves everyday white people who work with you, screen candidates at your job, live with you, walk dogs near your home, play with your kids, and sit at your holiday dinner table.

Real racists might even look like you. Or a real racist could be *you*.

When it comes to racism, what's in your heart and mind or your visualization and stereotype of who or what is racist is considerably less relevant than what you actually *do*.

At their core, white supremacy and racism are about two things:

1. Whether you *benefit* from an unfair system that advantages you based on race
2. What you decide to do or not do about the country's centuries-old biased system where *you* are personally a consistent winner

First, you need to understand the nation's history and appreciate its significance to develop empathy and nurture your allyship. Then, you must take action promoting material change.

People of color care a lot less about what you *think* and *feel* about them. They're more interested in what you're *personally doing* to maintain or remove your boot from their necks. What counts is how you're proactively purging your prejudices and institutional strongholds on their progress.

Let your understanding of racism evolve from burning crosses, pitchforks, hate crimes, and hate speech toward an enlightened, more accurate, and practical understanding of personal collusion.

In your heart, you can believe in equality in principle and still be racist. Feelings (or perceived feelings) and bigotry aren't mutually exclusive. If you sit back and do nothing to advance equity, address the wrongs of the past, and solve how the country's legacy impacts the present, that's *you* supporting white supremacy—that's *you* basking in the glory of white privilege.

Yes, that's *you* being racist.

No white hoods or Nazi uniforms are required to support the same racist power structures and systemic outcomes. It's just going covert—it's racism with a new wardrobe.

It's time to stop othering who you think can be racist.

If your modus operandi maintains the status quo, you're draped in bigotry. And *that's* what racism really looks like.

Silence, Complicity, Complacency, or Apathy = White Supremacy

Reframe how you see and understand racism. Stop deceiving yourself about your own role. Begin to see the white supremacy in your personal complicity, indifferent inertia, and daily collaboration supporting the status quo and racial regression where you live and work. Embrace doing a courageously fearless self-inventory because this form of subtle racism is a lot more dangerous and predatory to people of color than the Klansman with a pipe bomb could ever be.

This cunning form is what truly maintains systemic racism in every neighborhood, school, workplace, policy, law, and institution. And unlike the Vanilla ISIS, who openly terrorize people of color, most don't see nor fully recognize this subtle, more pervasive, and insidious version delivered with smiles, in meetings, and at the ballot box. Everyday racism relentlessly keeps people of color "in their place."

Status quo racism traumatizes people of color daily to advance White Welfare, white privilege, and the country's racialized caste system. This is why the racism reflected back in the mirror and present with those in your life is far more threatening. This is why your personal understanding of what racism really is—along with recognizing your personal role in upholding it through daily choices—is significantly more important to people of color and in dismantling racism.

HOW RACISM SHOWS UP IN DAILY LIFE

Racist behaviors and mindsets keep bigotry alive. They support a mentality where it's harder to see your own harmful behaviors, making it easier to think others are the racist ones who need to work on themselves. They support believing what matters are thoughts of goodness or performative acts instead of whether you're the beneficiary of White Welfare and privilege. Here are some examples:

- **Microinvalidations**—Momentary acts and unconscious interactions that invalidate people of color or deny that their experiences are racist. They perpetuate feelings of marginalization and invisibility. One example is refuting that a doctor's dismissiveness about symptoms is linked to the patient being Black, Latino, or Native American.

- **Knee-jerk defensiveness**—Deflecting criticism about engaging in racist behavior or saying racist things paired with statements like "But you know me. You know I'm not racist." Sometimes this accompanies saying their family didn't own slaves, slavery and Indigenous extermination happened before their family arrived, their grandfather marched with Dr. King, or they support XYZ charity. All these tactics try to snuff out the scent of personal racism. Defensiveness seeks to end discussions, promote self-absolution, and quiet white privilege accusations.

- **White centering and victimhood**—When the focus shifts to whites and how whites feel and their emotional wounds, this is textbook deflection and redirection. For example, when someone says something racist and gets called out, they respond with "I'm so embarrassed I said that" or "I'm hurt you think of me that way." But it ain't about you when you caused harm. Instead, respond with "I hear how my words or actions hurt you. Thank you for pointing that out to me. I will work on this." Then, actually do the work to improve to back up your statement.

- **Blank stares and ignorance**—Shutting down when confronted about your racism is another form of daily racism. Mentally checking out just invokes your privilege instead of facing and discussing what you did to become more racially aware. Alternatively, claiming ignorance without first taking personal ownership of overcoming knowledge gaps invites detachment. This trades looking inward for making the person of color take responsibility for bringing cultural and racial awareness to the surface.

- **Apologies and faux compassion**—When racism is being discussed (especially in planned discussions), it's vapid to say phrases like "I feel your pain" and "I'm so sorry." This reflective technique draws attention away from biased encounters. If you don't look inward to acknowledge personal participation in racist behaviors, ideologies, and structures, these phrases fail in being sincere. Instead say, "I'm here to listen and learn." But after you listen, spend time self-educating so you're not falling into the trap of expecting all the education to come from people of color. You must still take affirmative steps and not be lazy.
- **White guilt**—This form of guilt can encourage whites to try to comfort a person of color to make up for the indignities and oppression experienced by marginalized groups. Statements like "I feel terrible about police brutality" or "It's unacceptable how many people of color don't have access to affordable healthcare" don't quite get society closer to limiting oppression. Nor does this bring individuals toward a self-examination to raise personal awareness or drive solutions. What do these statements serve other than to placate white feelings and guilt (especially if you're doing nothing about these terrible and unacceptable realities)?

SELF-REFLECTIVE QUESTIONS

The questions below can help you see how whiteness positively impacts your life and how deciding not to proactively disrupt privilege supports white supremacy. They can also help you shift away from seeing racism in a good-versus-bad dichotomy. This viewpoint modification enables you to improve in recognizing the racism around you and in yourself. This knowledge can facilitate moving from status quo inaction toward choosing to actively disrupt racism.

Ask yourself these questions:

1. How does being white impact your life? How do race and racism positively *and* negatively impact your life?

2. What are you doing to personally address racism? How have desires for comfort and opportunity or to avoid feeling uncomfortable kept you from taking action?

3. Why haven't you said or done more to disrupt racism? At work? At home? In your community?

4. Do you see racists as being bad people? Do you see yourself as a good person?

5. If the choices you make at work or in your community support the status quo (which benefits you), isn't this upholding systemic racism? Does it matter if you're a good or bad person if the impact of your actions or inaction upholds white supremacy?

6. If your internal thought process or belief system supports discriminatory or status quo outcomes, are you open to making behavioral choices that contradict those thoughts if they support people of color or cause less harm (i.e., make choices that minimize the outward expression of internal prejudicial beliefs)?

7. Can you follow this book's Race Rules before you fully understand or agree with them to advance racism disruption (i.e., pursue anti-racist actions even if your mind hasn't caught up)?

8. What changes must happen in your life to become a consistent Racism Disruptor? What should you implement to hold yourself accountable?

Remember, what matters most isn't merely thinking that racism is bad. Replace believing in the "hearts-and-minds" framework. Instead, see what fundamentally advances white supremacy is making choices that negatively impact people of color and positively impact you and other whites.

> I am no longer accepting the things I cannot change.
> I am changing the things I cannot accept.
>
> —Angela Y. Davis, political activist and academic

White Liberals, Democrats, and Good White People Can Be Dangerous Racists

We should seek not a world where the Black race and the white race live in harmony, but a world in which the terms *Black* and *white* have no real political meaning.

—*Ta-Nehisi Coates, author*

RULE SUMMARY

"Good White People" and blue-state progressives can be tenacious supporters of systemic racism—the same petition-signing clicktivists who would jump to reelect Barack Obama for a third term.

White liberals, Democrats, allies, staff at social justice organizations, check-writing donors, and Black Lives Matter protesters can be progress-blocking status quo-ers. Comfortably enjoying privilege and unwilling to give it up, many are allergic to looking at their own prejudicial behaviors while hypocritically calling out others.

Woke whites and Democrats can be some of the most dangerous racists since they significantly outnumber self-realized racists and often absolve themselves from complicity, criticism, and learning while maintaining and benefiting from racism. White liberals have an unreliable commitment to anti-racism and civil rights yet frequently appoint themselves arbiters of what degrees of racial equity and progress are appropriate or too much given the circumstances.

Good White People who aren't *personally* doing anything to eradicate the country's racism are engaging in racism. This may sound shockingly harsh, but it's transparently candid. It shares what many won't say to your face. While people are on a racism spectrum with varying degrees of prejudice and inflicted harm, complacent coasting supports our racialized caste system.

There's no sitting on the fence. There are no neutral positions. Racism isn't passive. If you're not actively combatting racism in meaningful ways, then you're either upholding white supremacy through silent complicity and tacit approval or proactively protecting systemic bigotry. If you're a Good White Person but do little substantively in your own community and workplace to advance equity, then you can't claim to be as "good" as you think.

When thinking about racists, many often think of Confederate-flag wavers and white nationalists. That's too simplistic since most racists are ordinary people going about daily life—but with convenient blinders or limited interest in dismantling racism since privilege and White Welfare benefit them.

Viewing racism one-dimensionally gives good people an easy out—who can point the finger outward and never inward. This myopia means never having to critically evaluate their role and actions in amplifying racism and greenlighting its pervasiveness.

White liberals tend to scapegoat working-class whites for racism.

It's always other people who are the white supremacists—poor, uneducated whites, hateful Karens and Kens going viral, or deplorable Republican lawmakers. But this doesn't explain why schools and neighborhoods nationwide are more segregated than ever, including in blue states like New York and California, nor why it feels like a scavenger hunt when trying to find senior executives of color at companies across the country.

Racists don't have to consciously seek to hurt or dominate people of color. Racism doesn't require malice or verbally spewing obvious hate. But without self-reflection and personal accountability, few will see nor admit that through their actions and apathy they oppress, cause pain, and disadvantage people of color to maintain power and privilege—making trade-offs to advance selfish self-interests. Good White People's most effective racist tools are opportunity hoarding, microaggressions, denial, willful blindness, and passive complicity. Nice whites are the greatest threat to Black and brown progress, safety, and equality.

All whites are born into a system and societal structure that automatically benefits and privileges them through no additive effort—merely through birthright, skin color, and race. Our racial caste system advantages whites and promotes white entitlement. Whites don't have to do anything to *create* racist structures. They're preestablished. But whites can *maintain* the status quo. This system of white privilege and advantaged opportunity is the same privilege that benefits white liberals, Democrats, and Good Whites, which is why they vehemently uphold its benefits. Protecting white privilege is racist.

Becoming anti-racist is a process of personal deprogramming and proactive action to expand what you see yourself doing to uphold the country's racism legacy. To evolve, you must get past defensiveness. Change and expand what you think it means to be racist. Move away from an othering or exceptionalism understanding of racism to embrace a growth mindset. This is critical to disrupting racism. You can't change what you don't see.

Silence = Violence
Complicity = Racist
Inability to look inward = White-exceptionalism thinking

LIBERAL IN THE STREETS BUT NIMBY IN THE SHEETS

In New York City's heavily democratic congressional district represented by progressive Alexandria Ocasio-Cortez, a strong backlash came from white Bronx residents to upzoning efforts allowing taller buildings in an area with significantly fewer newly constructed affordable housing units relative to the rest of the city. New York has a housing crisis. Yet in the summer of 2022, a predominantly white group protective of low-density housing marched. Protesters harassed shoppers at the site of the planned development. Trying to spark fear, some said low-income drug houses will come to the community, along with crime going up.[1]

All these are euphemisms for Black and brown low-life invaders coming to ruin the neighborhood. White, Democratic racism was rearing its ugly head by blocking access—yet another form of modern-day restrictive covenants. It's the same old-timey game seeking an identical outcome played by nice white people.

Social justice and equality can come to a screeching halt the moment change comes to *their* neighborhood. White liberals don't set out to intentionally exclude people of color from their public schools or neighborhoods or dump all the undesirable power plants, highways, methadone clinics, homeless shelters, low-income housing, toxic waste, and correctional facilities in Black and brown communities.

But when it comes to where whites sleep and educate their kids, this is when they start blocking and opposing fairness through voting habits. It's the quintessential test for whites—when deflection tactics kick into high gear and Good Whites sound like the white racists they demonize. They're hell-bent on protecting their status, operating unconsciously but quite effectively at derailing racial equity. Deep down, equality is viewed as a zero-sum game, that by increasing Black and brown proximity to whiteness and sharing, whites will lose something like access to opportunities or resources.

Good White People and white liberals can be formidable barriers to attacking entrenched racism and change since it's harder to identify racism from supposed allies. They disguise racial hostility in innocuous-sounding terms—property values, zoning laws, taxes, neighborhood schools, qualified candidates, public safety, local control, colorblindness, and meritocracy. They use coded language and race-neutral phrases while writing checks, forming diversity committees, and voting for Democrats. They accept the status quo or see how it generally bestows privilege in society but fail to see how inherited advantage positively improves *their own* lives.

They lack a critical lens when it comes to their own backyards—sometimes sounding just like those racist Southerners when progress comes for their privilege or seeks to shift from white centering. Often, it's just a bridge too far when it's their turn to make room for people of color.

Not seeing the internal work feeds into misguided beliefs of white exceptionalism. It fuels white savior complexes of getting into what civil rights icon John Lewis called "good trouble."[2] If you're supporting progressive causes and voting blue down the ballot, then how could you be anything but anti-racist?

Too many white liberals spend too much time trying to earn a White Wokeness Gold Star for being a Good White Person who's not racist, or what Layla Saad calls ally cookies (i.e., the special praise sought by some whites for not being racist).[3] But cookie seeking is just *performative* and not true allyship since it doesn't disrupt racism and sustains the status quo.

We need to redefine how we understand racism and move away from relying on this false dichotomy of goodness versus wickedness as the determining factor that absolves people from being racist.

What matters most is the *impact* of your choices and *not* ideology, politeness, or intent.

IMPACT VERSUS INTENT TRANSLATOR

The impact of your actions and decisions is more important than what you intend. Saying or thinking "But I didn't mean it" falls flat when people of color are offended or harmed.

Your impact matters whether you're trying to be a helpful supporter of anti-racism or blissfully complicit through inaction. Don't let worrying about collateral damage deter pursing racism disruption. Instead, consider your choice's impact when acting, and refine decisions to minimize unintended consequences. See table 5.1 for examples.

Nice Whites use goodness, friendly views, and empathy as methods to deflect responsibility and protect white status. When you're willing to make changes impacting your own backyard—your schools, neighborhood, and workplace—then you've moved past symbolism and leveraging NIMBYism to block racial progress. Once you can take a hard look at *yourself*, you can start moving past verbal platitudes and earn claiming you're a good person or parent, especially if you're proactively trying to limit personally bequeathing racism to future generations.

Until we confront the harder issues, the country won't have a racial awakening. More importantly, those who avoid these discussions can't claim they're "Good White People."

Social change cannot be live streamed.
Racial progress isn't a moment but a movement.

WAYS WHITE LIBERALS AND GOOD WHITES PERPETUATE RACISM

Here are just a few of the many ways white liberals and Good Whites perpetuate racism:[4]

- **Kumbayaing for reconciliation**—One of the more popular deflection strategies is calling for racial reconciliation. White people use this technique to avoid feeling uncomfortable—because if there are angry Black and brown people, this provokes discomforting "white feelings," and then whites won't feel good about themselves. It's easier to gloss over racism with empty calls for reconciliation instead of the harder task of tackling restoring communities destroyed by racism—which requires whites to face facts and feel uneasy or even guilt. Instead of talking about unity, reconciliation, or national healing, focus on justice. People of color would rather hear about restoring communities than how to make white people feel comfortable again.

TABLE 5.1 Impact versus intent translator

What you did or said	What they experience or the result of your actions
Workplace	
You ask a Black business executive to become the new head of diversity—thinking you're strategically addressing company inclusion challenges and offering them a new leadership opportunity. **Intent**—Advance diversity.	You are glomming onto a random person of color and assigning them the task of solving systemic discrimination without expertise in specialized diversity work other than being Black, requiring a steep learning curve. **Impact**—Tokenize; undermine effectively advancing diversity and inclusion. **Alternative**—Hire experienced diversity expert with robust team and budget, reporting to the CEO.
Advertising and films	
Wanting to show diversity in commercials and entertainment, you cast an interracial couple where the female is white and the male is Black or where the female is light-skinned and the male is darker complected. **Intent**—Advance diversity and multiculturalism.	You're erasing Black women and signaling to women of color they're undesirable since they're not white, showing preferences for light skin. Rarely do we see dark women paired with a white man or man of color lighter than her. **Impact**—Render Black and brown women invisible; advance colorism; erode self-esteem. **Alternative**—Use dark women paired with lighter men of any race or men of the same complexion.

(*continued*)

TABLE 5.1 Impact versus intent translator (*continued*)

What you did or said	What they experience or the result of your actions
Community engagement	
You volunteer with a nonprofit providing college readiness programs to students of color. Eager to help, you arrive on day one with a list of ideas to expand operations that you propose after arrival. **Intent**—Support people of color; take action.	Before learning about organizational needs or previous efforts, you arrive as a know-it-all telling the "clueless" brown folks how the imperialistic white savior has all the solutions to impose on them, regardless of their feasibility. **Impact**—Paternalize. **Alternative**—Volunteer ready to learn about the group's interests, needs, and past efforts, and build trust over time before collaboratively suggesting changes.
Signaling of "common struggle"	
To identify with a person of color discussing racism, you talk about how you understand struggle having grown up in poverty or claim to be more disadvantaged than wealthy Blacks. **Intent**—Express commonality; introduce classism impacting life outcomes.	You appear out of touch and ignorant of the struggles faced by people of color *due to race* since whites may experience hardship but the adversity isn't *because of* race but classism. **Impact**—Marginalize; invalidate; advance white victimhood; equate classism with racism. **Alternative**—Listen; don't mention challenges experienced by white people.

TABLE 5.1 (*continued*)

What you did or said	What they experience or the result of your actions
Political discussions	
"I'm shocked. *We* can't tolerate the erosion of female reproductive rights. It's time to get more politically involved. What should we do about all these white men trying to control our freedoms?" **Intent**—Protect female body autonomy; express outrage; encourage political activism.	"Yet another white woman just focused on white women. Checked out when racists attack my civil rights but boohooing about *Roe v. Wade*'s demise when that was predictably coming next. FYI, *I've been* in the trenches *without you*." **Impact**—Prioritize white women's freedom; expose lack of interest in racial equality; reveal tone-deaf and obtuse insensitivity. **Alternative**—Complain to your white friends; work to protect civil rights of people of color too.
Personal relationships	
"I'm excited you can come to my dinner party. I need to jazz up my invite list. Know any hot Black guys to invite?" **Intent**—Advance diversity; increase pool of eligible bachelors.	"Hey, token Black friend, I want to leverage this 'friendship' so you can be a gateway to satisfy my fetish to date non-white men." **Impact**—Give off jungle fever vibes; tokenize. **Alternative**—Say nothing; explore why you're fetishizing Black men.

- **Selfish self-interests**—Another strategy involves protecting your own interests at the expense of racial equity in ways that uphold racism. This preserves privilege and access to power, wealth, and opportunities (e.g., advocating for racial diversity in schools while siphoning off funding by creating supposed merit-based gifted tracks, magnet programs, and specialized schools disproportionately benefiting white children and thus promulgating de facto segregated schools).
- **Coded language**—Another tactic involves hiding behind phraseology to mask racist views (e.g., Black-on-Black crime, good versus bad neighborhoods, devotion to order and civility over justice, white poverty and struggles, classism over racism, reverse discrimination).
- **Racial résumé**—Always ready to rattle off past efforts and loose connections, white liberals love to submit evidence they support "minority causes" and racial tolerance. "I voted for Obama!" "My Black friend . . ." "My town is racially diverse." "I volunteer at . . ." These efforts and alleged or actual friendships don't mean you can't be racially insensitive. This résumé can be used as a microinvalidation to deny a person of color's feelings.
- **Masochism**—Motivated by white guilt, whites can unconsciously seek self-punishment for historical oppression to appear racially sensitive. This perpetuates racism by simply becoming a receptacle for potential and actual abuse instead of examining racially biased behavior.

Whites need to pivot from thinking they're saviors, exceptional, and immune from racist thoughts, beliefs, and actions and don't benefit from privilege. Otherwise, they're contributing to the country's racism problem and never doing the critical self-reflective analysis to unindoctrinate themselves and advance impactful macrolevel change in society.

Here's a more productive approach—if someone says something you did was racist, *do not* get offended. Instead, pause. Think about how and why it could be perceived as racist by the other person. To grow, look within rather than going on attack. Look at yourself.

SELF-REFLECTIVE QUESTIONS

The following questions can help you not just understand yourself and your personal relationship with complicity, privilege, obstructionism, and upholding white supremacy, but also see areas where you need to augment your understanding and learn more. In addition, they can underscore where to take action to promote positive change at home, in your community and workplace, and at the ballot box.

1. What's an example of something constructive you did in an unfair, racialized situation? How did that action feel compared to when you did or said nothing?

2. What's something you did at work that you can admit was racist? In your family? Your neighborhood? Your kid's school? When voting in an election? Or in your quiet thoughts?

3. Following up on question #2 above and the racist behavior you recalled, how did your behavior harm a person of color? People of color as a group?

4. When your actions, decisions, or inaction harm people of color, does it matter if you didn't intend to harm anyone? What's problematic about focusing on intent over impact?

5. What's something you've done or avoided doing that advances white solidarity?

6. What actions will you take to address racism in your neighborhood? Local schools? Workplace? Family?

7. If you don't know how to solve racism or where to begin, why don't you know what to do to solve this? How have you grown into an educated, well-functioning adult without this knowledge? What have you done to remain ignorant? Why haven't you sought out information to know what to do?

8. Why do you assume it's other people who are the problem? Why don't you assume *you* could be part of the problem?

9. Would you support affordable housing built in your community? On your block? School integration (e.g., busing or changes to how kids are assigned to schools)? Racially equitable distribution of tax dollars to fund schools? At work, are you willing to decline

a promotion to create an opportunity for a person of color and elevate people of color?

10.   What do your responses to question #9 above say about you? How does supporting those initiatives and choices help you? Your community? Your country? People of color?

A productive way to counter innate tendencies to support existing power structures with disparate impact is to scrutinize choices you routinely make affecting your family, children, neighborhood, and workplace. The next time your community is planning new developments or considering changes to educational programs, evaluate how these could positively help whites and hurt people of color. Bring an especially critical eye to housing and school policies. Consider if you're protecting power and privilege, including with your voting and dollars. Ask what affirmative steps you can personally take to share the pie and create access to opportunities. And then go beyond noodling on concepts and act since action is the goal.

**What are *you* doing to dismantle racism—
to see *your own racism* so society can evolve?**

**People of color know you're often trying your best.
What this means is you have more work to do to tackle
your personal racist beliefs and prejudices to become
a better ally and transition into a Racism Disruptor.**

In this country American means white.
Everybody else has to hyphenate.

—Toni Morrison, author and academic

...5 YEARS LATER

...10 YEARS LATER

...30 YEARS LATER

...20 YEARS LATER

Racism Hurts Whites Too and Causes American Decline

A great civilization is not conquered from without until it has destroyed itself from within.

—*Will Durant, historian and philosopher*

RULE SUMMARY

Racism doesn't just hurt people of color. It harms whites too by limiting individual and collective economic opportunity. Racism facilitates American decline and prevents the country from achieving its potential. It derails our economy and global position. Bigotry squanders our competitive advantage as a racially diverse nation. Whites shoot themselves in the foot each time they cosign on white supremacy.

America needs to wake up from its racism slumber and solve its white supremacy problem or admit self-defeat and let another country become the world's new superpower. Already, we've lost critical ground on the global stage to China because we can't get over ourselves—China is strategically investing worldwide while America unwisely divests. Asleep at the wheel, we're conceding global influence and international presence with bigotry-entrenched distractions. Disillusioned "not-from-these-cold-dead-hands" whites cling to power and devise new oppression schemes. It's the 21st century, everything is global, and people of color are here to stay. Yet we're more focused on throwback domestic subjugation and complicity models—firmly keeping boots on necks of color since we're averse to change. Meanwhile, we're leaving money on the table as we destroy our economy and self-destruct.

Our domestic productivity and innovation are suffering. Our global impact is declining. We've chosen to amputate our future possibilities. The market signaled we must evolve with the times, shifting demographics, and demands for human rights, but we refuse to adapt. Apparently, collective national success isn't a priority if long-term economic American growth means "darkies and brown folks" will "get some freedom" and that darn equality malarkey. If we don't consider the big-picture impact of white supremacy, we will render ourselves obsolete—global dodo birds.

White America will deserve every moment of our downfall, with no one to blame but themselves when the real power game is lost. But unfortunately, those unwilling to sever ties with structural oppression in America are taking everyone else down with them on this sinking racism ship.

We need to stop this racial trauma nonsense, tackle White Welfare and privilege, and create access to opportunities and prosperity for people of color. This will enable America to thrive domestically and make room to focus on how we're slipping on the world stage. Racial diversity is America's unmatched competitive advantage.

Own dismantling racism in your community, family, workplace, and mindset. If a thriving economy and long-term American prosperity are important to you and the people you love, think critically about the policies, officials, and power structures you support.

In 2020, Citigroup economists estimated that over twenty years the US economy lost $16 trillion as a result of discrimination against Blacks from roughly 2000 to 2020. By comparison, US gross domestic product (GDP) in 2020 was $21.5 trillion. Failing to dismantle racism is costly, with Citigroup estimating our economy would feel a $5 trillion boost over five years if we tackled anti-Black discrimination.[1] If this is just the impact of anti-Black racism, imagine the lost economic value due to Native American, Latino, and AAPI (Asian American and Pacific Islander) discrimination.

According to a 2020 McKinsey & Company study that shows the upside of diversity on the economy, more diverse companies outperform less diverse companies—with racially diverse companies 36 percent more likely to perform better and earn higher profits (as noted in figure 6.1.)[2] This means we're squandering America's competitive advantage—racial diversity! If we committed to diverse workplaces, American companies could claim more economic value than less-diverse overseas companies.

The positive economic impact of racial diversity is also supported by a 2020 *Bloomberg* study. It found that hedge funds with more diverse fund owners and managers outperformed funds run by white men, with 6.6 percent investor returns on an annualized basis for funds run by people of color and women compared to 3.9 percent returns with white male fund managers over three years (as noted in figure 6.2). Yet, while diversity yields higher returns for investors, only 1.4 percent of US-based assets under management (AUM) were managed by diverse-owned firms in 2021 (i.e., non-white and women-owned firms).[3]

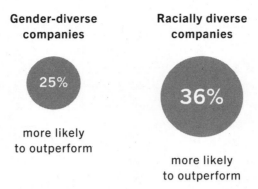

FIGURE 6.1. Diversity's value proposition. These data indicate the likelihood that companies in the top quartile for diversity financially outperform those in the bottom quartile for diversity in terms of profitability (i.e., racially diverse top-quartile companies outperform the bottom by 36 percent in profitability).

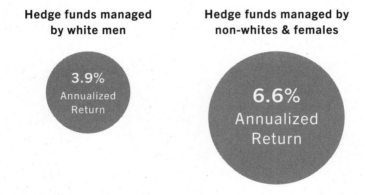

FIGURE 6.2. Diversity increases hedge fund returns and dividends. Hedge funds owned or managed by non-whites and women outperform white male peer groups. The data are the three-year total return of hedge fund strategies on an annualized basis.[4]

The business case for racial diversity and equitable access to opportunities is further bolstered when looking at technology, which is the cornerstone of a growing economy. According to a 2016 analysis from Intel and Dalberg Advisors looking at diversity in the technology sector, our innovation hub is losing economic value. If the tech sector were more racially diverse, this could lead to $300 to $370 billion annually—consisting of higher revenues and market value (as noted in figure 6.3).[5] Racial homogeneity is a lost economic opportunity for companies, the industry, and the US economy. Failing to realize our full potential by throwing away hundreds of billions of dollars in revenues and market value in the tech sector alone translates into a lower American GDP.

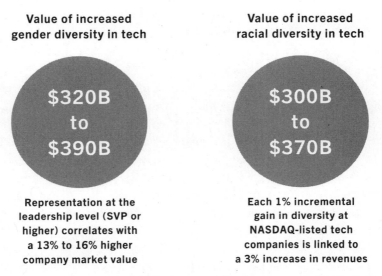

Value of increased gender diversity in tech

$320B to $390B

Representation at the leadership level (SVP or higher) correlates with a 13% to 16% higher company market value

Value of increased racial diversity in tech

$300B to $370B

Each 1% incremental gain in diversity at NASDAQ-listed tech companies is linked to a 3% increase in revenues

FIGURE 6.3. Annual economic impact of boosting diversity in tech. More diverse companies are 14 to 17 percent more likely to earn revenues above industry medians. This growth takes place as an effect of changes in labor and consumer markets, which increases job creation and the development of better quality products.[6]

Collectively, while these studies aren't scientific, this research suggests that companies, universities, and the entire country—which are typically led by powerful whites—are leaving massive sums of money to the wayside by not maximizing the benefits of diverse talent and access to opportunity for all Americans. We're letting other countries eat our lunch because we don't want all Americans at the dinner table.

To illustrate the point beyond the impact of diversity and anti-Black discrimination, let's break down some fundamentals of what boosts economic growth. Proven pillars of prosperity to ensure strong economic performance are innovation, trade, and talent. This includes a healthy, educated population able to get to work, create, and innovate and return to a quality home. We can't do this effectively if we have failing schools. And where do we underfund and overcrowd schools? We know the answer: communities of color.

We have intentionally blighted schools in communities of color and let educational quality decline for everyone. Our international education rankings have been falling for the past three decades. According to a 2017 Pew Research Center analysis, the United States ranked thirty-eighth globally in math and twenty-fourth in both science and reading.[7] Not a good look if we value innovation and inventing. We're not investing in cultivating future domestic talent. Educated immigrant talent makes up for our shortcomings, but this solution isn't sustainable long-term.

It's the same story for housing and healthcare. A quality standard of living with healthy citizenry is important for economies to flourish. Like a broken record, people of color live in crappier homes, are more likely to be homeless and lack health insurance, and have shorter life expectancies. We're incapable of developing a decent healthcare system while other industrialized nations have better systems. In the United States, we celebrate squabbling over and thwarting universal access to basic and preventative healthcare—all because we're entrenched in protecting a racist caste system and resistant to change.

> **Remove your blinders to see racism as a pervasive cancer on American progress and prosperity. Racism encompasses negative macro impact on all Americans, not just the individual harms to people and communities of color.**
>
> **Unlearn viewing racism in a bubble exclusively hurting Americans of color to absorb, value, and prioritize the business case for diversity and equitable access to opportunity. Begin to see how it harms you.**
>
> **Disrupting racism is critical to America's survival.**

We can't grow and be ready for the future, modernize, and maintain our global position because we're stuck on this destructive path of white supremacy. Meanwhile, China is replacing us around the world in markets and industry. Russia is back to its Cold War tactics. Iran is working on its nuclear capabilities. North Korea loves blasting off missiles. Cybercriminals are attacking the infrastructure necessary for commerce and our quality of life. And the world is deeming us less relevant and useful and is less inclined to listen when we speak or peg its economies to the US dollar. Why? Because we care more about thwarting racially equitable access to housing, education, jobs, healthcare, and capital to build wealth. Because we're prioritizing racism and prefer to concentrate on maintaining white privilege at all costs.

American racism makes us vulnerable and easier for our enemies to manipulate. Russia takes full advantage to influence our elections—using social media to fuel racial tensions. Except this time, it's not the "Southern strategy" used by Ronald Reagan to increase white voter support appealing to anti-Black racism. It's Vladimir Putin's international Machiavellian power move. As a racist country, we're ripe for manipulation. This makes us susceptible to foreign control and threatens national security.

You'd hope national pride and collective interests would prompt a focus on sustained innovation and growth. But no. People are distracted and can't look further than their status quo noses. As a result, we drive on shitty roads and dangerous bridges, send kids to crumbling schools, drink dirty water, and don't provide healthcare and the social infrastructure necessary for us to prosper and focus on creating and inventing. We rely on immigrants to come up with some of our new ideas—depending on migration to fuel growth and sustain America's economy—because we're following the racism bouncing ball, trying to keep a grip on white power and privilege. This is domestic suicide.

As you can see, we don't stop at just destroying communities of color and making life harder for only them. To make sure racism wins, we make things worse for *everyone*, whites included. A classic example is our postal system. Mail delivery is critical for a functioning modern society and efficient commerce. But since we don't want people of color to vote, we systematically started dismantling our US Postal Service infrastructure—blowing up another pillar of prosperity. Blinded by racism, in an attempt to slow votes arriving on time, we traded away medicine getting to veterans and the elderly, businesses' ability to send out packages to customers in the United States and overseas, and stimulus checks arriving in the mail. We swapped an important component of global competition, trade, and industry that keeps goods moving and traveling to hold Americans of color down. In a society where whites are already advantaged in the richest nation in the world, an insatiable taste for white-centered power and political avarice promotes collective self-destruction when prosperity aligns with unpalatable, racially equitable outcomes. As singer, songwriter, and reggae pioneer Bob Marley said, "In the abundance of water, the fool is thirsty."

Wise countries respect the value of underwriting the future. Instead of investing in America to compete, we opt for divestiture and self-harm. We opt for jumping off the top of the global food chain. We choose not to produce a 21st-century workforce that embraces equality and diversity or a society that follows other fundamental aspects of the dollar. We stifle economic growth and improved infrastructure because sharing the pie with people of color is repulsive for many whites.

If we take this analysis another step further and acknowledge that part of the lifeblood of America is immigration, we're placing ourselves behind the eight ball. Racism is now a deterrent. We will lose out on future foreign-born inventors, innovators, and investors if people around the globe fear anti-Asian hate and deadly police encounters for Black and brown people. Immigrants of color are opting to go to other countries out of racial fear. Plus, as we decline economically over time and become replaced by more attractive and competitive options, America will generally lose its allure.

We must invest in homegrown talent, and not just because of increased overseas competition and racism discouraging immigration. Our global brand as an international pillar of freedom is tarnished. We've lost credibility. We're less inviting and enticing. Our democracy is failing because white supremacists are clinging to power—prompting the rise of voter suppression, antiabortion laws, book banning, racist school curricula overhauling, the January 6 attempted government overthrow, and human rights abuses at the border. And when you throw in our gun culture threatening the right to life, countries increasingly warn their citizens about traveling to America.

Our country is in trouble. The pernicious effects of racism and discrimination will cripple our economy and scope of possibilities if we insist on leaving certain people behind. This is cannibalization. It's time we started listening to the Fall-of-Rome wake-up calls and course correct before it's too late. Let's hope this isn't too high an emotional hurdle for you and those in power.

Why point this out? So you recognize how racism also hurts you and all whites and you actually do something about it. You've got skin in the game. In your selfish self-interest, you should prioritize dismantling racism before it dismantles your way of life and the "American Dream." Push toward equality and anti-racism so America prospers. Take steps to purge white privilege in your home and workplace so we can maintain our global position.

More specifically, what can you do personally? Don't just be an ally but a Racism Disruptor by proactively combatting voter suppression in your community. Advocate for changes impacting your neighborhood, housing policies, and schools. Support affirmative action, reparations, and expanded access to healthcare. Vote for infrastructure investments. Kick out politicians upholding the status quo since old-timey approaches stifle growth.

It's time to clean house. Fund campaigns and organizations supporting anti-racist policies, social justice, and change. This will promote democracy and economic progress. You can't tackle racism without thinking of macroissues and taking microaction in your own community. This is how you dismantle racism—a multiprong approach locally and nationally. This is what being a Racism Disruptor looks like.

You can't hold down people of color without simultaneously holding yourself and your country down.

SELF-REFLECTIVE QUESTIONS

These questions are designed to help you see how racism hurts everyone, not just people of color, and what you might do to disrupt racism:

1. How important is eradicating and disrupting racism to you?
2. How do you feel about the notion that racism hurts America's economy and global position? Are you willing to make choices and personal sacrifices for the greater good of the nation?
3. Do you see how decisions made in your daily life and community have societal and macroeconomic impacts? If so, what are they? How to they impact people of color? The US economy? Our global relevance?
4. How do racism and white supremacy negatively impact you? Your family? The next generation?
5. If personally taking actions and making decisions to disrupt racism (i.e., prioritizing personal gain) isn't a priority for you (or important enough to implement personal change), what does this say about you? Whether you're living your values?

6. Do you think there's a connection between segregation in your local school and divergent life outcomes for people of color relative to whites? Do you see how school policies taken collectively across the country impact the country's declining educational levels over time? How do the country's educational global rankings impact the country's competitiveness over time?

7. When supporting local initiatives, candidates, and workplace decisions, how often do you think about the racial and economic consequences of those decisions? How have your past decisions hurt people of color? The country? You and your family?

8. What could you do today to counteract racism in your community? Workplace?

> When you allow racial disparity and institutional inequity to affect one part of the country, eventually it's coming back to get everyone.
>
> —Tim Wise, author and activist

PART 2

Abolish White Welfare and White Supremacy

PART 2 is critically foundational by providing the knowledge base underscoring and informing other parts of this book. It concentrates on understanding the history, policies, and societal infrastructure that create America's racialized caste system, which are essential to sustaining systemic white supremacy. It covers what you may not have learned in history class or while consuming mainstream media. It introduces the term *White Welfare*, which is linked to privilege, wealth gaps, and America's racist social construct of haves and have-nots.

People have been socialized to buy into racism or casually go along with it. Disrupting it requires debunking myths, countering whitewashing, and getting continual reminders to go against the mainstream current of what you've been conditioned to believe is normal, acceptable, reality, and equal opportunity.

Be open to surrendering to this transformational process. Trust and believe in what's explained. Reject any reflexive tendencies to make excuses or introduce comparisons to other marginalized groups (e.g., women, LGBTQ, overseas atrocities). The journey isn't about oppression porn and calculating who suffered more. It's about specific, ongoing harms connected to race. Measuring sticks are distractions, along with seeking credit for past improvements.

This section helps you learn to unlearn racism and engage in vital education to disrupt racism. Caring about people of color involves caring about the history, policies, and structures that form the scaffolding of their current condition. It will contain some hard truths about your social status and past choices but will help you develop empathy and humanize people of color.

Acknowledge All White People Benefit from Privilege and White Welfare

I'm speaking as a victim of this American system.
And I see America through the eyes of the victim.
I don't see any American dream; I see an American nightmare.

—*Malcolm X, civil rights activist*

RULE SUMMARY

White Welfare unfairly benefits *every* white person in America—rich and poor, homegrown and immigrant, liberal and conservative, learned and uneducated. White Welfare is racism's wealth redistribution mechanism. It's America's ultimate entitlement program for whites—securing financial gain, promoting white privilege, and fostering a mental state of feeling entitled to limitless winning.

White wealth, opportunity, and power are built on America's original sin of genocidal African enslavement for free labor and Native American extermination for free land. America's origin story—with these two central pillars of American capitalism—means whites win, while Americans of color suffer through a caste system unfairly transferring wealth and opportunity to whites.

Historical facts detailed below prove this Race Rule. This knowledge is foundational to understanding White Welfare—critical context that informs the rest of this book. It may be hard to swallow, but you need to hear hard truths to drive behavioral change and racism disruption.

There's psychological safety in whiteness. This is ultimate white freedom. Whites aren't required to consider their whiteness when living life.

Don't ask people of color to "get over" the past or "move on" when they and their families are still living with the negative effects of their ancestors' oppression and related present-day discrimination and systemic racism. These impact their career prospects, wealth, education, housing, access to healthcare, life expectancy, physical and mental health, treatment from law enforcement, and personal safety. Every aspect of their lives is related to the past.

More importantly, our historical legacy is America's present—disproportionately advantaging your life, well-being, bank account, career, neighborhood, and local schools 24/7/365.

Your full citizenship is at the expense of people of color enduring second-class status. Every advantage in your life is connected to and built on White Welfare.

Doing nothing about inherited wealth-and-power windfalls and leveraging heirlooms for modern-day opportunity hoarding through complacency is harmful. White Welfare without corrective action is infuriating and traumatizing, especially for descendants of America's Forced Founders (i.e., the Native Americans and enslaved Africans who built this country into a superpower). The status quo maintains contemporary white supremacy.

It's irrefutable that whites benefit from White Welfare. It's not about good or bad, if your family owned slaves, or if you just got here. The system is set up for you.

As a beneficiary, it's time you personally addressed White Welfare and the pillars of white supremacy. In your community, do this through reparations and policy change. In your daily life, do this by counteracting natural tendencies toward opportunity hoarding.

THE MYTH OF THE AMERICAN DREAM

Everything America is today exists on the rotten foundation of forced unpaid African labor and stolen Indigenous lands. This enabled unprecedented financial opportunities to flow exclusively to Europe's peasants flocking to America's shores (i.e., White Welfare). Anyone living in and coming to America today is an enriched beneficiary of modern-day societal structures built on Black and Native corpses. This historical looting is linked to discriminatory government policies and business practices unfairly promoting current white prosperity, wealth, power, and comfort (i.e., white supremacy). Without asking, you receive a perpetual handout and leg up.

White Welfare is marketed as the American Dream, bootstrapping, and meritocracy. That false storyline—that white achievement solely results from skill, grit, and hard work—is a lot easier to stomach than the truth and making amends. Even whites who feel flashes of white guilt for inheriting systemic advantage typically don't feel accountable enough to change anything impacting their lives, communities, neighborhoods, schools, and workplaces in transformational ways. The intoxicating taste of privilege is just too sweet no matter how anti-racist whites feel.

When you're dealt a better hand—relatively free from comparable hardship, suffering, and overpolicing—while others routinely face endless structural hurdles, racial trauma, and predator cops, people of color don't want to hear a single word about their need to move on from the past, how they need to work harder, nor how your granddaddy achieved everything on his own without help from anyone or anything. Your *entire* lifestyle and livelihood are predicated on White Welfare.

While you may have faced adversity, it's not the same as enduring the catastrophic consequences of centuries-long racism and institutional barriers thwarting you at every turn. Denialist comments demonstrate a lack of sensitivity, self-awareness, empathy, and accountability. They're grounded in white supremacy.

As the rapper Tupac Shakur said, "Somebody gotta explain why I ain't got shit!" White Welfare is why.

WHITE WELFARE

White Welfare is the society- and government-sanctioned policies and benefits that privilege whites by discriminatorily fast-tracking them to obtain jobs and land, secure control over resources, develop intergenerational wealth, gain political power, and elevate whites' general condition either directly or indirectly through systemically disadvantaging people of color and taking their sweat equity, land, and resources to unfairly advantage whites, artificially fabricate pro-white market conditions, and create a society of white-centered opportunity and unfair competition (i.e., white entitlement).

It leverages past oppression, present-day discrimination, and social norms for contemporary power-and-wealth windfalls of white privilege and supremacy built on unjust wealth redistribution and theft.

White Welfare is how America was built and still exists today. It's how white Americans got *everything* they have by synthetically skewing political power and resources in their favor *at the expense* of people of color. It's the unjust transfer and enrichment of wealth to whites often achieved through racial violence, genocide, intimidation, government policies, oppression, and systemic racism. These instruments are frequently accompanied by denialism, gaslighting, revisionist history, and modern-day adherence to the status quo.

Some examples include voting laws, hiring procedures, mortgage lending practices, eminent domain, property-tax-linked school funding, zoning laws, redlining, education policies, anti–affirmative action efforts, agribusiness, and the 1921 Tulsa race massacre.

Being white doesn't make you immune to difficulty. This is where many whites get twisted up—leaning into personal struggles; claiming reverse discrimination; believing in white victimhood; or clinging to tokenized success stories, like Barack Obama or Oprah Winfrey, as proof we're in a post-racial world. Lacking an evolved inclusive perspective manifests profound misunderstandings of white supremacy and prompts opposition to dismantling structural racism beyond performative, perfunctory steps.

This myopia buys into the pyramid scheme of white supremacy, that if you play along with white power structures and racial subjugation, you'll be rewarded with more than people of color.[1] When the promise of the American Dream seems elusive and life isn't financially easy, many whites get angry and feel powerless. They blame people of color, bundled with hostility that can turn violent.

What they fail to see is they're still quite privileged. But relative to some *other* whites, the white supremacy hustle that requires buy-in from average whites ain't working out as they hoped when they voted for the status quo and bought into America's racialized social contract. They feel cheated due to an underlying sense of entitlement anchored to white supremacy.

Having white privilege just means your struggles aren't *because* you're white. You still have a manufactured, race-based leg up. Cops aren't coming to kill you when you're jogging. You're more likely to get a home mortgage. Your home loan is likely to have a better interest rate compared to a Black person with a higher income and credit score. Your neighborhood school is probably better funded. Doctors listen more attentively when you speak. If you grew up qualifying for free lunch at school, your poverty was about class and not your whiteness. And you benefit from the psychological safety of white-centering—being able to speak, exist, and live life with more dignity and fewer dehumanizing attacks on your self-esteem.

Because you're white, you have more access to opportunity and less emotional stress. This is why the past being the past and bootstrapping comments are insulting. People of color get it that you don't want to think about racialized dynamics of wealth and achievement since the game is manipulated in your favor. That's the luxury of blissful, complicit indifference.

EVERYDAY WHITE PRIVILEGE

People of color live in a rigged societal system that needs to change. It's designed and operated *by* whites *for* whites. Whites built this environment, and it's whites' personal and collective responsibility to dismantle white supremacy, white privilege, systemic racism, and White Welfare.

Privilege is about the advantages you inherit as a birthright, continue to cash in throughout life, and grow to bequeath to heirs as your racialized legacy and estate.

Race is the reason why things play out differently.

Outcomes differ not just because you're white but also because others are *not* white. This can manifest itself in several ways:

- **Upward mobility**—Whites are more financially capable of sending their children to college, buying a house, and getting family support because of White Welfare. People of color typically can't rely on intergenerational wealth to become homeowners and college graduates, invest in business opportunities, and get help during financial emergencies.

- **Mediocrity and support structures**—Whites have the freedom to be mediocre while simultaneously believing their achievement is solely due to merit. When they're new or underperforming at work, they may get a pass or mentorship. There's a support structure fostering belonging on day one. Employees of color are routinely measured and tested for what they're doing and not doing—left on their own to figure things out under critical, watchful eyes whose default is to find the bad before supporting the good. They must outperform and be exceptional for a shot at promotions above mediocre whites.

Considering the lifelong impact on opportunities, would you choose to be born Black or white? Chances are you picked white. The road is easier. This validates the undeniable presence of white-centered, engineered, uncompetitive advantage.

White privilege is a byproduct of White Welfare. And White Welfare is a byproduct of white privilege. As they feed into each other, White Welfare becomes foundational to privilege.

HISTORICAL OVERVIEW— AMERICA'S WHITE WELFARE CASTE SYSTEM

To truly appreciate this Race Rule and the absurdity of denying White Welfare, we need to kick-start learning to unlearn with a tour down memory lane. Let's revisit America's legacy of Native American extermination and Black enslavement.

This American History 101 refresher is the unvarnished—not white-washed—version. It lays the groundwork for absorbing the truths behind this book's Race Rules and explores how and why the United States' existence is saturated in white supremacy and cosigned daily by its people to maintain White Welfare today. This knowledge is foundational to unlearning racism.

White America's economic growth and resources derive from theft from Blacks and peoples here before us—taken for whites-only giveaways and Manifest Destiny's westward expansion. Because of stolen lands and free labor, America was able to build a strong middle class and become the richest country in the world.

This still-thriving White Welfare caste system maintains the perpetual transference and redistribution of land, money, resources, and employment from people of color to whites. Being born with a discriminatory birthright to unscrupulous winning fosters an entitlement mindset allergic to dismantling racialized uncompetitive advantages. It triggers strong rejections of revisiting history that could prompt recalibration and uncomfortable introspection.

Nothing happens in isolation. All things are connected. History doesn't start when you wake up in the morning (see table 7.1).

Undeniably the most radical redistributive policies in US history, the Homestead Acts provided the descendants of peasants, convicts, Puritans, and freedom-seekers of Europe with unprecedented access to the American Dream. Supplementing the exponential national wealth made in the North and South from slavery, American progress has been a nonstop journey in whites taking from others. There's a systemic pattern of whites receiving government welfare as a foundational platform to build intergenerational wealth, coupled with falsely claiming whites didn't steal a leg up and that they supposedly achieved homeownership and accumulated assets through grit and merit. This myth enables whites to ignore receiving tremendous race-based government assistance to thrive.

Without a base upon which to generate wealth, Blacks and Native Americans never had a fair chance at overcoming the economic and psychological blight caused by slavery, Indigenous genocide, ethnocide, and federal policies. America's legacies of enslavement and extermination are lasting—along with land-looting other conquered communities. White

TABLE 7.1 What you may not have learned in history class

Native American extermination: *Implementing genocide for land theft*	African enslavement: *Engineering systemic racism for free labor*
Indian removal and ethnic cleansing—stealing land for white wealth creation • 1513—Europeans arrive on America's shores. From the late fifteenth century to 1900, we wiped out over 95 percent of the Indigenous population. Today, American Indians and Alaska Natives are less than 3 percent of the population.[2] • 1830—Indian Removal Act lays the foundation for the 5,043-mile-long Trail of Tears and the federal government's forced relocation of roughly 100,000 Indigenous peoples on foot to "Indian Territory," with an estimated 15,000 dying en route.[3] • 1924—Indian Citizenship Act is passed, granting Native Americans citizenship and the right to freely travel within the United States. • 1965—Pursuant to the Voting Rights Act of 1965, Indians finally gain the universal right to vote.	*Slave trade—creating intergenerational White Welfare* • 1526—Spaniards bring slaves to our shores, before the Dutch-English ship *White Lion* brought enslaved Africans plundered from a Portuguese slave ship to Virginia in 1619.[4] All thirteen original British colonies had slaves. • 1520s to 1860— Transatlantic slave trade was banned in the United States in 1808 (nearly 300 years after the first slaves arrived in the country), but New York–based slavers dominated the illegal slave trade. The *Clotilda* was the last known slave ship to arrive in the United States in 1860. Its last known survivor died in 1940. • Early 1500s to 1860—12.5 to 20 million Africans were snatched and shipped to the Americas. As many as 10 million Africans died along the Middle Passage. At least 463,000 slaves were shipped to what became the United States. By 1860, the United States. had nearly 4 million slaves.[5]

TABLE 7.1 *(continued)*

Native American extermination: *Implementing genocide for land theft*	African enslavement: *Engineering systemic racism for free labor*
• 1970—Forced sterilization of Native women is formally institutionalized and funded through federal law, resulting in sterilizing roughly 25 percent of Native women of childbearing age until this was stopped in the late 1970s.[6] • 2023—There are 574 federally recognized Native American and Alaska Native tribes and villages as of September 2023.[7] Not all tribes are federally recognized, excluding many Native communities from tribal sovereignty rights and governmental relationships with the United States. *Extermination for homesteaders— elevating the White Man through Manifest Destiny* • 1862—The Homestead Act of 1862 becomes one of the more impactful pieces of US legislation, leading to Western expansion and land ownership for white Americans. Roughly 1.6 million deeds in 30 states were granted, with 10 percent of US lands claimed and settled by Americans. The final land patent was granted in 1988.[8] Lands were taken and redistributed for white property ownership to build homes, start businesses, and accumulate intergenerational wealth.	• 1520s to 1865—Slavery was a Northern *and* Southern way of life and business. Laws protected returning escaped Northern-captured slaves to Southern enslavers, legitimized by the US Supreme Court in 1842. Massachusetts was the first British colony to legalize slavery in 1641, and Congress passed its first Fugitive Slave Act in 1793. • 1865—The last slaves in New Jersey and Delaware were freed, pursuant to the Thirteenth Amendment ending slavery nationwide. • 1520s to present—Slavery established a caste system enabling the US economy to flourish, with state-sanctioned Northern *and* Southern slavery used to build cities, infrastructure, and exclusive white wealth and upward mobility. This slavery-era caste system created today's American racialized caste system. *US Constitution—legalizing racism* • 1787—US Constitution supports increased Southern power by counting slaves as three-fifths of a person and establishing two senators per state regardless of population.

(continued)

TABLE 7.1 What you may not have learned in history class (*continued*)

Native American extermination: *Implementing genocide for land theft*	African enslavement: *Engineering systemic racism for free labor*
• 1862 to present—The government augmented homesteading policies to further enrich white citizenry. It built land-grant colleges to teach farming and engineering, provided county agents to improve expertise in agriculture, and provided low-interest loans to mechanize farms. Today, billions of dollars in federal subsidies go to predominantly white farmers annually. • 1863 to 1988—Congress gave hundreds of millions of acres of Indigenous lands to white settlers through the Homestead Act for coast-to-coast White Welfare to uplift whites, while refusing reparations for Black enslavement. • 1860s to late 1970s—To make room for white homesteaders building little houses on the prairie, Native Americans were violently displaced onto reservations, raped, kidnapped, enslaved, separated from children via boarding schools, forcibly converted to Christianity, banned from cultural practices, and exterminated. Genocide and land grabs had started by the early 1500s.	• Today—Roughly one-quarter of the US Senate represents 60 percent of the population.[9] White voters in low-population states have power over the country's majority in populous states, which is increasingly Black and brown. *Slavery, Reconstruction, and Jim Crow—engineering pervasive systemic racism* • 1810s to 1860 (pre–Civil War era)—Slaves represented 15 to 20 percent of total US wealth with enslaved people worth more than all the factories, stocks, bonds, and currency combined, with each male slave roughly twenty years old in the 1850s worth as much as $250K in today's dollars.[10] • 1865—Civil War ends nearly 340 years of chattel slavery, but prison labor strategically secures free Black labor through the Thirteenth Amendment, fueling chain gangs and prison industrial complex (i.e., modern-day slavery).

TABLE 7.1 (*continued*)

Native American extermination: *Implementing genocide for land theft*	African enslavement: *Engineering systemic racism for free labor*
• 1500s to present—Centuries of land dispossession resulted in Indigenous peoples losing upward of 99 percent of their lands. Today, the lands they were forcibly migrated to are more vulnerable to climate change and have fewer resources.[11] • 1962—President John F. Kennedy remarked that the Homestead Act was "probably the single greatest stimulus to national development ever enacted."[12] More accurately, it's one of the greatest American White Welfare policies to unjustly and disproportionality elevate whites and transfer wealth to them.	• 1865—Black Codes and the Jim Crow era begins and continues until roughly 1968. Jim Crow facilitated arbitrary incarceration and post–Civil War servitude through "convict leasing" of Blacks, which continues today in places like the cotton-production prison farms in Louisiana and Arkansas. • 1865 to 1877—Reconstruction lasted only 12 years, with rights and opportunities quickly reversed through Jim Crow laws, segregation, and ritualized domestic terrorism. • 1870s—Jim Crow laws are enacted to mandate segregation and discrimination and disenfranchise Black voters while increasing whites-only political power through poll taxes, literacy tests, and grandfather clauses.

(*continued*)

TABLE 7.1 What you may not have learned in history class (*continued*)

Native American extermination: *Implementing genocide for land theft*	African enslavement: *Engineering systemic racism for free labor*
Today, Indigenous peoples face discrimination and are hate-crime victims, and many live in abject poverty. Their intergenerational trauma, economic position, poor health outcomes, incarceration rates, and limited political power are a result of past malfeasance. Their current condition is directly linked to this devastating history of conquest achieved through land seizure, genocide, forced assimilation, ethnocide, psychological warfare, and the destruction of a way of life and culture. Since the arrival of European colonizers, Native populations have been decimated. Many tribes are extinct, and cultural legacies are lost forever. To build a country and wealth, you need land. White Americans stole land to become wealthy.	• 1865 to mid-1960s—Post–Civil War era is followed by 100 years of lynchings (premise for seizing Black-owned assets and quashing Black competition); Jim Crow; and discriminatory government-backed policies excluding Blacks from building wealth, with lasting economic impacts shaping today's standards of living and policy implementation. Today, people of color are disadvantaged with a diminished economic base, fewer opportunities, and less assets resulting from institutionalized racism implemented as slavery's legacy. To maintain White Welfare and wealth transfers, America foreclosed Black opportunity and access to capital by implementing segregation, ghettoization, and state-backed institutional discrimination continuing today. To quickly build a country and grow the economy, America pilfered free labor (i.e., wage theft through human, child, and sex trafficking).

TABLE 7.1 (continued)

Native American extermination: *Implementing genocide for land theft*	African enslavement: *Engineering systemic racism for free labor*
As Keri Leigh Merritt, scholar and historian, said, "The number of adult descendants of the original Homestead Act recipients living in the year 2000 was estimated to be around *46 million people*, about a *quarter of the US adult population*. If that many white Americans can trace their legacy of wealth and property ownership to a single entitlement programme, then the perpetuation of [Black] poverty must also be linked to national policy. Indeed, the Homestead Acts excluded [Blacks] not in letter, but in practice—a template that the government would propagate for the next century and a half."[13]	

Welfare is at the root of Black, Indigenous, aboriginal, and Chicano poverty, low wealth, and inferior access to quality housing, education, and jobs.

These were just the preliminary pieces of America's discriminatory oppression quilt sewn into the fabric of countless policies giving whites freebies and entitlement to wealth-generating programs funded with tax dollars. These taxes were also paid by Black and brown people and represent additional transferences of wealth—forcing people of color to pay for programs largely excluding them and funding their own oppression.

This now brings us to the government's 20th-century White Welfare. It too was a breeding ground for ensuring strategic, inequitable playing fields—white affirmative action elevating the advantaged, dominant group. Discriminatory policies attacked every foundational component of life success, driving deeper racial opportunity gaps and keeping white supremacy contemporary.

THE NEW DEAL: REDLINING WHITE SUBURBAN AMERICAN DREAMS AND BLACK GHETTOS

The New Deal was really a White Deal. It supported white Americans while intentionally and strategically leaving people of color behind. Its policies were structured to promote discrimination and further expand racial wealth and opportunity gaps. From the New Deal's design and implementation, its housing policies were not race neutral but explicitly racist. Here are some examples:

- As the Great Depression in the 1930s drove homesteaders into bread-lines, President Franklin D. Roosevelt's New Deal rescued white Americans through low-interest, government-backed home mortgage refinancing for indebted, disproportionately white borrowers.
- The government created our modern-day public housing system, designed to increase and segregate housing. It provided white families housing in new suburban communities and pushed people of color into urban housing projects—promoting white flight and suburbanization.
- The federal government advanced segregation through redlining and refusing to insure mortgages in Black neighborhoods. It subsidized building whites-only suburban subdivisions to depopulate cities and offered access to loans to build wealth. This created America's ghettos.
- Redlining created color-coded racialized human topography zones concentrating people of color and excluding them from homeown-ership programs. These zones were reinforced by restrictive covenants making it illegal to live or own property in certain areas. The government's refusal to insure mortgages meant banks deemed communities of color as lending and investment risks.
- Large demarcated geographic areas were blighted by disinvestment, further impoverishing communities of color in concentrated poverty zones. Redlining wasn't outlawed until the 1960s and 1970s. But redlining exists today through discriminatory banking and appraisal practices.

Roosevelt's mortgage bailout was one of the most impactful New Deal policies with present-day ramifications on equality—with a racially disparate impact on shaping neighborhoods and divergent wealth outcomes. It rescued white homeowners while foreclosing access to opportunity for people of color. In creating white suburbs and ghettos for Black and brown communities, the federal government's mortgage-crisis package fueled today's wealth gaps, affecting intergenerational wealth, access to quality education, and college and retirement affordability.

THE G.I. BILL—MIDDLE-CLASS BOOM FOR WHITES AND POVERTY BUST FOR BLACKS

Amplifying the racist implementation and impact of the New Deal, the G.I. Bill created lasting repercussions for white America and people of color. Similarly, the implementation of its programs were discriminatory against Black veterans, further driving a wealth wedge between Black and white Americans. Here are some examples:

- The 1944 G.I. Bill of Rights put higher education, job training, homeownership, and business financing within reach for millions of veterans. But its promises were an illusion for Blacks.
- The government backed low-cost and low-interest loans for homes, farms, and businesses—shaping intergenerational socioeconomic, political, suburban, urban, and rural landscapes.
- The G.I. Bill drove postwar prosperity and an economic boom. While it promoted suburban capital investment and development, communities of color were increasingly blighted through divestiture and blocked from home loans and the right to move due to legal segregation, restrictive covenants, and redlining.
- In providing the working class unprecedented tuition for college and vocational school, it's considered one of the most significant modern developments in education history.
- Veterans of color were nearly shut out of educational benefits due to racist implementation and discrimination, along with related increased earning potential and lifelong career opportunities.
- Considered one of the most successful government programs in US history, the G.I. Bill helped build America's white middle class and their accumulated wealth in skilled jobs while strategically leaving behind veterans of color, thus providing epic intergenerational White Welfare.
- Many believe there was no greater postwar instrument for widening an already large wealth gap than the G.I. Bill, as employment, college admissions, and wealth surged for whites.

By the mid-1950s, nearly 4.3 million home loans worth $33 billion were issued through the G.I. Bill (i.e., 20 percent of postwar home purchases).[14]

From 1934 to 1968, 98 percent of *all* government-backed home loans were given to white families.[15] Thus, Blacks gained no home equity even though ownership *was* affordable for Blacks back then *if* allowed government mortgages.

The G.I. Bill insured roughly 67,000 mortgages in New York and northern New Jersey, while *less than one hundred* were issued to non-whites due to the government's and banks' racist policies.[16]

By the 1990s, veterans who took advantage of the educational subsidy earned on average $10,000 to $15,000 more annually than those who didn't.[17]

Today, the United States has huge racial wealth gaps, with the median income in 2021 at $77,999 for white households and $48,297 for Blacks, according to the US Census.[18]

CONSEQUENCES OF WHITE WELFARE

Collectively what these racist government policies—the New Deal and the G.I. Bill—meant for *all* Blacks regardless of military service is they couldn't buy a home or start a business. They couldn't relocate out of redlined neighborhoods starved of affordable seed capital. Neighborhoods became impoverished by design.

Once white flight to the suburbs created whites-only enclaves, Blacks were blamed for the decline of areas when they had few affordable options and often higher housing costs. They faced predatory, price-gouging landlords, higher home prices due to *blockbusting*, exploitative homeownership through *contract buying*, and the inability to get a mortgage at a fair price. This further decimated the property tax base funding schools, creating a downward spiral of increasingly impoverished schools and substandard public services. Today's ghettos were created by the government and financial institutions and cosigned by white citizens thriving on White Welfare— generating a financial windfall still benefiting *all* whites today.

As figure 7.1 shows, it's nearly impossible for Blacks to catch up. It would take over two hundred years for Black families to attain the *same* wealth white families have *today*.[19]

By the time laws were passed in the 1960s and 1970s allowing Blacks to buy homes anywhere and get government-backed loans, homes were

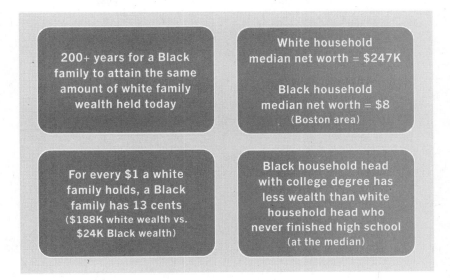

FIGURE 7.1. Data and statistics—wealth gaps

no longer affordable to families of color. With the wealth created through New Deal programs and the G.I. Bill, white families sent their children to college with their home equities and were able to care for elderly parents. Today, whites disproportionately have higher home values, better-funded schools, and de facto segregated communities that attract more investment. The increased desirability further fuels local economies, property values, and wealth.

Fifty years after laws banned discriminatory lending, 2018 data show Black and Latino households are still denied conventional mortgages at rates significantly higher than whites. This modern-day redlining persists even when controlling for income, loan amount, and neighborhood.[20] Borrowers of color pay more than whites for loans regardless of wealth or credit score and are more often victims of predatory banking practices regardless of income.[21]

Race is *the* determining factor. Given the domino effect of institutionalizing White Welfare and discrimination in the housing market, past legal changes barely make a difference. Today, the Black-white homeownership gap is wider than during the Jim Crow era.[22]

WHITE WELFARE INTERGENERATIONAL WEALTH REALITY CHECK

Exactly where and how can people of color accumulate intergenerational wealth in this engineered white supremacist system?

This isn't about if people of color work hard enough. It's about the past controlling the present with whites winning and non-whites losing.

Think about this when you walk into your home and down your streets, send your kid off to school, get financing, and discuss meritocracies.

Are you starting to see why Blacks "ain't got shit"?

History and data show *no white person* in America is a real bootstrapper. Nearly every aspect of American society has been and is currently impacted by legacies of racism and modern-day structural and institutional racism advancing White Welfare—land grants, housing, farming, banking, education, healthcare, you name it.

Starting with our birth defect of enslavement and extermination, much of America's wealth has been snatched by putting a boot on the necks of Black and brown people. Continually tipping the scale away from equality—from land grabs and free labor through Jim Crow, the New Deal, the G.I. Bill, the civil rights movement, farming policies, government bailouts, tax policies, and stimulus packages all the way to today.

When government programs are developed to assist Americans, those programs have either uplifted whites at the exclusion of people of color or been strategically managed to skew benefits to whites. When these policies leave cracks that could diminish white privilege, white supremacy intercedes to ensure racism plays a pivotal role in government oversight and regulations or through the private sector in implementing company practices. This is White Welfare at work, fueling a white superiority mindset.

GENERATIONAL WEALTH BEQUEATHS UNFAIR ADVANTAGE TO WHITES

White Welfare enables whites to be born into and receive generations of privilege, wealth, comfort, and opportunity enabling them to buy homes, bequeath property, bestow access, pay for better educations, fund wealth-expanding investments, secure employment, launch businesses, grow companies, and build intergenerational family empires—unburdened by the shackles of structural subjugation and psychological warfare.

Society's engineered and structural uncompetitive advantage gives whites and some new Americans a real chance at the illusive American Dream. This has created a warped view that their achievement is linked to a free market meritocracy and has been wholly earned by their own efforts and qualifications.

Any whites claiming they and their family never got a handout in America and was a bootstrapper is opting for willful denial. Any immigrant claiming no one handed them anything while they followed the yellow brick road to opportunity—an access road paved on Native lands and built by Black bodies before their arrival—is being conveniently dishonest.

American history has strong factual receipts to prove otherwise.

Yes, you work hard for what you have. But all your life achievements and assets are enhanced *because* you're white. You're living on White Welfare.

This historical overview is necessary for learning to unlearn. The country's present is a continuation of a white supremacist origin story. Failing to understand factual US history as it relates to people of color and your own achievement means you can never dismantle racism and get closer to understanding perspectives and experiences of color. Nor will you be equipped to fully appreciate this book's Race Rules and drive solutions as a Racism Disruptor.

If you do nothing to tackle White Welfare, you're complicit in advancing the racial status quo. If you proactively combat power structures in your community, workplace, and family, then you're walking toward anti-racism and racism disruption. And if you're actively or passively supporting white supremacy in your actions and choices (e.g., at the ballot box, through the workplace or governmental policies you support, to whom you consistently give business and job opportunities, and through the words coming out of your mouth), then you're supporting the same end goal as the Ku Klux Klansman. You're both cutting down Black and brown competition and advancement for your selfish self-interests.

Frankly, what's more dangerous than the neo-Klansman is the status quo, complicit collaborator. This Trojan horse *thinks* they're not racist, but they actually are racist through elective inaction. If this is you—the complacent—then you're inflicting far more widespread racist damage. You're reinforcing our current system and granting political power to perpetuate white supremacy and White Welfare.

WHAT NOT TO SAY—
AVOID TRIGGERING WHITE WELFARE PAIN

Avoid conjuring up and amplifying the baggage of historical racial pain. It's offensive. You will be viewed as an ignorant person who doesn't get it, just doesn't care, or is deeply committed to maintaining white supremacy. Here are some examples of what not to say:

- **Post-racial hypnotism**—People who say "Let's move on" are really saying let's move on so *they* can do it again without taking responsibility and feeling uncomfortable. They're asking, "Can we just forget this happened so I can enjoy my privilege in peace?" It's a strategy asking for no accountability.
- **"It wasn't me" or "fresh off the boat" deflectors**—Claiming you had no personal role in slavery, Indigenous genocide, or events or policies from over one hundred years ago is irrelevant. You're here now living off of the legacy. Plus, if you're not doing anything to address the past baked into our present, then you're not a part of the solution but the problem.
- **Poor white people**—Poor whites have suffered too. But their struggles are about classism, not racism. Adversity faced because of racism is nearly impossible to overcome without radical social and

institutional change. *White privilege doesn't mean your life hasn't been hard. It just means it hasn't been hard because you're white.*[23]

"Move on" and "I didn't create this system" mindsets are corrosive and invalidating. They lay the foundation to strategically thwart efforts to correct the past as being "reverse discrimination," which doesn't exist when considering who has the institutional and societal power as a group.

A BETTER APPROACH

Instead of making "Get over it" or "It's not my fault" statements, acknowledge you're the beneficiary of *past and present* White Welfare. Accepting the existence of White Welfare in your life is critical to understanding the journey and struggles of people of color. It's hard to identify with people of color if you're blind to how the past guides your and their present condition.

You could say, "I understand it doesn't matter that my ancestors weren't here during slavery and Indigenous genocide. My family piggybacked on their misfortune. I have wealth and opportunities that people of color don't have because of this legacy and discrimination today."

The important next step is to do something about this. Knowing White Welfare helps you and harms others isn't enough. To be a Racism Disruptor, you need to act.

SELF-REFLECTIVE QUESTIONS

If the refresher on American history infused with an intentional layer of critical race theory to cover what your high school teacher and textbooks strategically glossed over does little to sway you, then ponder these questions to expand your perspective:

1. How has the upside of America's origin story benefited you and your family (i.e., enslavement and extermination)?
2. How have government policies like the Homestead Acts, New Deal, and G.I. Bill helped you?
3. How did policies during the COVID-19 pandemic or 2008 credit crisis bailout help you? Were they discriminatorily implemented?

4. How does your family's current wealth directly result from being white?

5. What has America specifically done to atone for or redress slavery and taking Native lands? How has your current job, community, and the home you live in been impacted by slavery and conquering Native Americans? What about taking land from Mexico, Native Hawaiians, Alaska Natives, Puerto Ricans, or Guamanians?

6. What have you personally done to balance benefiting from the upside of oppression at the expense of others? If nothing, then why is it appropriate to think others should "move on"?

7. If you think people of color should "get over the past," then *how*? What's your solution for how they should do this? How can they get over something so systemic and pervasive?

8. Would you want anyone to ask you to "move on" if you, your people, or your ancestors experienced genocide and still live through the aftermath?

9. If Blacks and Native Americans are supposed to get over their past, then why is it okay for whites to cling to their Confederate past and celebrate slavery-sympathizing ancestors?

10. Do we ask Jews to get over the Holocaust? Is that appropriate?

WHAT TO DO ABOUT WHITE WELFARE
AND DISRUPTING RACISM

Take these steps to learn about and transition to becoming a Racism Disruptor who takes direct aim at addressing America's original sin and ongoing systemic racism. This guidance addresses three levels of proactive action and will help you claim ownership of your personal responsibility to dismantle White Welfare:

1. **Individual level**—Recognize White Welfare exists and identify how it impacts your life. Learn more American history to understand how marginalized groups are impacted by land grabs and exploitation to build the country. Learn about current government policies and workplace practices with racially disparate outcomes. Open doors for people of color. For example, you could start

locally. Learn about on whose Indigenous land your home sits, what happened to those peoples, how slavery touched your community, what the racial wealth gaps in your town are, and how local policies widen these gaps. When you have an opportunity to hire someone or purchase products, be intentional and proactively find opportunities to support and hire businesses and people of color. Avoid opportunity hoarding.

2. **Community level**—Identify opportunities to create equitable access to housing, education, and jobs in your community and through your workplace. Seek to disrupt policies with discriminatory impact, including with hiring and business practices where you work. For example, learn about pending zoning or city planning measures, proposed changes to your school district, affordable housing projects, or if your community is banning books. Push for policies that won't expand racial wealth gaps but create opportunities for people of color, even when policy solutions directly impact your neighborhood. At work, advocate for improved diversity hiring and retention efforts.

3. **Societal level**—Reparations. Reparations. Reparations. This is the only pathway to enable people of color to catch up and close massive wealth gaps. Proactively support reparations. Call your elected officials advocating for federal legislation on reparations. Push for reparations commissions in your town, county, and state. Demand solutions beyond studies. And when reparations are proposed, vote for cash payments since reparations compensate for past harms (including wage theft with slavery). Policies shouldn't be paternalistic.

> There is a difference between remembrance of history and reverence of it.
>
> —Mitch Landrieu, former mayor of New Orleans

Oppose White Supremacy—Voting Restrictions Are Racist

I'm sick and tired of being sick and tired.

—*Fannie Lou Hamer, voting and civil rights activist*

RULE SUMMARY

Any attempt to suppress the vote and encourage Jim Crow 2.0 is white supremacy—the modern-day cousin to old-school Jim Crow. Any person, policy, or entity supporting restrictions to voting access is engaging in racism. This is especially true if choices disproportionately impact voters of color.

With our democracy at risk, you need to actively fight the dangerous expansion of disenfranchising voters of color. Now isn't the time to sit on the sidelines.

You either are on the side of democracy or stand on the wrong side of history against equality. Either you believe in freedom or you don't. There is *no* gray area when it comes to America's most sacred right of its citizenry—the right to vote.

Proactively ensuring universal access to voting is one of *the most important actions* you can take to dismantle white supremacist power structures and be a Racism Disruptor.

Turning a blind eye to voting restrictions actively promotes an American society where whites predominantly control society in a diversifying nation. Recognizing that practices are discriminatory isn't enough. You need to take action through (1) personal choices, (2) who you vote for and donate to, (3) not remaining silent when companies fund campaigns of harmful politicians, and (4) vocal activism and lobbying.

Avoid de facto participation in racial subjugation and supporting a caste system.

Voter suppression is a clever tool to hold all the power for whites, which is textbook institutional and systemic racism. If you control who's in government, then you can engineer who are the real beneficiaries of that government. You can block change. As a foundational pillar, manipulating voting is at the heart of building and reinforcing White Welfare.

Equal participation in the political process is a fundamental tenet of a functioning democracy. People of color and low-income Americans have a right to freely participate in our system of government. It's what full citizenship means.

Voter restriction has been at the epicenter of our democracy for centuries. It's never fully gone away. It's merely transitioned to covert iterations and is on the rise. To combat and disrupt it, you need to understand history. Background and context are critical to seeing today's sinister tactics at play to marginalize voters of color.

Contemporary policies serve one strategic purpose—to keep non-whites away from voting polls to diminish their power and silence their voices.

Too much of America's voting system is intentionally racist. Election practices that are entrenched in white supremacy weren't rendered obsolete when Jim Crow was abolished in the 1960s. Modern voter suppression efforts subversively advance strategies that appear race-neutral on their face but have disparate impact to discriminate in their application and effect.

Since the passage of the Voting Rights Act of 1965 (VRA), we've been on a steady path of neutralizing the VRA's power. The 2020 voter suppression tactics mimic bigoted measures employed through the mid-1960s to stop Blacks from voting during the Jim Crow era. Reforms seek voter disenfranchisement. What we're experiencing today is Jim Crow 2.0—a repeat of the Southern strategy electoral campaign scheme to increase white political support by appealing to anti-Black racism.

There is *only one* acceptable pathway forward. To secure our democracy, there must be an unequivocal rebuke of these policies and their masterminds. We must take proactive steps to chase these people out of office and dismantle their prejudicial policies. We must rebuild our voting system to ensure equal and unfettered access to voting.

MODERN-DAY VOTER SUPPRESSION AND JIM CROW 2.0 RESURGENCE TIMELINE

Since the 1700s, America's voting history is a story of intentional disenfranchisement and exclusion, not quite a true representational democracy of one person, one vote. It's a journey of institutionalizing and codifying white power and supremacy. Today, blocking universal voter access is expanding.

For a longer overview of America's voter suppression timeline starting from the 1700s, visit FatimahGilliam.com/RaceRulesDownloads. The following are the main milestones of modern-day voter suppression:

- **2000s**—There is a significant resurgence in voter suppression. States implement ballot-box barriers with strict voter identification laws, cut voting times, restrict registration, and purge voter rolls.
- **2006**—President George W. Bush signs a twenty-five-year extension and reauthorization of the Voting Rights Act, strategically overcoming strong opposition through extensive public support from major corporations and business groups expressing a need for the law's extension.
- **2013**—A US Supreme Court landmark case weakens voting rights. *Shelby County v. Holder* declares a clause in the VRA unconstitutional, enabling states and local governments to change voting laws and practices without federal preclearance approval enacted to limit racist voter suppression. This immediately sparks widespread voter suppression to lower turnout for voters of color (e.g., closing polling places, making cuts to early voting, purging voter rolls, and imposing strict voter ID laws).
- **2021**—The US Supreme Court further weakens the VRA by making it more difficult to challenge discriminatory voting laws, which effectively cripples legal challenges to laws with disparate impact on voters of color and renders the law on life support (*Brnovich v. Democratic National Committee*). This decision makes congressional action through new legislation one of the sole remaining pathways to counter aggressive tactics to suppress votes and protect universal suffrage rights.
- **2021**—Georgia passes a throwback Jim Crow voter suppression law, prompting nationwide backlash. An assault on democracy, the law limits absentee voting, imposes strict voter ID requirements, scales back ballot drop boxes, bans mobile voting centers, makes extending voting hours burdensome, empowers the legislature to suspend local election officials (facilitating manipulation of election results), and criminalizes giving food or water to voters in strategically created long lines.
- **2021**—Legislatures in forty-eight states introduce 389 bills with restrictive provisions to limit voting rights, and 28 are signed into law by mid-June.[1]

- **2023**—In January, state legislators in thirty-two states introduce or pre-file 150 restrictive voting bills and 27 election interference bills, which is an increase in the number of restrictive bills introduced in the same timeframe in 2021 and 2022. On top of typical efforts to require voter IDs and restrict absentee ballots, bills include proposed laws to allow partisan actors to overturn election results, criminalization for routine election activities and human error, and mandated, less accurate hand counts.[2]

Efforts to disenfranchise voters are exploding, not slowing. Without federal intervention and an updated Voting Rights Act to supersede the impact of *Shelby* and *Brnovich*, America's Jim Crow 2.0 will suppress votes of people of color and younger, urban, elderly, and disabled Americans. Citizens are being stripped of their freedoms.

When you can't win on the issues and your policy platform isn't compelling to a multiracial society, you change the rules to cheat at the ballot box.

As Kimberlé Crenshaw, legal scholar and creator of the term *intersectionality* said, "Some of the worst racist tragedies in history have been perfectly legal."

JIM CROW IN NEW CLOTHES

Voting is a right, not a privilege, and is enshrined in the US Constitution. When you don't have easy and universal access to voting, you don't have freedom for all but instead freedom for the privileged and powerful.

Unfortunately, many don't care about racist voting laws since they think the system works for them. It reinforces their power as a white person. They prefer election guidelines that disenfranchise voters of color and support white supremacy. This desire to unfairly maintain power is racist.

Understanding how voter suppression shows up today (see table 8.1) will help you identify and disrupt it in your community and vote against it and its supporters.

TABLE 8.1 Discriminatory voter-suppression tactics

Jim Crow era	Jim Crow 2.0
Poll taxes Required payment of voting tax for the right to vote, precluding poor Blacks and whites from voting or charging Blacks a higher tax.	**Government-issued IDs** Require driver's licenses or photo IDs to vote, which is tantamount to poll taxes, especially when 29 million citizens lack ID (i.e., 12 percent of voting-age citizens) and getting ID is costly.[3] **Result:** De facto poll taxes—people are forced to pay for their right to vote. A solution in search of a problem—voter fraud is *not* a real thing.
Literacy tests and civic exams with obscure trivia Gave illiterate and literate Blacks complex legal documents to read while enabling uneducated whites access to voting; asked little-known facts and trivia in mandatory tests for Blacks, like the number of windows in the White House.	**Confusing absentee ballot rules to void ballots on technicalities** Impose intentionally complicated rules requiring careful reading of directions with increased complexity to disproportionately impact voters of color, new and less-educated voters, and voters with low literacy skills, with ballots rejected without notice or opportunity to cure (e.g., voter wrote name in cursive instead of printing name; submitted a "naked ballot" by forgetting to place absentee ballot in additional secrecy envelope). **Result:** De facto literacy tests with unnecessary hurdles.

TABLE 8.1 (*continued*)

Jim Crow era	Jim Crow 2.0

Voter purges
   White officials purged voter rolls, removing names so Blacks' names wouldn't be on registered voter lists on election day.
	Voter purges
	   Used to disproportionately remove names of Black and Latino voters from voter rolls—often without notice. By 2019, at least 17 million were removed from voter rolls since 2016; in jurisdictions previously subject to VRA "preclearance" before the *Shelby* case, 2016 to 2018 saw a purge rate 40 percent higher than places previously not covered by Section 5 of the VRA.[4]
	   Result: Fewer eligible voters able to vote. One person, no vote.

Former prisoners
   Prohibited former prisoners from voting—Blacks were often arrested on trumped-up charges for minor offenses to keep them from voting, along with forcing Blacks on chain gangs as unpaid farm, factory, and mining labor.
	Former felons
	   Many states prohibit former felons from voting (including after voters pass supportive ballot measures), which predominantly impacts people of color given structural racism in criminal justice system and racial profiling with police practices. This impacted an estimated 4.6 million people in 2022 (i.e., 2 percent of voting-age Americans).[5]
	   Result: De facto poll tax—felons are required to pay court fees and fines to reinstate suffrage rights (backdoor voting rights cancellation).

(*continued*)

TABLE 8.1 Discriminatory voter-suppression tactics (*continued*)

Jim Crow era	Jim Crow 2.0
Jelly bean test and similar ridiculous hurdles Required Blacks to guess the number of jelly beans in a jar to gain access to voting.	**Criminalization of voter support** Make it a crime to give nourishment like food and water to those waiting to vote in hours-long lines (in Georgia). **Result:** Voters are intimidated, which deters voter turnout.
All-white primaries and practical voting barriers <ul><li>Precluded Blacks from voting in what were the most important elections (i.e., primary elections) given how Southern races were effectively decided in primaries before the general election.</li><li>Put up roadblocks and physically blocked the ability to enter polls.</li><li>Closed voter registration sites to Blacks at random times to prohibit voter registration.</li><li>Accompanied Blacks into voting booths to make sure votes were cast "properly."</li><li>Allowed Blacks to vote but required voting for a specific political party.</li><li>Stacked local, state, and federal courts with white supremacist judges to deny legal challenges seeking to enforce voting rights.</li></ul>	**Nefarious logistical and practical voting barriers** <ul><li>Dismantle postal service infrastructure and slow down mail so absentee ballots or voter registrations miss deadlines, targeting areas with high populations and people of color, all with the goal to stop counting actual votes.</li><li>Engineer long lines for voters of color and short lines for whites (e.g., closing polling locations in Black areas while opening polling sites in white communities with less people).</li><li>Shorten the number of days to request absentee ballots.</li><li>Deprive election officials in communities of color of resources and underfunding them.</li></ul>**Result:** Create and expand systemic voting barriers. Policies make it harder for communities of color to vote while supporting easy white voter access, which unfairly favors white voter turnout.

TABLE 8.1 (*continued*)

Jim Crow era	Jim Crow 2.0

Gerrymandering and congressional redistricting
  Arranged and manipulated election districts to give whites unfair advantages—diluting the voting power of people of color, rigging the system to keep white incumbents in office, and limiting the ability of people of color to challenge racist laws given their lack of power and recourse.
	Gerrymandering and congressional redistricting
	  Still an effective form of voter suppression—marginalize Black and brown votes, used to dilute votes or hyperconcentrate votes by diluting them elsewhere into a handful of districts. This was further amplified by changes to the 2020 US Census process prematurely ending completion deadlines and adding citizenship questions to deter responses and dilute political power in Congress of people of color.
	  Result: Steal legislative seats, political power, and federal appropriation dollars. Race-based gerrymandering unfairly skews representation toward whites, and census undercounting redirects federal fund allocations and programming dollars away from people of color (i.e., White Welfare).

HIDDEN AGENDA OF "NEUTRAL ON ITS FACE"

This is where self-actualized white supremacists suck you in, by dangling the argument that the rules apply to everyone regardless of race. We all have the same voter identification rule and registration deadline. Each of us must trek to the polls or mail our ballot. The paperwork says we all must sign the absentee envelope and then place the enclosed ballot in another envelope. That's what the rules say. They're all the same for everyone, right? No!

Race-neutral policies seek to appear benign and written for everyone, yet they miraculously disproportionately apply to people of color. The neutral-on-its-face rationale falls apart when you consider the following:

- The rules aren't always applied uniformly from county to county with racist officials subjectively clamping down on voting districts of color while giving leeway in white areas.
- Polling sites and ballot drop boxes have been strategically removed to disenfranchise voters of color and engineer long voting lines in those neighborhoods.
- Election officials have removed countless names from voter lists after people properly registered to vote, often targeting—well, we know who they targeted.
- Studies keep showing us these regulations disenfranchise marginalized communities, making it harder for them to vote.
- Poor people who are disproportionately voters of color, elderly, less educated, young, and disabled have a harder time paying for and obtaining identification cards, have less flexibility to take off time from work to vote, and have fewer affordable transportation options to travel to voting sites and identification-issuing agencies.

The Jim Crow 2.0 game is clever. Giving these rules the *appearance* of being fair—that's part of the plan. Don't be fooled by "neutral" policies shrouded in bigotry. They won't say, "Hey! Navajo citizens, you can't vote." That's a get-tossed-by-the-court-before-the-judge-even-raises-the-gavel rookie move. Instead, they conceal countermoves and regulatory impact in words that look neutral and universal but have an intentional discriminatory impact when implemented. For example, North Dakota prohibited post office box addresses for absentee ballots even though state officials know many Native Americans living on reservations don't always have traditional street addresses to easily receive mail at residences.

SELF-REFLECTIVE QUESTIONS

Ask yourself these three questions:

1. Should we keep laws that are more harmful to specific races of people?

2. Does it matter if the rule's written text appears fair and universal but doesn't work that way in real life?

3. If the rule doesn't alter your life but makes voting more difficult for someone else, is that okay?

VOTER FRAUD AND VOTER ID—
SOLUTION SEARCHING FOR A PROBLEM

Some argue that we need to revise regulations to limit voter fraud—claiming the ballot boxes are rampant with hordes of people impersonating others to cast more than one vote or to vote in multiple jurisdictions. Research shows there is virtually no voter fraud in America. Equally important, studies show when voter identification requirements are added, it makes it harder for people to vote—especially people of color, the elderly, the disabled, younger voters, the poor, and non-English speakers.

Deciding to strengthen identity verification requirements is a conscious decision to disenfranchise and limit the suffrage rights of the most vulnerable and least powerful citizens. It's a deliberate choice to support white-centric outcomes.

VOTER FRAUD DOESN'T EXIST

The Brennan Center for Justice at New York University School of Law found voter fraud incident rates of 0.0003 to 0.0025 percent, and most reported incidents of voter fraud actually traceable to other sources, like clerical errors or bad data matching practices—concluding an American is more likely to be struck by lightning than impersonate another voter at the polls.[6]

Five states have mail-in voting as the primary voting method (i.e., Colorado, Hawaii, Oregon, Utah, and Washington). Since 2000, over 250 million votes have been cast by mail, and in 2018, over 31 million people voted by mail (i.e., 25.8 percent of election participants).[7]

Virtually none of the states whose elections are primarily conducted by mail had voter fraud. Oregon sent out over 100 million mail-in ballots since 2000 and documented only about a dozen confirmed fraud incidents—0.00001 percent of votes cast.[8]

SELF-REFLECTIVE QUESTIONS

Having looked at the numbers that clearly show virtually no one is sneaking into the ballot booth, if you still think we need stricter identification laws, ask yourself these questions:

1. Why do you *really* want others to have IDs?
2. What's in it for *you?*
3. How much is *race* playing into your decision?

If the facts and data don't change your thinking, you're leaning into racism.

ELECTION INTEGRITY—ADDING SECURITY TO A SECURE SYSTEM AND THE BIG LIE

Supporters of new voting regulations say these bills are needed to improve public confidence in election results. This implies we have problems like untrustworthy voting equipment, secret ballots, voter fraud, corruption, vote-rigging, and other malpractices causing flawed counts. America doesn't have this problem. The issue we have is not letting everyone who wants to vote vote and placing burdensome obstacles in voters' path. Jim Crow on steroids is America's *true* election integrity issue.

The 2020 election results were accurate, despite false claims to the contrary (i.e., the "Big Lie"). Biden won. The other guy lost. That should have been the end of the story.

**If there's widespread voter fraud, why aren't votes for senators, mayors, and governors on the *same* ballot questioned?
Why is just the presidential line item for a Democrat problematic?**

What's most notable about the Big Lie is that the votes where there was alleged fraud and rigging are mysteriously localized in swing states. Interesting. Is it a coincidence all the supposed shadiness is in districts where people of color live? Why weren't there Big Lie lawsuits in the states where Biden decisively lost and 90 percent of the population is white, like Iowa?[9] Because the fraudsters must be those genetically criminal Blacks and Latinos in places like Atlanta and Phoenix—you know, where President 45 didn't have a shot at winning or lost by a large enough margin for it to be a decisive defeat.

The undercurrent is that people of color are untrustworthy, lie, cheat, steal, and are otherwise incapable of casting legitimate votes. They're incompetent and undeserving of the right to vote. What all these "darkies" and "little brown ones" need is an overseer to make sure they don't break the law, to do what they're told as the master race holds their hand through the voting process.

The verbiage about election integrity is code talk for white supremacist ideologies and strategies. These euphemisms are anchored in the belief that people of color are a threat to a white zero-sum racial political game. And the way to maintain power is to nullify the political potential of Black and brown voices. Hence, we get Birth of a No-Black-or-Brown-Vote Nation.

SELF-REFLECTIVE QUESTIONS

When it's irrefutable that our election counts are accurate, ask yourself these questions:

1. Why design voting policy around securing the already-secure system when it's a pretext to disenfranchise marginalized groups?
2. Is it wise to follow the election reform advice of politicians waging a coordinated attack on voting rights?
3. When officials are clearly targeting people of color, do you want to associate yourself with those politicians and their policies? What does it say about you?

Disrupting Jim Crow 2.0 is one of the most singularly important anti-racist actions you can take in your community to oppose white supremacy and to support people of color. There's no neutrality. Either you support *everyone's* right to vote or you don't.

In thinking of voter reforms and suppression, why join the Jim Crow Caucus? Even if you didn't think it's advancing white supremacy before, after reading this chapter and asking yourself the questions above, now you should know better. You've been educated on how and why these voting rules are racist, including that their proponents and campaign funders oppose freedom. It should be clear you shouldn't actively support these prejudicial laws, nor should you quietly endorse them through nonaction since the outcome is the same. The stakes are too high when democracy is on the line.

If you still approve of these restrictive voting laws knowing they're racist, then it's hard for many people of color not to conclude you're a self-aware white supremacist dangerously close to playing footsie with white nationalists—and your loungewear comfort clothing at home is a white hood and robe.

> A man without a vote is a man without protection.
>
> —President Lyndon Baines Johnson

Never Say or Tolerate the N-Word!

Race Rule #9 applies to all derogatory and pejorative equivalents for other races, ethnicities, and groups of people.

This rule is equally important when hearing offensive terms. Tolerating hate speech is an act of complicity. For a chart demonstrating the application of the Bedrock Race Rule for deciding to speak up when you hear the N-word, go to table 1.1 in the Bedrock Race Rule chapter.

> The word nigger . . . sums up for [Blacks] all the bitter years of insult and struggle in America.
>
> —*Langston Hughes, poet and author*

RULE SUMMARY

Nigger is a derogatory racial slur directed at Black people. Its goal is to insult, terrorize, and maintain domination over an entire group of people. The word is directly linked to racist anti-Black caricatures, tropes, and violence. It's an instant reminder of being sold into bondage as human property with family structures strategically destroyed.

American slavery represents over five hundred years of oppression, inhumanity, and violence that started in the Americas in the 1500s, before 1619, with the enslavement, kidnapping, human trafficking, and transport of upward of 20 million Africans to the New World, with as many as half dying en route.[1] At least nearly half a million human cargo crammed into ships surviving the Middle Passage were "imported" to what became the United States. With stunted life spans, slaves were bred like livestock to a population of nearly 4 million by 1860.[2] Countless died and were tortured, raped, and ripped from parents by the start of the Civil War. This word reminds Blacks that while their blood and sweat built this country, they're not and never were the intended beneficiaries of America's false promise of freedom, prosperity, wealth, and opportunity.

Nigger is used to belittle, demean, impose feelings of superiority over Blacks, "put them in their place," threaten, and instill feelings of fear and intimidation. This term is frequently used when committing hate crimes, murders, lynchings, and racially motivated rapes. Sometimes it's used by the police when racial profiling and interacting with Blacks.

Keeping this pejorative alive is a form of abuse that simultaneously unearths reminders of centuries of violent subjugation and links to present-day inequality, injustices, harassment, police brutality, violent attacks, and institutional racism. It reminds Blacks of the daily racism they face. It's a traumatizing verbal weapon that seeks Blacks' perpetual submission and incessant suffering from PTSD (post-traumatic stress disorder) as a walking-wounded racial cohort of mentally and structurally oppressed.

Using this word instantly labels you as a racist. If you're lucky, you'll only be viewed as ignorant, culturally insensitive, or an idiot. It's a glaring red flag for bigotry, aligned with domestic terrorists trying to repeal the 20th century.

If you hear it and do nothing, you may be viewed as a white-nationalist sympathizer. You're not in the clear just because you don't personally vomit this word. Your silence is tolerance. Doing nothing is an act supporting white supremacy. Consuming media and content using this term breathes new life into it, keeping it and its racial harm contemporary and immortal.

Speak up when you hear it used. Tune out from supporting its monetization. Vocalize opposition to its cavalier use in social media, music, films, and other forms of entertainment and media.

Even if the white person using it *thinks* they're "cool with Black people," it's still racist. Just because the person using it is a person of color doesn't mean it's appropriate or acceptable. However, if you're white and they're Black, evaluate if speaking to them is culturesplaining.

Given its offensive nature, replace it with the "N-word" when wanting to discuss the term. This lessens its racial impact and limits appearing racist. Substitute N-word in conversations.

Don't say or cosign on the N-word. It's deeply offensive and unearths America's bloody legacy of slavery and racism. It can cost you friendships, your reputation, and your job.

Most importantly, this word traumatizes Black people. It's a tool of psychological warfare.

This singular word is the summation of the Black experience in America—bundled into one term. Its power serves as a potent undercurrent that supports bigoted ideologies and racism's ability to permeate throughout and toxically infect many aspects of American society. Its prevalence historically corresponds to the increasing use of stereotypical Black imagery and offensive racial caricatures (e.g., coon, sambo, mammy, pickaninny, Mandingo, jigaboo, savage).

The lexicon of exclusion is linked to discrimination and used to perpetuate negative stereotypes of Blacks being lazy, stupid, subhuman, genetically inferior, filthy, criminal, dangerous, violent, dishonest, athletic and animalistic beasts, sexual objects, rapists, thieves, low-down leeches, and welfare queens posing a threat to American society and its way of life who siphon off government funding. This is some of the false and white supremacist thinking intertwined with the N-word. Racist vernacular triggers the pain of the past and present trauma. Arguably, it's the ultimate American insult—promulgating a racial hierarchy with whites at the top and Blacks at the bottom.

No level of taking back this term by Blacks divorces the word from its bloody legacy. The term is irrevocably linked to its history of enslavement, rape, violence, lynching, oppression, claims of genetic and hereditary inferiority, and degrading treatment of Blacks in America. Nor can efforts to reclaim this term eliminate reminders of present-day discrimination against Blacks. Even if you're Black, many other Blacks still find the use of this epithet by other Blacks abhorrent and offensive (e.g., in everyday language, songs, movies, comedy routines, literature).

Today, it is still seen as a highly offensive racial slur connected to prejudice, racism, violence, hatred, and systematic and institutional oppression. This is why "N-word" should be used instead in conversations.

ICE CUBE TO BILL MAHER ON MAHER'S N-WORD JOKE

On his late-night show in 2017, Bill Maher was interviewing a conservative politician who invited him to "work in the fields" in Nebraska (which could have meant supporting on-the-ground political activities and not alluding to the state's farming industry). Maher jokingly retorted, "Work in the fields? Senator, I'm a house nigger."[3]

Bill Maher saying the N-word illustrates how a white liberal who believes he's one of the good whites is part of the problem as a vector for racism and hate speech.[4] Ice Cube's response, shared below, summarizes what many Blacks felt about Maher's behavior. Some still reject Maher's apology, seeing him as a white supremacist with a global platform. Ice Cube told Maher,

> I knew you [were going to mess] up sooner or later. . . . You've got a lot of Black jokes. . . .

> What made you think that it was cool to say that? . . . We need to get to the root of the psyche because . . . a lot of guys . . . cross the line because they [are] too familiar. . . . They think they can cross the line and they can't. . . . It's a word that . . . you can use it as a weapon, or you can use it as a tool. It's been used as a weapon against [Blacks] by white people.

Figure 9.1 highlights a litany of typical yet troublesome excuses people use when called out for dropping N-word bombs. These vapid justifications double down on being racially offensive.

IF *THEY* USE IT, WHY CAN'T I?

Yes, we hear the N-word often in rap music, movies, stand-up comedy routines, and sometimes even when overhearing a group of Black people on the subway or young kids on the playground. But most likely, you're not *them*! Plain and simple. It's just like how you get to talk smack about how your drunk, trifling uncle keeps ruining Thanksgiving. But when your next-door neighbor chimes in with a snarky comment—repeating what you've said or thought one hundred times—your blood boils, and you start rolling back your sleeves preparing for a brawl. You can trash-talk your uncle, but you'd be damned if your neighbor could get away with it!

People from a specific group are allowed more leeway and get a pass—albeit limited—because they're in a classification in which *only* that group of people are. It doesn't make it right, and it's irrelevant whether it's fair. They're given more latitude by the very nature that they're a card-carrying member of a group when you're not, so they can say it and you can't. *Them's the rules!* Whether they *should* say it is a separate issue.

Some oppressed people take a pejorative and embrace it to preserve their dignity. Some Blacks argue that by using the word, they're taking it back and eviscerating the word's centuries-old power to denigrate them. However, how can anyone truly reclaim something when it *still* causes pain today when spoken by non-Blacks? It's still a censored expletive for a reason. It gives further license to racists to use it. And there's no neutralizing it by softening the ending "er" with "a" or "ah" when its meaning is clear. Mere linguistical magic and dialectical pronunciation shifts don't alter the

N-word Excuse Bingo			
"It's just a word."	"Black people say the N-word, but I can't. Is it because I'm white?"	"We shouldn't give one word so much power."	"Here come the PC Police."
"People are so easily offended. Why are you so upset?"	"There's a difference between Black people and niggas."	"They pushed me [to use the N-word]."[5] —former Papa John's CEO John Schnatter	"She's old and from a different time. Just ignore her."
"He didn't mean it like that. Besides, he apologized right after."	"But my relative/friend is Black. And I've dated lots of Black guys."	"They use it in rap and hip-hop."	"What about freedom of speech?"
"It's so much worse to be called a racist."	"I was just singing along to the song."	"I said 'Nigg-A' not 'Nigg-ER.'"	"I was young and dumb when I said that."
"Nobody should use it."	"Those are old tweets."	"Well people call my race/ethnic group _____, and I'm not bothered by it."	"I was joking. Learn to take a joke."

FIGURE 9.1. Typical N-word excuses and defensive retorts.

word's literal and historic meaning. Its use, even by Blacks, perpetuates and promotes the ongoing harm this word can do in advancing racist beliefs today.

Thanks to the prominence of the internet and social media, the word has found rebirth with modern-day racists in spreading anti-Black hostility and hatred. The collateral damage of the internet is how it foments a toxic platform for white nationalists to spread evil and hate to increasingly larger groups of impressionable people worldwide. #Charlottesville

Failure to remove the N-word from our collective language promotes its ongoing usage by non-Blacks who may not be obvious supremacists but otherwise can lean on the weak and trite excuse that they didn't know better and didn't mean any harm when repeating the word. The term's use serves no legitimate purpose other than keeping its harmful impact continually alive.

Its use confuses a younger generation of people and those in other countries into thinking the term's meaning has changed over time, is no longer offensive, or ceases to have power against Blacks.

Yet this is far from the truth. It's terrorist terminology.

TIPS AND ADVICE

The advice below will help you not just transition away from using offensive language but encourage you to see the toxic role silence plays when failing to act upon hearing hate speech. Also, it provides guidance on what to say and do when you witness someone using the N-word to support and help you develop your racism disruption skills. These tips will also help you determine and navigate when it's appropriate to hold back and when to speak up.

YOU—SAYING IT

When it comes to saying the N-word, don't. Instead, follow these rules:

- Just don't use "nigger," "nigga," "niggas," or "nig" no matter who you are. Definitely *do not* call someone a "nigger bitch." These are all fighting words and need to be canceled.

- If you're having an intellectual conversation with someone about the word, substitute the N-word version.
- When singing along to rap songs, censor yourself! Just remain silent when the lyric is sung. You don't want to be *that* person. This same rule applies if reading aloud lines from *Adventures of Huckleberry Finn* or *To Kill a Mockingbird*.
- Don't literally call someone "N-word" and think you're making progress because you didn't fully say nigger. If the intent is to insult, demean, intimidate, or simply be a jerk, then you've voluntarily outed yourself as a racist. Don't complain or whine when you must pay a high price for its usage.
- Don't assume just because there aren't any Black people around that you can say the word. All this does is feed into your own prejudices and limit your personal evolution.
- By no means does using the word make you cool. You shouldn't call your friend one even in a friendly way as some people do—including non-Blacks in speaking to their non-Black friends. This isn't mere tomfoolery but ignorant behavior supporting racism, racial animus, and racist power structures in American society.

YOU—WHEN YOU HEAR IT[*]

When you hear someone else say the N-word, this advice will give you the tools, words, and guidance on what to do or not to do:

- If you hear someone use the term, speak up and say that you "don't use that word in your vocabulary and appreciate it not being used around you, and preferably not at all." If you say nothing, then you're participating in keeping the word alive and harming Black people.
- Consider having heard the word as an opportunity to educate about the term's history and engage in a discussion about why you and others find it offensive. If you opt for the teachable-moment route, please try to avoid sounding patronizing or holier-than-thou.

---

[*] To see an analysis of aplying the Bedrock Race Rule's three-step process to decide how to react and take action when hearing the N-word, see Race Rule #1 (Bedrock Race Rule: Choose to Disrupt Racism Every Day).

- When hearing it, if the person using the term is Black and you aren't, consider remaining silent to avoid culturesplaining unless it's your Black biracial child or adopted Black kid or you're the adult in the room supervising children. If you correct a Black person, you're inviting an argument.

> You don't choose the times you live in.
> But you do choose who you want to be,
> and you do choose how you want to think.
>
> —Grace Lee Boggs, author and social activist

PART 3

Disrupt Credible Threats— Racial Violence, Weaponizing Whiteness, and Karens

PART 3 focuses on threats to Black and brown lives and how white decisions and ignorance contribute to jeopardizing their physical safety. While some people deservedly are canceled since actions have consequences, this section provides a coaching culture by teaching what egregiously endangers lives. This guidance will help you prioritize the security of people of color. Racism Disruptors ensure their decisions don't cause bodily injury or death. The human right to life is safeguarded when all people experience full citizenship, equality, freedom, and protection under the law.

Before you fully understand or agree, follow these Race Rules. This is a racism-avoidance guidebook. People of color prefer your choices and behaviors change before your brain catches up, compared to no change and inaction. Incremental improvement is still progress. When in doubt, implement them. Take a leap of faith.

Here are some tips to navigate feeling overwhelmed, discouraged, or angry. Complicated feelings are normal. This work involves coping with and managing your emotions to receive and accept the Race Rules.

Go for a walk. Meditate. Listen to relaxing music. Make a cup of tea. Do breathing exercises. Take a nap. Let information percolate. But return. Don't disappear. Remain open to trusting the material, being present, and changing how you see yourself through unvarnished truths.

Remember, this book provides rare access to help you grow and understand racism. Transitional processes require listening to uncomfortable realities that could make you feel shame, guilt, sadness, or outrage. Be patient and forgiving of yourself. Unlearning racism takes time.

Avoid False Equivalencies— Capitol Siege Was an Insurrection, and Black Lives Matter Rallies Are Protests

When you're so deeply invested in your privilege, and in this case white privilege, racial equality feels like oppression.

—*Anthony N. Morgan, racial justice lawyer*

RULE SUMMARY

One of the most pernicious examples of racialized false equivalencies is comparing the Black Lives Matter (BLM) protests to storming the United States Capitol Building.

Months after demonstrators rallied around the world in support of the BLM movement, a right-wing mob sieged the US Capitol on January 6, 2021.

Comparing the unlawful January 6 attack to BLM protests is a false equivalency.

Using false analogies to try to draw similarities when there's no valid correlation seeks to delegitimize genuine grievances of people of color while simultaneously aiming to acquit or ignore racist behaviors carried out by whites. This attempts to leverage the guilt of white bad actors to transfer it onto or condemn reasonable and appropriate actions of people of color.

Specifically with BLM and January 6, this false comparison enables you to turn a blind eye to the racism entrenched in insurrectionism. This false flag allows you to easily dismiss efforts demanding the public and government equally value Black lives.

There is no legitimate comparison between a seditious rebellion seeking to prevent Congress from carrying out its constitutional duties and exercising constitutional rights to peacefully protest for police reform. One is about government overthrow and revolution saturated in white supremacy, and the other is about saving lives and advocating for human rights and social justice.

Their motivations are relevant, along with their diametrically divergent objectives and methodologies.

BLM marches are based on a visible truth that Blacks are murdered by the police at alarming rates, seeking an end to systemtic racism. Storming Capitol Hill was based on a demonstrable lie, striving to undermine a free and fair election. The goal was to suppress the voices of the majority of American voters.

We shouldn't even dignify January 6 by referring to it as a "riot." It was a violent *insurrection*.

Bringing up this logical fallacy is insulting. It demonstrates an utter lack of understanding of Black and brown deaths at the hands of the police and belittles the struggle for equality. It reveals a lack of caring for Black and brown people and exposes your underlying prejudices.

Equating the Capitol siege to Black Lives Matter protests is offensive to those caring about equality, life, liberty, democracy, the rule of law, and freedom from white supremacy. The BLM movement is grounded in factual data that Blacks die at statistically significant higher numbers than whites. There's chronic undervaluing of Black lives.

The BLM movement draws attention to police brutality, systemtic racism, and society's failure to equally protect the civil rights and freedoms of Black people. Its goal is to improve American society—using the US Constitution's First Amendment right to free speech and peaceful assembly to apply political pressure to reform existing laws, institutions, and practices. It's a quintessentially American movement since its bedrock methodology is peacefully protesting to amplify voices of the unheard to government. Working within the American legal framework toward our country's collective progress, the movement wants to eradicate bigotry and promote equal protection under the law.

In contrast, the January 6, 2021, US Capitol Hill insurrection was a planned, coordinated siege sacking the Capitol Building. It was based on confirmed lies and baseless conspiracy theories of a "stolen" 2020 presidential election, with an underlying racist belief in the nefarious illegality of votes from Black and brown communities. It was an attempted coup d'état—an effort to overthrow the United States government, our democracy, and the free will of the people to elect our leaders. An armed violent mob of racist radicalized domestic terrorists sought to assassinate the vice president of the United States and Speaker of the House of Representatives to stop the certification of the presidential election (i.e., prohibit the installation of Joseph R. Biden as the democratically elected 46th president).

Table 10.1 debunks ignorant counterarguments people make about January 6 in trying to draw comparisons with BLM.[1]

TABLE 10.1 Capitol Hill insurrection versus summer 2020 BLM protests

Capitol siege	BLM protests
Political activities	
• The siege was an illegal incitement to riot—not free speech. • This was not a protest but a rebellious uprising centered on violence—a hostile, military-style, coordinated assault to take over the US Capitol Building. • Some insurrectionists called for revolution (aka Civil War secession déjà vu), arguably treason.	• Lawful protesters used the right to free speech and to peacefully assemble as guaranteed in the First Amendment to the US Constitution. • This effort and movement aimed to reform and improve practices and policies as they function *within* existing power and governmental structures.
Violence	
• Participants were violent from start to finish, and deadly. • Elected officials and Capitol staff ran for their lives—many sending final goodbye messages to family. • Police officers were blinded, impaled, beaten with American flags, tasered, trampled, crushed, and pepper sprayed.	• There was little evidence of widespread violence, yet any violence was grossly sensationalized by the media. • At least 93 percent of over 7,750 BLM protests in 2,400 locations nationwide were peaceful with no destructive activity—no violence, looting, or vandalism.[2]

TABLE 10.1 (*continued*)

Capitol siege	BLM protests
Vandalism	
• Offices were ransacked, government documents and public property were stolen, feces were smeared, hallways were urinated in, and historic statues were defaced. • The US Speaker of the House's laptop was stolen with the intent to sell it to Russian intelligence.	• Minimal destruction occurred as less than 7 percent of protests involved violence, property damage, destructive activity, or looting.[3] • Statues of our country's legacy of racist violence were specifically targeted (e.g., Confederates).
Participants	
• Thousands of the participants were radicalized extremists and domestic terrorists. • Those in the mostly white crowd were adherents of white supremacist and white nationalist hate groups, supporters of subversive and antigovernment organizations, and conspiracy theorists.	• Protesters comprised millions of people in all 50 states and Washington, DC—from coast to coast. • These demonstrators were advocates of anti-racism, equality, and social justice of all races and ages. • There was no significant presence of anti-fascist Antifa supporters.
Rallying cries	
• "Hang Mike Pence!" • "Stop the steal!" • "This is our America!" • "Where is Nancy [Pelosi]?" • "USA!"	• "I can't breathe!" • "No justice, no peace!" • "Hands up, don't shoot!" • "Black Lives Matter!" • "Get your knee off my neck!"

(*continued*)

TABLE 10.1 Capitol Hill insurrection versus summer 2020 BLM protests (*continued*)

Capitol siege	BLM protests
Event gear	
• At the violent event were guns, pipe bombs, chemicals, pepper spray, gallows, pitchforks, tasers, tactical clothing and riot gear, body armor, police shields, hockey sticks, bats, batons, a noose, etc.	• At the protests were signs, bullhorns, whistles, face paint, tambourines, music, strollers for kids, anti-COVID face masks, milk to treat being tear-gassed, phone numbers of civil rights legal groups, etc.
Intended beneficiaries	
• White Americans.	• Everyone, especially Black and brown people.
Goals and mission	
• Insurrectionists wanted to overthrow votes and stop Congressional certification of the valid democratic presidential election, overthrow the government, and replace the American government with authoritarian rule (i.e., a coup d'état). • They wanted to maintain the superiority of white Americans through violence.	• Protesters wanted to end senseless killings of Black people by law enforcement and civilians, end police brutality and abuses of power, accountability for cops, and enforce Blacks' human and civil rights. • They wanted to reform police practices and the justice system that disproportionately negatively impact people of color by advancing anti-racism.

This false-equivalency linkage diminishes the struggle and realities of being brutally killed by the police. It trivializes the legitimate terror many people of color have of law enforcement—that when they walk outside *each and every day*, it could be their last. Just like with the murder of George Floyd—where a trip to the convenience store results in a police officer pressing his knee on your neck for 9:29 minutes, you cry out for your mother as your life flashes before your eyes, and you have the terrifying conscious realization that you're dying as you unsuccessfully beg for your life.

Your last day dying without feeling basic love, respect, dignity, and humanity—you're never on vacation from this daily, traumatic anxiety. This is what it means to be Black or brown—on high alert in survival mode, which negatively impacts your mental and physical health.

George Floyd's killing is not unique. It's all too common. The difference was merely that *this* time when it was caught on camera, the world watched. Whites were collectively forced to pay attention for once, during mandated COVID lockdowns. Floyd's murder sparked an overdue awakening for white Americans, who were unable to look away. Simultaneously, it pushed communities of color to a breaking point for what was an ordinary Monday for them.

It's demeaning, dehumanizing, and disrespectful to claim that the January 6 lawless, seditionist mob of fanatics hell-bent on maintaining white supremacy are analogous to people who want the basic human right to life, as if government overthrow orchestrated by whites is the same as white Americans protesting in solidarity with Black and brown people and those from AAPI communities. Bringing up their similarity demonstrates your quiet, bigoted belief that Black lives don't actually matter to you—at least not as much as white lives. *But don't get defensive; rather, accept that you can do better.*

ORIGINS OF THE BLM MOVEMENT

The phrase "Black Lives Matter," the BLM movement, and the hashtag #BlackLivesMatter or #BLM were born out of the profound pain, shock, and trauma of the July 2013 George Zimmerman verdict when he was wrongfully acquitted of murdering seventeen-year-old high schooler Trayvon Martin. Martin was merely walking home from the corner store with candy. This child was pursued and shot by a twenty-eight-year-old grown man for the noncrime of walking in his own neighborhood.

Martin's murder is deeply rooted in white supremacy, unfounded fears of Black people, and bigoted beliefs about who "belongs" in any given neighborhood. Racist othering of Blacks emboldens brazen vigilantism, unequal valuations of Blacks' lives, and murder acquittals for killing them.

The phrase inspired a movement. Now it's a rallying cry for social justice, equality, valuing Black lives, and ending the senseless killing and brutalizing of Blacks by civilians and police.

Efforts to position BLM as subversive seek to reinforce white superiority and the subjugation of people of color. In 2021, the movement was nominated for the Nobel Peace Prize.

The core of what BLM activists seek is to save Black lives. It's literally a life-and-death struggle for Black and brown folk.

DECONSTRUCTING KNEE-JERK REACTIONS

If you equate the Capitol siege and Black Lives Matter protests, on some level you prefer society's default position of white superiority, racist violence, and the unjustified murder of Black and brown people. Otherwise, you'd stop resisting changing the status quo. You wouldn't respond with countervailing comparisons rationalizing the indefensible behavior of violent white nationalists as a distraction technique. You'd be less complacent about social justice and less complicit. Reaching for the false parallel reveals tacit indifference to the objectives of the BLM movement (i.e., protecting lives).

This is knee-jerk racism. People need to be honest with themselves. Explore why bringing this up was a natural go-to response or almost was. Anyone can change *if* they're willing to put in the work.

SELF-REFLECTIVE QUESTIONS

Feel free to explore these questions with a group of white friends, knowing the discussion might get heated. Be selective about whom to invite and include if you explore these questions in a group setting. It's best to focus on white invitees.

1. Why is your natural response to compare January 6 to BLM protests?
2. When you saw news coverage of the Capitol Hill insurrection, were you outraged? If not, why?
3. Do you think that January 6 was a protest? Was it unlawful? Were the participants trying to overthrow the government? Are they fascists? What are the definitions of *fascism* and *authoritarianism*?
4. Why did the media show so many stories about looting and riots linked to BLM protests?
5. When you hear "Black Lives Matter," does it make you think "All Lives Matter" or "Blue Lives Matter"?
6. What comes to mind when hearing "defund the police"?
7. Do you think the strong emotions at BLM protests are identical to the rage displayed in storming the Capitol?
8. Why are you more focused on *what* BLM protesters were doing versus *why* they were doing it (methods versus reasons)?
9. The last few times you encountered the police, was it a positive or neutral experience? How does your experience influence your views on BLM? How much do you consider the role of race in benign traffic stops that result in bodily harm to civilians?
10. Do your responses to these questions imply that you actually don't value the lives of Black and brown people as much as whites? Are you being brutally honest with yourself in answering this question?

TALKING POINTS FOR WHEN YOU OFFEND AND TRY TO RECOVER

You've already dug yourself into a hole when mentioning problematic false equivalencies. Recovering will be challenging but not impossible. Even though the person hearing you compare January 6 to BLM protests may conclude you're racist and their impression of you may not change, you should still try to repair the relationship. Your words will go over better when signaling you have a growth mindset.

Here are some suggested talking points:

- "I'm sorry what I said was offensive and hurtful. It wasn't my intent, but I know it's less about what I intended. This is about how I made you feel and my blind spots where I need to learn more."
- "I admit that I probably don't understand this topic and the underlying issues with policing Black and brown communities. I need to better educate myself."
- "I plan to take steps to learn more."
- "I have some work to do on myself but will *start* doing better." (You need to actually start doing better and not *try*. Saying you will try is hollow and meaningless without subsequent action.)
- "I'm going to research some films and books on this topic to learn more."

WHEN YOU HEAR WHATABOUTISM

To rebut specific arguments people make, refer to the side-by-side comparison in table 10.1 to shape your responses. Also, weave in some of the reflective questions listed above—forcing the person to consider why their go-to is a false equivalency. This could help spark their broader thinking.

Striking at the heart of flawed BLM-vs-Capitol-siege false equivalencies or criticism of BLM, you could use these tactics and talking points:

- **Point out racism**—"Have you ever considered how that could sound racist?"
- **Encourage self-reflection**—"I truly believe that you should ask yourself why raising this comparison is important to you."

- **Counter belittling the cause**—"When you say that, it trivializes what the BLM movement stands for—protecting lives from abuses of power and pushing for equality. Basically, it's saying that Black and brown lives don't matter."
- **Acknowledge the racist Capitol siege racism**—"If they weren't racists, then why did they have the paraphernalia from the Racist's Handbook—Confederate flags, nooses, swastikas?"
- **Challenge clinging to "All Lives Matter"**—"White people aren't in danger of being killed by the police. There's no need to point out something that's a given. But when people respond with 'All Lives Matter' or 'Blue Lives Matter,' they're basically saying that the people in real danger—Black people—don't matter."
- **Be helpful**—"If you're open to it, I could suggest a few resources on the topic. You could read XYZ book."
- **Exit stage left**—When things break down, you don't feel it's your job to enlighten them, you just don't have the energy, or you want to cut ties and run, you could do any of the following:
  - Say, "I need to take a step back. I found that offensive and I feel uncomfortable continuing this discussion."
  - If needed (without a nasty tone, raised voice, or including "Sorry"), you could add, "I don't know when my impression of your worldview will change, if ever. There's an undercurrent of prejudice. But I'd need to see a significant change before I could spend time with you again. It's just not the kind of energy I enjoy being around." Some people are in your life just for a reason, season, or lifetime. It's acceptable to limit exposure to people whose values don't align with yours, even if they're your own family.
  - If this discussion becomes too hot to handle, continue to speak in a calm tone and leave—especially if you feel your safety is in danger.

> Either we shall have to make democracy work for every American or in the last analysis, we shall not be able to preserve it for any American.
>
> —Loren Miller, civil rights attorney

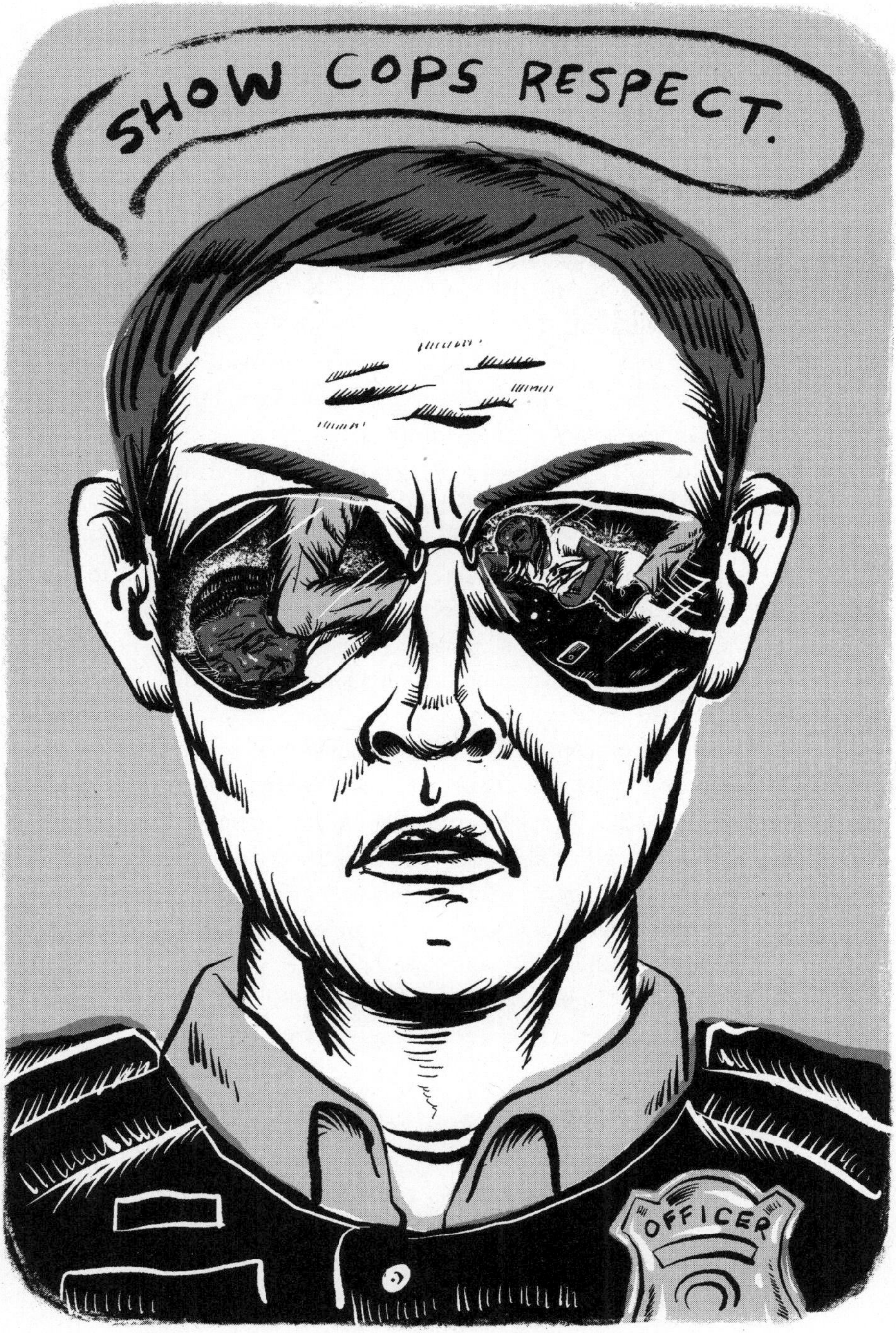
SHOW COPS RESPECT.
OFFICER

Black and Brown People Fear the Police— Because Cops Kill Them with Impunity

Until the killing of Black men, Black mothers' sons,
becomes as important to the rest of the country
as the killing of a white mother's sons, we who believe
in freedom cannot rest until this happens.

—Ella Baker, civil rights activist

RULE SUMMARY

Many people of color don't trust but rather fear the police—feeling cops are predators and people of color are their prey. This is a *life-and-death* issue. It's about survival.

Many whites unrealistically expect people of color to have similar police encounters as they have. Many whites get indignant when marginalized groups view cops as murderers, criminals, and human-rights violators. This thinking is unreasonable and anchored in racism.

Why should they trust cops? Have the police *earned* their trust? How does blind trust promote survival? Why must they even like or respect law enforcement when paying the salaries of the people and government agencies victimizing, traumatizing, and killing them?

People of color have a prolonged history of negative interactions with law enforcement—stemming back to when Slave Patrols terrorized Blacks and eventually evolved into today's police forces. While patrols and Night Watches aren't rounding up slaves and Native Americans anymore, the same white supremacist mindsets persist along with equally dehumanizing methods of apprehending, hog-tying like animals, arresting under false pretenses, and siccing dogs on them.

Some cops are linked to antigovernment and antidemocracy domestic terrorist groups because police departments attract bigots. Police forces provide safe harbor for and foment white supremacy.

Communities of color are overpoliced, overprofiled, and underprotected. Driving a car, lying in bed, crossing the street, buying candy, and playing in a park can result in taking a final breath.

Community trust in law enforcement erodes because of racist police-involved killings and a lack of institutional accountability.

Low confidence and nonexistent accountability are due to police unions, qualified immunity, and whites enabling this system.

If all you have is a hammer, then everything looks like a nail. Some cops pounce on people of color, who they routinely and erroneously perceive as dangerous threats—constantly exhibiting trigger-happy poor judgment. They prejudge people of color based on racist assumptions. This racial profiling has deadly consequences, which is why many Americans of color feel terrorized by law enforcement.

These fears aren't detached from reality. They're backed by statistical data. According to a 2020 Harvard University study, Blacks are up to six times more likely than whites to be killed by the police (ranging from three to six times, depending on geographic location). Causes of death at the hands of the police regardless of race include gunshot wounds (94.2 percent); tasering (3.4 percent); asphyxiation, bludgeoning, or pepper spraying (1.7 percent); and other causes (0.7 percent).[1]

We must stop operating based on feelings of *how we would like* things to be versus *what they actually are*. The police are disproportionately killing Americans of color—fact, not hyperbole.

If you don't recognize the predatory threat police officers and law enforcement culture pose to people of color, then you're paralyzed in demanding needed change. You're blocked from understanding the role white supremacy plays in the personal safety of Americans of color. This makes you part of the problem and unable to dismantle racism in community policing and effectively demand reforms. It also makes it easy for you to discount real Black and brown experiences and shrug when another Philando Castile is murdered without cause.

Failure to understand life-and-death issues impacting people of color signals a major disconnect with their lives. It's hard for them to trust or befriend you when you're blind to their realities.

If this issue isn't a priority for you, the message you're sending is Black lives don't matter.

In the first eight months of 2020 alone—during a global pandemic when most people were stuck indoors—the police killed at least 164 Blacks. That's roughly five people *per week*! In 2022, the police killed 276 Black people.[2] Whites don't live in constant terror of a militarized police state. If they did, we would've implemented transformational reforms years ago. Instead, many whites feel empowered to openly carry guns unapologetically without fear they'll be shot and presumed criminals by the police—a freedom unavailable to people of color.

Unacceptably, we can't even say *exactly* how many Blacks were killed since we don't track police shootings, only how many cops die. Organizations must reverse engineer and collect their own imperfect data to approximate deaths. *We measure what we value.*

It's become a rinse-and-repeat routine—officers are put on paid administrative leave or desk duty. Afterward, they face no consequences for what's later conveniently deemed "justifiable homicide." Police forces and district attorneys are biased in policing themselves. Often, they withhold evidence and material information yet ask the public to have blind faith that their findings are legitimate.

Blacks are entitled to safety in neighborhoods and protection by police departments spending their tax dollars. This includes the right to be safe from cops posing a deadly threat and a judicial system that delivers equitable justice.

DANGEROUSLY RACIALLY DIVERGENT THREAT-LEVEL ASSESSMENTS

The deadly reality facing people of color is deeply misunderstood by whites. This is why a 2023 ABC News and *Washington Post* poll found only 12 percent of Blacks think the police treat Black and white people equally while 48 percent of white Americans do. And only 20 percent of Blacks think the police are adequately trained to avoid excessive force compared to 46 percent of whites. This illustrates how different races face divergent policing experiences.[3]

These alternate realities are underscored by a 2020 Pew survey that found 45 percent of Black adults felt they'd been unfairly stopped by the police (64 percent Black men and 32 percent Black women), compared to 9 percent of white adults.[4]

The fact-based, genuine fear of death is why Black parents have "the talk" with their children about how to survive random police encounters with a pulse and vital signs.

If you see cops as threats to your survival, you're likely to carry significant anxiety, pain, PTSD, anger, and accumulated racial trauma at the mere *sight* of law enforcement. This fear and panic multiplies when cops approach, pull you over, or speak to you. Encountering a predator, you may experience survival mode kicking in. And when you and your people are hunted daily, your natural reaction could be to run from danger.

If Black and brown people flinch, tense up, look stressed, pull out a phone to record, and start mentally calculating how to flee, this is *logical*. Survival instincts are turbocharging into action. Fight or flight might be how to stay alive—except natural Black and brown reflex responses to threats aren't socially tolerated nor considered justified.

Murder-by-cop is sometimes a modern-day lynching protected by a badge and backed by the state. Cops have a license to kill.

Given how frequently police encounters turn deadly for non-whites, it's *rational* for people of color to not just distrust cops but even *hate* them.

Are all cops bad? No. But are they all good? Definitely not.

Where's the *quantitative* data to prove there are more good cops than bad cops? We always assume this without evidence and won't verbally malign our police since it sounds "un-American." We give cops the benefit of the doubt, but it's time you challenge this.

A code of silence infects police culture and perpetuates white supremacist outcomes where Black and brown lives have lesser value than whites. When police officers cover for each other and fail to report or testify against criminal behavior, the *entire police department is immoral*. Law enforcement has created a dangerous ethos where even wannabe good cops can't be good. They knowingly work in places posing a public danger and turn a blind eye when their literal job is to prevent criminal conduct. Even the late conservative televangelist Pat Robertson said the police need to "stop this onslaught" and "open their eyes to what their public relations are." He went on to say that "we don't have the finest in the police department . . . [and] it's not a question of training . . . but hiring a more superior workforce . . . and we cannot have a bunch of clowns running around . . . who really are not the best and brightest."[5]

It's time to weed out the riffraff and clean house. Demand better for your community.

If your loyalties lie with the police on this issue, then you stand for murder and against life.

No one is above the law, including the "thin blue line." It's a very dangerous position to be in when your only recourse is to call the police *on the police*. Good luck with that.

Death by cop coupled with killer cops sidestepping justice is an epidemic. Yet the police have an unfounded fear of Black and brown people linked to white supremacy. Their prejudicial fear is deemed socially acceptable, while people of color's *legitimate* fear as a rational means of self-preservation is considered baseless—racist hypocrisy.

Police brutality is producing generations of children of color who grow up believing and experiencing that cops are dangerous and not there to help. Imagine how that impacts your psyche knowing that because of your race, the government is threatening your life and you're perpetually vulnerable to state-sanctioned danger, that a white person can get a flat tire or become lost yet find aid while Americans of color might get pummeled by bullets. Misdemeanors turn into trial-by-cop with street injustice since it's open season on non-white skin. Cops can do no wrong. Is this the America and life lessons you want?

When you're silent about police conduct and reforms, you're endorsing and participating in these wrongs. If you overlook this systemic problem, you personally pose a threat to people of color through deadly complicity.

DEREK CHAUVIN—NOT A REFERENDUM ON POLICE REFORM AND PROGRESS

Don't assume just because Derek Chauvin was convicted of murdering George Floyd we've solved America's policing problem. That's too simplistic. Like clockwork, the very day his guilty verdict was announced, another Black person was murdered by the police. There's never a reprieve from racist cops.

This case shows the bar to get a conviction is too high. Sadly, video alone of nine minutes and twenty-nine seconds with a knee-to-the-neck hold on a prone-positioned body isn't enough for a slam-dunk murder indictment and guilty verict. This trial involved a rare evidentiary package. A guilty verdict required a perfect storm of witnesses, prosecutors, public outcry, and worldwide protests for courthouse justice.

Now that Chauvin is a convict, many whites act like the police brutality problem is solved. There's an undercurrent of willful ignorance. They've tuned out. Instead of going back to their insular lives—blissfully sipping caramel macchiatos at the dog park—understand Blacks are still being killed and cops are going unpunished for murders.

This conviction isn't a marker of systemic progress, widespread accountability, nor increased trust. When people of color witness institutionalized courtroom injustice and acquittal after acquittal, this further undermines confidence in policing and the judicial system.

This case is an anomaly.

SELF-REFLECTIVE QUESTIONS

In considering why Blacks fear the police, ask yourself these questions:

1. Which triggers stronger feelings and why: (a) people of color loathing cops or shouting "Black Lives Matter" at law enforcement, or (b) people of color being shot and officers going unpunished?
2. Do you think the police are there to protect you? Protect people of color?
3. Why do you think death by cop happens to Blacks, Native Americans, and Latinos at a higher rate than for whites?
4. Do the police seem to *protect* communities of color or just *patrol and monitor* them like overseers?
5. Do you think cops living outside the communities where they work negatively impacts their ability to identify with and humanize the people they're supposed to protect and serve?
6. Why should Black and brown people believe cops are there to help them? Do you see *why* they logically perceive the police as a constant threat to their survival, why they may *run* from police?
7. Why should we give officers the benefit of the doubt when data keep proving how racially trigger-happy they are?
8. What role do you play or have you played in upholding racially discriminatory policing practices?
9. If you're not doing anything to protect the safety of community members of color, why wouldn't they logically conclude their lives don't matter to you?
10. What are your plans to help keep your friends, neighbors, and colleagues of color safe from police misconduct?

> It is not possible . . . to hold another man down
> in a ditch without staying down there with him.
>
> —Booker T. Washington, founder of Tuskegee University

Taking a Knee Isn't a Protest against the Flag nor Veterans

The ultimate measure of a man is not where he stands in moments of comfort and convenience, but where he stands at times of challenge and controversy.

—*Dr. Martin Luther King, Jr., civil rights activist*

RULE SUMMARY

As much as folks like to get worked up in a tizzy over silent "Taking a Knee" protests during the national anthem at sporting events—claiming it's unpatriotic and antiveteran—this peaceful form of a First Amendment protest is *not* about the American flag nor our military. It's about Black Lives Matter, police brutality, and the criminal justice system.

If you didn't realize Taking a Knee was about BLM, well now you know. Armed with this knowledge, if you still cling to the antimilitary or antiflag retort, you're knowingly throwing out what looks like racist fodder. You're failing to acknowledge the truth behind BLM messaging or the merits of the movement's goals.

If you insist on talking about disrespecting our military or dishonoring the flag, then *you're not listening*—by choice. This is intentional. As you harp on this and ignore the underlying reason for Taking a Knee, you'll sound increasingly racist by the minute—demonstrating that you don't value Black and brown lives nor equality for all.

It's time to quiet your outside voice and work on your inside voice.

There's nothing more patriotic than protesting for freedom in a country founded on protests for freedom.

Former National Football League (NFL) quarterback Colin Kaepernick clearly stated *why* he was Taking a Knee—the unrelenting police violence against and oppression of Blacks. His quiet protest prompted similar protests from professional and college to child sports leagues. Refusing to *recognize* the protest's purpose or ignoring it by focusing on symbols more than lives twists political acts into commentary on the flag, military, or patriotism. This behavior is a racist distraction. It's an attempt to run interference, throwing out diversion grenades blocking the path of legitimate life-or-death concerns and advocacy work by changemakers seeking police reforms.

Did you hear Kaepernick mention the military? Is anyone talking smack about veterans or flags? That would be a hard *no*! So why focus on a totally different topic?

More importantly, if your grievance is over the *method* or *venue* of their protest, ask why you're more focused on *what* people are doing versus *why* they're doing it?

People are dying! There is strong reason to be urgently concerned about this, as evidenced by the statistics on Blacks killed by cops and causes of death discussed in Race Rule #11. Kneeling draws attention to this life-and-death issue—even if you'll be upset. That's what protests do—push buttons in the most visible places since they challenge norms. Maybe your family was in the military, making you angrier. But you're not alone. No one has a monopoly on claiming service. Lots of Black and brown people are veterans. Nearly half of active duty servicepeople are people of color, who return to typical American bigotry on the homeland.

SELF-REFLECTIVE QUESTIONS

If you're offended because you feel the flag is being disrespected, ask yourself these questions:

1. When was the last time you did something to improve the daily lives of veterans?
2. Does protest by kneeling cause systemic deaths?
3. Why does your outrage warrant priority above human life?
4. What message do you send when you ask people to silence their pain?
5. How appropriate is it to require people to physically stand for a country that doesn't stand with and for them?
6. Why ask people whose country violates their civil rights to swallow injustice?

Keeping it real—isn't liberty a main reason our roughly 20 percent Black military goes to war?[1] To protect freedom? Free speech and protesting come with the right to say what others don't want to hear and in ways some don't want to see. While this means you can freely complain about them, first you should get their motives right so you're not hurtful—making them feel invisible over death by cop.

"THE STAR-SPANGLED BANNER" IS A RACIST PROSLAVERY SONG

"The Star-Spangled Banner" is dripping in white supremacy. Its author, Francis Scott Key, was a wealthy slaveowner viciously opposed to abolishing slavery who spoke of "a distinct and inferior race" and shipping Blacks back to Africa.

Here's the part of the song we don't sing:

> No refuge could save the hireling and slave
> From the terror of flight or the gloom of the grave,
> And the star-spangled banner in triumph doth wave
> O'er the land of the free and the home of the brave.

The song was meant to threaten Blacks helping the British during the War of 1812. Making it the official national anthem in 1931 was a neo-Confederate political victory—celebrated with a "stars-and-bars" victory parade. As a presidential advisor, Key helped shape the US Supreme Court. He helped get his brother-in-law Roger Taney appointed chief justice. Taney penned the awful landmark 1857 *Dred Scott v. Sandford* decision, ruling Blacks weren't citizens or protected under the US Constitution and upheld the institution of slavery.

While people are standing up for BLM by kneeling, it's fitting that it happens specifically to this anthem, even though people aren't protesting it. It's written by this staunch bigot who memorialized his racist belief that Black lives don't matter in a theme song. His lyrics symbolize slavery, white supremacist violence, and law enforcement hunting and killing runaway slaves.

This example reminds us how many aspects of American society and culture—widely accepted as normal, innocuous, or simple with many unaware of their origins—aren't simple. Some may decide not to stand when it's played not just because of Taking a Knee but since it's an anthem glorifying slavery and the engineer who helped indoctrinate it into law.

Continuing the history lesson, Kaepernick initially sat down during the anthem. Then fellow football player and former Green Beret Nate Boyer told Kaepernick that he felt it was more respectful to kneel than sit since soldiers often take a knee in front of a fallen soldier's grave. Afterward, Kaepernick started kneeling instead of sitting to support BLM. Arguably, kneeling is more respectful of those who are sensitive to this form of protest as a compromising concession.

Even if you still contend the anthem represents the military or flag and it's disrespectful not to participate in pledging allegiance, it's offensive to prioritize cultural norms and public displays of contrived patriotism above deaths. Patriotism isn't about performance art but protecting freedoms enshrined in the Bill of Rights.

You can claim you have a right to how you *perceive* Taking a Knee. That's true. But you're still valuing symbols over lives if you get riled up. Vocalizing this may be *perceived* as racist and coded language for supporting police brutality. #BigotAlert! It's the truth, like it or not.

At some point, to move beyond supporting white supremacy, people need to move past performative idolatry and revering totems above survival and freedom. Objecting emits a strong racist vibe. It's best to let the anger go. The optics and priorities are bad. No one's forcing you to kneel. Why don't you do you and let them do them. Better yet, focus on how to *improve* society.

Or you can continue sounding insensitive and place greater value on connections to a piece of cloth and an old-timey antebellum song. What's more important? Acting and being racist? Or human lives?

The answer should be obvious. If you reject this advice and you're called a racist, you were warned. You walked into it. That's on you.

> White feelings should never be held
> in higher regard than Black lives.
>
> —Rachel Cargle, author

Stop Dialing a Cop for No Reason

Those who can make you believe absurdities,
can make you commit atrocities.

—*Voltaire, philosopher*

RULE SUMMARY

Police alert! Do *not* call the cops for nontransgressions or when little brown girls sell lemonade without a permit. Mind your own business! Don't be a Karen or Ken.

This also applies if someone is having a barbeque in the park, swimming at the local pool, sitting at a café, entering their home, waiting in their car, birdwatching, asking you to follow the law, jogging, walking down the street, golfing, taking photos in a park, babysitting, napping in a dormitory common room, legally buying a gun, riding an elevator, exercising at the gym, dog walking, delivering a package, turning around in your driveway, or living daily life.

If something can't be categorized as criminal behavior by any stretch of the imagination or is a mere misdemeanor, then stop meddling.

Calling the police for fictitious infractions could permanently alter the trajectory of a person's life or sadly be the catalyst for their death. Dialing the "five-O" for benign behavior will deservedly get you labeled a racist. And if caught on video, you may go viral as a "Worldstar."

Are you the county's licensing agency? Does your job involve enforcing specific rules? If the answers are no, then don't dial the cops and focus on you. Stop trying to regulate another person's behavior.

Do not appoint yourself the community conduct monitor or neighborhood watch. You're not being a good Samaritan but a town nuisance—the local bigot about whom everyone will talk.

This rule equally applies when you insert yourself into places, spaces, and discussions you don't belong but then dislike how things unfold, like when overhearing a stranger's conversation in public and you interject to verbalize your unsolicited thought bubble. A heated debate sparked by your interference still isn't cause to bring in the authorities. Learn to modulate your behavior and let things go. Don't channel your white privilege. #WhiteCallerCrimes

Calling the police, store managers, and those in positions of authority on people of color when legitimate taboo behavior isn't taking place treads into racist waters, especially if you have no direct connection to their activities. It's what some white people quickly do when Black and brown people are near—presumably invading perceived exclusive whites-only spaces or challenging whites by not submitting to white wishes (i.e., white superiority). It's "white people white peopling," which is code for just being racist. The undercurrent is a belief in white entitlement and Black and brown illegitimacy.

SELF-REFLECTIVE QUESTIONS

If you're inclined to call the po-po, here are the bigger questions to ask yourself:

1. Why do you think the person of color doesn't belong there, have a right to do what they're doing, or that it's not their own property?
2. Why is your go-to calling the police? What's your real motivation?
3. Do some soul-searching and be honest with yourself—would you call the police if the person were a different race or skin color?
4. Are you sweating the small stuff? Is this *really* a police issue?
5. What are you afraid will happen if you do nothing?
6. Is there a whiff of prejudice involved that *others* would see?
7. If the person is angry or animated or argues back after you meddle, do you have a legitimate and reasonable fear or just a *perceived* fear of a threat? Are you merely afraid or uncomfortable since it's a person of color (i.e., you see them as a threatening brown person just because they're not white)?

The best option is to do nothing! Do not call the authorities to enforce nonrules that smell like a racial pretext. And if you decide to speak to the supposed rule-breaking brown people (*not* recommended!) and insist on being an obnoxious busybody, if and when things escalate—probably due to your pesky intrusiveness—defuse the situation. Use basic mediation and deescalation skills. Calmly walk away. You have a duty to leverage conflict resolution skills when you're the debacle's architect.

> The way to right wrongs is to turn the light of truth upon them.
>
> —Ida B. Wells, journalist and NAACP cofounder

PART 4

Cease Overstepping Boundaries—Caucasity, Cultural Appropriation, and Tokenization

PART 4 delves into shamelessly bold white behaviors, like taking without permission and leveraging people of color to strategically block equality. This section removes blinders by explaining how certain choices harm people of color and create a mainstream culture of entitlement to exploit and steal, which invigorates White Welfare.

If you find yourself frequently having knee-jerk reactions or countering with whataboutism, slow down. Accept instead of refuting. Embracing or rejecting these Race Rules is your choice. But by dismissing them, you're derailing your ability to learn to unlearn and evolve into a Racism Disruptor.

This book concentrates on people of color's experiences—how behaviors, choices, and apathy impact them. Avoid rabbit holes about your own negative experiences. Don't unearth how you or other whites had hard lives, when you were offended, or what they should do. Race Rules are about *your* actions. Focus on your transformation.

If you feel blocked and unable to cease opposing what's written, then pause. Ask yourself why your go-to is litigating comments instead of welcoming transparent candor. Then return. You can hop around to different Race Rules and sections to continue your self-discovery and learning. If you need an activity, find a local organization supporting people of color. Volunteer there this weekend. Meet new people. Exposure to people who don't look like you could provide the boost needed to resume reading. Volunteerism facilitates how learning and self-reflection must be accompanied by positive action—with the three-prong approach toward disrupting racism: learn, reflect, and act.

Cultural Appropriation Is Theft

Preservation of one's own culture does not require contempt or disrespect of other cultures.

—*Cesar Chavez, labor leader and civil rights activist*

RULE SUMMARY

Cultural appropriation is capturing ownership and monetizing intellectual property that's not yours. White people are taught they have a right to everything, but they don't.

Cultural appropriation involves plundering or adopting the elements of another culture or identity by people not a part of that heritage, often done without permission by those in the dominant culture (i.e., whites) by appropriating cultures of color outside of the original cultural contexts so traditional significance gets distorted and lost in translation. It's commonly done in ways that advance racist tropes and stereotypes or fail to give credit to the original source. Not to be confused with mutual cultural exchange, it's *colonization* since the taking culture has more societal power than the copied culture—often imitating or grifting expressly against the wishes of people of color.

In its egregious forms, the dominant culture leverages its position to loot power, privilege, perception, portrayal, economic opportunity, or money from people of color. This pillaging further strengthens whites' power, privilege, and societal position to remain dominant.[1]

Cultural appropriation is trying to own what is not yours and you didn't create. It violates the intellectual property rights of people of color. It can include monetizing what's stolen and developing power from theft. This includes heritage commercialization carried out by people who don't understand the ethnicities nor share any generated wealth or income from cultural commoditization. It's ethnic gold mining.

Cultural appropriation threatens cultural preservation. Often, what's copied would be looked down on when used by the original community but is considered cool, funny, or high fashion when the privileged appropriator uses it for their own pleasure or goals.

Wanting all the rhythm but not the blues, white interlopers who never experience racial oppression are allowed through cultural appropriation to temporarily play an "exotic" other without experiencing any of the daily discrimination and trauma faced by people of color.

It's the social equivalent of plagiarism with an added dose of denigration.[2] By educating yourself, you can raise your antenna and be more alert to when you're treading into heritage appropriation.

Aim for cultural sensitivity when adopting elements of another group's culture. Remember, culture isn't a costume.

Cultural appropriation can include exploiting cultural and religious traditions, customs, dance steps, fashion, art, symbols, language, music, food, hairstyles, tattoos, intellectual property, wellness practices, and tribal names. White appropriators often perceive what they're emulating as avant-garde and exotic. But cultural appropriation is an act of oppression that fetishizes while it simultaneously alienates and others.

It's the epitome of whiteness and a white-centered imperialistic mindset to brazenly take what doesn't belong to you and feel entitled to imitate since America's dominant white culture teaches whites few boundaries and racial home training. Our society grants license and free rein to think cultural appropriation is a part of white freedom and expression. It fuels White Welfare and its underlying mentalities.

SELF-REFLECTIVE QUESTIONS

Wanting to appreciate, explore, and elevate other cultures is a positive goal. Appreciation happens when you seek to understand and learn about another culture to broaden your perspective and connect with others. You shift to deeper appreciation and authentic expression when you actively engage in dialogue with those from that culture to underscore your self-education about other peoples, cultures, and traditions.

When trying to determine if you're crossing a line, use these questions as your guide.[3] They will help you decipher whether what you're considering doing or your actions are cultural appreciation or exploration versus cultual appropriation.

1. **Goals**—What's your objective? Is it following trends, exploring a culture's history, or trying to look cool? Are you culturally borrowing as a joke or part of a costume (e.g., Geisha girl, tribal clothing, "urban" rapper, hula dancer, sports team mascot)?

2. **Education**—Have you educated yourself about the culture, history of that heritage and its people, and item's importance? Are you ignoring the deeper cultural significance to follow fads or seem exotic?

3. **Disrespect**—Would this insult someone's culture or cause others racial pain? Are you plucking at historical wrongs or using a sacred item that honors a heritage's people in a flippant way (e.g., headdress as an accessory)?

4. **Tropes**—Are there any stereotypes involved with what you're doing (e.g., thug or farmworker)? Does it include painting your skin or altering your features (e.g., blackface or blackfishing)?

5. **Monetizing**—Are you making money, gaining power or influence, or otherwise propping yourself up or amplifying your brand or reputation? Would someone from the copied community benefit less than you if they did the same thing (e.g., a fashion label borrowing a Mexican Indigenous design for its latest apparel line, a social media influencer Columbusing "new foods" already popular in the Global South as an opportunity to grow followership and attract sponsors)?

6. **Profiteering**—Are you purchasing directly from the cultural source, or are you buying a mass-produced item from a big retailer (e.g., online retailer selling West African clothing made in China by a non-Black vendor)? Is it listed as Indian but not made by or the proceeds going to any Native Americans? Is it a reproduction, or is it an original (e.g., artwork, artifacts, crafts)?

7. **Hijacking and Columbusing**—Are you giving credit to the source or inspiration, or are you claiming it as your own original idea or creative invention (e.g., dance steps, hair-care products, cooking recipes, or decorative fingernail art)? Are you borrowing from an ancient culture and pretending it's new (e.g., Eastern medicine)?

8. **Co-opting**—Does this result in or advance cultural erasure or exclude those from the original community (e.g., white versus South Asian yoga instructor)?

9. **Hypocrisy**—If someone from the culture you're emulating were doing the same thing, would they be viewed as cool or could they face discrimination (e.g., white person freely wearing braids or cornrows when a Black person faces racial profiling or job discrimination or termination)?

10. **Litmus test**—How have people from that community responded when their culture has been similarly copied in the past? Are those supporters outliers (i.e., tokens) or the majority view?

When you have an opportunity to monetize but you defer to the original source, that's honoring another culture. When your actions aren't offensive to that community and they don't feel robbed, that's cultural exploration. When you ask for permission and don't perpetuate stereotypes, that's respecting a culture. When you're learning about others while positively engaging with and elevating them, that's cultural appreciation.

Here are some examples of positive cultural appreciation:

- Buying Native American art or jewelry from a Native artist.
- Frequenting a Mexican restaurant owned by Mexican Americans instead of dining at a corporate chain restaurant.
- Speaking about the #MeToo movement, giving credit to civil rights activist Tarana Burke as its originator instead of white women.
- Wearing a sari to an Indian wedding purchased from an Indian designer or store.
- Dressing like Tina Turner or Michael Jackson for Halloween as a fan of their music but hard-passing on altering facial features or skin color.
- Listening to any music genre you enjoy, but skipping white musicians who exploit Black culture for profit since this only encourages future grifting (e.g., listening to Bobby Caldwell, who was a cultural practitioner possessing an appreciation and respect for Black culture and music genres).

WORD APPROPRIATION AND SEMANTIC BLEACHING

Words can also be co-opted, diminishing their original meaning. This happens when whites use terms originating in communities of color—often terms of pride or self-empowerment—but willfully or inadvertently distort the original meaning.

Woke is an example of cultural word appropriation. It's mutated from a social justice term in the Black community implying a racially conscious person. Whites started misusing it as a badge proclaiming they're "one of the good ones," while others weaponized it as a pejorative against people of color to dismiss and stigmatize racial issues and grievances. Watered down by well-intentioned whites and commandeered as a negative earworm, the initial meaning was stripped. Semantically bleached, now *woke* means anything relating to race or progressivism.

COMPLICITY WITH CELEBRITY CULTURAL APPROPRIATION PERPETRATORS

Purchasing products, supporting celebrities, and following social media personalities engaged in cultural appropriation is moving from passive bystander to personally and directly advancing and participating in cultural theft. By voting with your dollars and social media endorsements, you're providing a platform and marketplace for grifting to thrive. You're messaging that thieving is encouraged and has consumers. Countless celebrities like the following cultural vultures have millions of customers and fans cosigning on appropriation:

- **Elvis Presley**—His success was built on copying Black music and mimicking dance moves to become the "King of Rock and Roll," but he never adequately gave fair credit on his path to fame and wealth.
- **Gwyneth Paltrow**—This wellness and lifestyle "guru" markets and arguably fetishizes Eastern traditions to the wealthy customers of her "science" brand.* She even boldly claimed *personal* responsibility for popularizing yoga. Her product line has included thousand-dollar yoga mats and Ayurvedic herbal formulas sold under the Organic India label. Her cultural exploitation whitewashes the wellness industry while earning her a fortune in ways South Asians cannot earn since they're not white.
- **Addison Rae**—This social media personality known for her dance videos and tens of millions of TikTok followers, making her the second-most-followed person on the platform by early 2021, has been accused of performing dance moves taken from Black creators without giving credit to the original choreographers. Her influencer brand is a million-dollar earning machine. She's an example of a non-Black person profiting and elevating her career off the creativity of Black talent.

These examples are relevant because everyday global citizens have purchasing power, influence as consumers, and control over their daily choices.

---

* Randomly tossing out *guru* is offensive language appropriation. This Hindu and Buddhist title refers to a spiritual leader. Cease referring to industry mavericks or wellness personalities as *gurus*.

You can demand companies and entertainers credit sources, pay talent of color for their creations, and cease borrowing without permission. What happens in industries and commerce has implications for establishing guardrails of acceptable behavior for society. You become complicit with brands and public personalities when you fuel the marketplace and support the careers and profitability of cultural carpetbaggers. If you don't buy what they're selling, they'll respond to market conditions. This is about personally playing a role in a larger framework and economy facilitating racist cultural appropriation (i.e., you directly advancing white supremacy).

TIPS AND ADVICE

In daily life and the workplace, look for opportunities to personally avoid being a cultural appropriator and guilty of heritage theft:

- **Going viral**—When making videos or participating in the latest online dance video craze, know the inspiration's source. Give proper credit when posting online.
- **Killjoy**—Before doing something like hanging a dreamcatcher or referencing your "spirit animal," know if that's offensive behavior desecrating or honoring traditions.
- **Retail colonization**—Be cognizant when products use tribal names or references. For example, when shopping for a car, avoid vehicles commodifying tribal names (e.g., Jeep Cherokee).
- **Fashion crimes**—When buying clothing, don't cosplay someone's culture or purchase "ethnic" clothing from major retailers or fashion houses unless the designer is from that community.
- **Mascots and tropes**—If attending sporting events, don't wear symbols or support mascots that mock, including doing dances or making noises, chants, and hand-chopping gestures offensively associated with Native peoples.
- **Corporate gold mining**—At work, be mindful when developing marketing campaigns or products if you're stealing cultural intellectual artifacts from others. This includes using white artists performing music attributable to cultures of color. Hire the originators instead.
- **Key benchmark**—If you profit or advance professionally from another culture, immediately evaluate if you have permission, are

being culturally sensitive, and are *fairly* sharing the wealth. Otherwise, you're offering a master class on stealing.

ETHNIC FRAUD AND PRETENDIANS

One of the more shameful forms of cultural appropriation is when it goes full deviant into ethnic fraud, race faking, and con-artist identity theft. This involves racial charlatans fraudulently claiming to be a person of color, often for professional gain and financial reward. It can include claiming it in résumés, bios, or job, college, scholarship, or grant applications to work the system around the falsified identity. It's reverse-passing. In its lowest form, it's deceptive box-checking to gain a potential advantage. *Pretendians* are people who falsely claim to be Native American but lack legitimate links to tribes.

These might seem like extreme cases, but this happens daily when whites check boxes for college admissions and other affirmative action programs designed to address systemic racism. This practice unjustly engineers undeserved professional access—robbed at the expense of actual people of color.

It's immoral. People of color have long histories of discrimination, and racism has negatively impacted them and their ancestors and families. Whites don't get to parachute in and helicopter out of being a person of color when it suits their needs—snatching the *very few* professional benefits for marginalized groups. This behavior steals opportunities and access away from genuine people of color who've suffered due to racism. These "Great Pretenders" leverage their privilege to expand White Welfare dividends.

Pretenders who steal identities of color simultaneously erase them. Ethnic fraud isn't harmless nor victimless. Identity hoaxers threaten communities of color. In particular, Pretendians endanger tribal sovereignty.

How many times have we heard someone say they have some Cherokee in them? Where's the proof? If you're relying on family folklore and have no tribal ties, you're a Pretendian. This behavior feeds the yearning for a romanticized "drop of the exotic"—except they don't want the poverty, racism, and accompanying reservation life, just the cool street-cred factor.

It's just more of that "all rhythm and no blues." This is the colonizer mentality of takers: line crossing as momentary tourists.

By the way, if you took a DNA test proving there's a drop of African, Native American, or East Asian in your genetic code, don't start claiming you're a person of color. Don't rush to buy a dashiki, moccasins, or a kimono. Don't try to get your company designated as a minority-owned business. Identity isn't just about DNA when you lack connections to the history and heritage, nor can you point to any specific relative or tribe other than Native. It's too many generations back. At that rate, we could all declare we're African by reaching back three million years to "Lucy" and the other *Australopithecus* in Ethiopia.

As philosopher Hannah Arendt reminded us, lying tears holes in the fabric of factuality.[4] It's perfectly acceptable to be an ally. Do support racial equality and people of color. Embrace disrupting racism. Just don't claim to be what you're not. #WhiteLiesMatter

> We will be known forever by the tracks we leave.
>
> —Dakota Sioux (aka Santee Sioux) proverb

Stop Hue-Jacking and Blackfishing

Racial superiority is a mere pigment of the imagination.

—*Unknown*

RULE SUMMARY

Hue-jacking is the offensive practice of comparing suntanned or olive-toned skin color to a person of color's skin tone as if it were the same thing as being Black or brown—as if all it takes to be a person of color is a few hours on a tanning bed or roasting in the sun.

Whites often pridefully hue-jack like it's bronzification show-and-tell, but this behavior is demoralizing, doesn't establish sameness, trivializes the prejudicial realities faced by non-whites and lighter-skinned people of color, and is rooted in ignorance.

Are you a person of color (e.g., Black, brown, or *non-white* Latino)? If not, hue-jacking is thoroughly off the table! You're getting way too casual with your friend, acquaintance, or colleague of color by engaging in unwelcomed behavior linked to racism. It's time to put your filter back up before you act.

A word to the wise: please don't crank it up by physically putting your arm next to their arm to compare skin color. They're not interested in playing this game no matter how much summer baking you've done. And especially don't do this to your light-skinned friends as it's deeply infuriating, implying you're somehow Blacker or more POC than them because of a tan or bronzer in a bottle.

Hue-jacking happens to people of color of all shades, but let's unpack specifically why some Blacks are light-bright, high yella, red boned, light skinned, light brown, or even bronze or caramel. Let's dive into why they're not all a lot darker.

Pray tell, why do many Foundational Black Americans whose families have been in the United States for centuries come in a spectrum of shades and skin tones? One word: rape. If the enslavers hadn't violently raped so many Blacks in bondage, many would be darker. While rape isn't in every Black person's family lineage, it's part of every Foundational Black American's collective history.

Light-skinned Blacks are still considered Black because of the "one-drop rule." This rule is a throwback social and legal principle of racial classification from slavery days and the Jim Crow era asserting a person with even one Black ancestor is considered Black (i.e., one drop of Black blood). It's tethered to methodologies to keep Blacks classified as slaves no matter how much sexual violence. This effectively allowed open season for sexual predators boldly strutting to the slave quarters since the enslaver's children would still be stuck in the fields in subjugation, frying in the sun, melanin-challenged as the product of rape and oppression.

Although truth be told, due to *colorism* some would have ended up "in the big house" as house slaves since lighter slaves were sometimes assigned domestic tasks instead of harder manual labor. This just meant rapists didn't have to commute to their prey—like pedophile sex trafficker Thomas Jefferson violating his wife's half-sister Sally Hemmings, who was his sex slave. But we won't overly touch on issues around colorism and why it was more socially acceptable to pluck the lighter ones from the fields and hold them hostage in "Massa's house" (i.e., prejudice or discrimination against individuals with darker skin tones).

You can debate America's blurred and confusing racial classifications if you like, but that won't change our history and how hue-jacking is offensive. For some, hue-jacking conjures up why many Blacks have different shades through rape by enslavers. Many Black and brown people generally aren't interested in privileged whites pretending a beach vacation wiped away their differences and racial oppression. It's invalidating and offensive.

COLORISM AND THE TOXIC-FUME FANTASY WAFTING FROM HUE-JACKING

Hue-jacking advances the hypocritical and racist fetishization of tanned skin in society. This plays out with consumer products and marketing that praise the sun-kissed look while simultaneously rejecting Blackness or brown-skinned people and advancing a preference for whiteness through skin-bleaching creams, hair-straightening products, light models, Eurocentric imagery, and other media messages around purity and beauty standards that reinforce white supremacy and ideals of white beauty standards.

This includes routinely pairing white women with Black men in advertising and films, rendering Black women invisible. It's acceptable in society to be a tanned white person, just not an actual person of color. If you're actually Black, then you must de-Blackify as much as possible to try to get even close to skating the periphery of the "mainstream."

Whenever we approach the tanning months or when returning from a holiday, know that Black or brown people don't want to hear "I'm almost as dark as you" or "Funny, I'm now Blacker than you." Naw, Becky and your cousin Karen, people of color don't want to hear this nonsense. In fact, when you do it, more colorful names for you and where you can go will probably come to mind. Cue the eye roll. No matter how much you think your actions are harmless, hue-jacking is upsetting.

Did your family pick cotton? Were your ancestral lands stolen? Did this country commit mass genocide against your people?

If you said no, don't hue-jack. It isn't just invalidating your friend or coworker, but it's also a demoralizing way to mock their people's history and struggles. It's a reminder that it's your white world, and according to power structures, they're just tourists in it.

This brings us to a more perverted form of brown-skin fetishization that's hue-jacking adjacent and infused with cultural appropriation, ethnic fraud, and neo-blackface: *blackfishing*

RULE SUMMARY

Blackfishing is a subtle form of blackface combined with cultural appropriation where non-Blacks take steps to appear Black and alter their facial features, body, or skin tone or otherwise quasi reverse-pass as Black, play into racial ambiguity, or visually present as Black without taking the bigger step of racial identity theft and living as a Black person.

Blackfishing is often achieved by wearing makeup darker than your natural complexion, using products to mimic Black hair, thickening lips with lips injections, getting plastic surgery to become or using padding to appear more curvaceous, wearing "Black clothing," faking a "blaccent," or otherwise aesthetically or culturally aligning with racist stereotypes of Blackness to create a public persona or personal brand built on ethnic fraud. This is commonly done for financial gain, career advancement, street cred, and increased social media followership and online impressions. Typical transgressors are white women on social media platforms (e.g., celebrities, influencers, wannabe virtual stars, fans) monetizing impersonating Blacks. Blackfishers tend to deny their actions are racist or that they're even blackfishers when called out for their manipulative exploitation of Black culture and dragged in the news or online. Anyone engaged in this form of neo-blackface is a blackfisher.

Anyone supporting blackfishing influencers and celebrities by buying or developing their products, following them on social media, promoting their ad campaigns, or supporting their personal brand and companies are blackfish accomplices by proactively endorsing or otherwise complicitly amplifying and cosigning on white supremacist behavior. Blackfishers and their supporters are engaging in racism.

Blackfishing is another example of whites leveraging their white privilege to take from Blacks. This identity hoaxing and race shifting cheapens the experiences of those who've suffered real racial pain and trauma. It's anchored in racist tropes and white supremacy.

It's another vehicle for whites to do what many whites often do: exploit Blacks for profit—a centuries-old American and European tradition. It promulgates White Welfare. Blackfishing is an opportunity for white women to financially benefit from a twisted practice of cosplaying as Black women.

This virtual and celebrity phenomenon is social media minstrelsy—blackface 2.0 for the modern age, just less coonified, but it's definitely the privileged capitalizing off the looks of the oppressed. While there's no more white gloves and Al Jolson sing-alongs, we've moved from shoe polish to bronzer with lots of fish-face selfies rockin' dark skin, cornrows that some grifters ignorantly call boxer braids, big lips and hips, headwraps, animal prints, acrylic nails, big-hoop earrings, and "urban" clothes. It's disgusting and racist as Black femininity is commodified and reduced to a caricature of what whites think being Black looks like or what Black culture includes.

The *caucasity* and harm of blackfishing is more apparent when thinking about misogynoir and how impactful Black cultural theft and appropriation are on society.

A white identity requires a fantasy of Blackness.

There's a love-theft dynamic—a thirst for things considered desirable in Blackness and the fear in having to deal with the downside of being Black in Western societies. This isn't just about blackface or blackfishing but a general white fantasy of Black culture—a fetishistic desire for temporary Blackness or the benefits of it that triggers deep shame since people know it's wrong on some level. This is why ethnic identity theft has been condemned for decades yet persists. Where blackface was meant to entertain, blackfishing is meant to somewhat pass as or have the patina of being at least half-Black or make money off racial ambiguity. It's indisputable race hoaxing as celebrities and internet personalities try to look non-white—they transform from white women to light-skinned Black women with style and fashion derived from Black hip-hop culture.

Blackfishers don't really want to be Black; they want only the upsides of mimicking being Black when the social norm is that Black people are incapable of financially benefiting from being who they naturally are. The advantages are just for White Girl Culture Vultures. Grifting blackfishers want to seem less white-looking and racially vague in the latest craze of Black exploitation. Being a Black woman is to create without credit and support others without personally benefiting from critical support systems. Appropriation thieves want the culture washed clean of the ancestry and struggle that birthed it and instead cherry-pick the commercially marketable components.[1]

Black culture is extremely profitable if it's out of the hands of Blacks. Companies shaping fashion and generic American culture give infinite professional opportunities to whites and not Blacks—feeding into Black exploitation and the country's thirst for Blackness repackaged by Imitation-of-Life white blackfishers. Together, they're stealing in response to this ravenous culture of consumption where what Blacks invent and create is marketable but where white women and white-led corporations get paid.

Why has this cultural blackfishing phenomenon exploded? High-profile celebrities.

THE DANGEROUS INFLUENCE OF THE KARDASHIAN-JENNER BLACKFISHERS

The biggest perpetrators and profiteers of blackfishing are the Kardashian-Jenner family. Their behavior is hazardous since they leverage their platform for financial gain. The public gobbles it up. What's equally important about why they're dangerous is their fame enables them to influence American society and shape what the dominant white culture deems socially acceptable and desirable. By being CEO blackfishers, they fuel normalizing cultural appropriation along with a mentality that it's attractive for whites to steal and cosplay being Black while Black women would be penalized since misogynoir persists. Celebrities promote white supremacy, and through the vicious cycle with their social media reach, they export this mindset globally.

As a family and individually, most of Kris Jenner's children habitually borrow and steal from Black culture; from excessive plastic surgery to transform their bodies and alter their features to look more Black to Kendall Jenner trivializing Black Lives Matter in a Pepsi ad and then facing backlash. Each year, it seems Kim Kardashian becomes a shade darker and curvier. This posse of racial shapeshifters has been accused of blackfishing and stealing ideas for their brands and products from Black businesses. But they face no consequences, teaching other whites they too should steal from Blacks and can build a thriving career and business empire from theft.

Given their global reach as influencers and businesswomen and ability to guide behaviors of everyday people and lure corporate partnerships, they pose a significant threat to people of color in advancing racist tropes and endorsing mass-scale heritage profiteering. The Kardashian-Jenner family facilitates white supremacy going viral. You'd hope they would have learned more about what's acceptable behavior having dated and married several Black men and birthed Black babies, but it's an example of how having a Black friend or Black relative doesn't immunize someone from exhibiting or engaging in racist behavior, sitting in white supremacy, or basking in white privilege. #ChaChing

Why does this matter? Why are these celebrities relevant? Because they influence young girls and maturing adults. Because blackfishing fuels more blackfishing with cohorts cribbing off each other to keep this insidious and nefarious racist practice alive and maintain white-centered societal power. Because social media is a booming treasure trove of seemingly benign yet menacing influencers shaping society and courting corporate dollars. They send messages promulgating white supremacy and are rewarded for exploiting Black and brown trauma as culture vultures.

This goes beyond endorsement from hundreds of millions of online followers. Nice whites become collaborators in the monetization of blackfishing when supporting their fame and brands. In keeping black-fishing profitable and thriving, everyday whites create the marketplace for cultural theft. As the public idolizes blackfishing celebrities, good whites mimic this behavior. They too get plastic surgery, lip injections, implants, and fillers and bronze their bodies. They rock braids and wear "urban" clothing. When copying beauty standards and fashion trends, some feel empowered to showcase their personal metamorphosis on social media. This promotes a perpetual blackfishing cycle.

The vagueness and subversive nature of blackfishing compared to old-school blackface is that this contemporary iteration is harder for most people to decode that they're consuming bigotry. This makes it easier to turn a blind eye or brush it off as something other than what it is: white supremacy. Famous blackfishers can claim they're not appropriating directly from Black culture and hoodwink you into thinking this is just mass American culture going viral and global. In turn, this blinds you from seeing your complicity or active participation in blackfishing.

You can appreciate Black culture without stealing and hoaxing. You can participate, but participating, appreciating, and respecting doesn't mean you should "become Black."

There's no respect in theft and cultural appropriation. Blackfishers have no incentive to stop transforming into poor imitations of Black. This will continue until we hold whites and companies accountable for neo-blackface.

TIPS AND ADVICE

To stop blackfishing and supporting blackfishers, take the following steps:

- **Unlike and unfollow**—If you see blackfishing online, don't "like" the post or follow that person, brand, company, influencer, or online content. It's important you don't support this practice or imagery online.
- **Boycott**—When celebrities blackfish, call them out and the brands sponsoring them. Don't buy their products or anything they endorse. Encourage others to stop supporting entertainers and companies monetizing cultural theft and racist stereotypes.
- **Educate**—Speak to your friends about the impact of blackfishing when they share racist blackfishing content so they understand why it's harmful to people of color and that it advances racist tropes.

- **Object and scrutinize**—Evaluate and challenge messaging in the media that reinforces skin-color preferences, blackfishing, and white imposters' ability to profit off Black culture, including looking at advertising campaigns that support blackfishing and elevate white supremacy as whites earn from Black culture.
- **Self-assess**—Think about if you're *personally* proactively involved in blackfishing by not celebrating Black culture but instead mimicking it or perpetuating tropey racist versions of what you think Blackness means.

> You want to continue to believe in the rightness of whiteness, and that is a lie.
>
> —Jane Elliott, diversity educator and schoolteacher

CHIEF EXECUTIVE OFFICER
CEO
SINCE 2000

CHIEF OPERATING OFFICER
COO
SINCE 2000

CHIEF FINANCIAL OFFICER
CFO
SINCE 2000

CHIEF MARKETING OFFICER
CMO
SINCE 2005

CHIEF TECHNOLOGY OFFICER
CTO
SINCE 2008

GENERAL COUNSEL
GC
SINCE 2010

CHIEF CUSTOMER OFFICER
CCO
SINCE 2011

CHIEF HR OFFICER
CHRO
SINCE 2017

CHIEF DIVERSITY OFFICER
CDO
SINCE JUNE 2020

Tokens and Having Black Friends Doesn't Mean You're Not Racist

Most men today cannot conceive of a freedom
that does not involve somebody's slavery.

—*W. E. B. Du Bois, Pan-Africanist and NAACP cofounder*

RULE SUMMARY

A *token* is a person of color who is included in (or held out as an affiliate of) a majority-white group to give the false impression of that group's fairness, equal treatment, and racial inclusivity. Tokens are used as superficial markers for diversity and racism shields, often to avoid criticism and appear anti-racist.

Tokens can also be present on an individual level in actual or alleged friendships.

Tokenism is believing in and acting on the myth that proximity to Blackness or people of color immunizes whites from having attitudes rooted in racism or engaging in racist behavior. It leans into racism by hiding behind familial ties or actual or perceived friendships, including giving more credence to acquaintance relationships that aren't real friendships.

Tokenization involves how people of color are treated by whites, used as props, sequestered to specific divisions or roles in organizations, and leveraged to block including additional people of color or silence them. It's a form of racism.

While your goal should be to improve diversity by increasing underrepresented groups in your private life and at work, the mere presence of people who don't look like you won't eliminate discrimination or prejudice. Diversity isn't the same as inclusion and can be performative.

POC presence isn't proof positive you've done the work to credibly claim allyship. Having people of color in your family or circle of trust doesn't symbolize you can't be racist nor tokenize them—even if you have a Black child, East Asian spouse, Native American best friend, Latino doctor, or Arab colleague or client you like and respect.

Acquaintance ≠ Friend

Even if someone is truly your friend, it doesn't mean you aren't a habitual line crosser who says racist things or subjects friends of color to microaggressions. And note that if the person works for or receives income from you, you're probably *not* friends (e.g., nanny, gardener, home health aide, housecleaner, hairdresser, personal assistant, or trainer). You need clear crossover events where you spend time together offsite and hear about *their* life story and issues instead of just data dumping your problems in one-sided exchanges. If it's not mutual, then it's not a genuine friendship.

Whether you volunteered in developing countries, work in an underserved community, or attended high school with many students of color, none of these degrees of separation automatically translate into being woke. Your exposure to people of color just lowers the likelihood and frequency of your choices being racist. It doesn't signify that you're impervious to racist thoughts and behaviors, no matter how deep your friendships and connections might be.

This is even more apparent if you're prone to fist bumping with your supposed friends of color when you don't use this salutation with your white friends. Are you just high-fiving your homies? Interesting.

How often do we hear the "Some of my best friends are Black," "My boyfriend is Asian," or "I don't have a racist bone in my body, and the Mexican guy I hired on my team can attest to this" defenses? These trite deflection tactics are tokenized bigotry-denial red flags, often tossed out as preemptive-strike distractions when white guilt bubbles up or you need punchline ammunition to escape accountability after crossing a line. These proclamations are often accompanied with an insistence to "not see color" or declare "racism has no place."

The Black friend excuse is reminiscent of old-timey slavery days when white enslavers fancied the false narrative that oppressed Blacks "jus luv dem some Massa!" This warped view helped rationalize white supremacist racial hierarchies. By painting the illusion of relationship harmony between dominant whites and subordinated Blacks, it fabricated a license and consent to subjugate. Today's Black friend variant claims are similar nonsensical word salads trying to head fake others into seeing friendships as significantly more meaningful than merely tenuous to escape accountability and avoid acknowledging prejudicial personal shortcomings.

Besides, integration and socially mixing alone aren't the solution if you do nothing additive to understand people of color, their history, and their journey. You need to unlearn antiquated views and bad behaviors. You need to *see* them, develop empathy, and nurture sensitivity to what's offensive. This limits the chance you will make tone-deaf statements and racially rude comments that cause others pain and invite warranted criticism.

Even when you take the time to form strong interracial bonds, it's still hard to overcome society's subliminal and overt messages creeping into our thoughts. You can develop close ties with people of color and still feel superior and harbor racist stereotypes. Society is centered on whiteness, making it difficult to deprogram yourself to thwart racist tendencies and being prejudiced.

TIPS AND ADVICE

Here are some strategies to circumvent slipping into tokenism and develop genuine cross-racial friendships:

1. Consciously increase the scale and scope of your friends of color while simultaneously broadening your knowledge of inclusive, accurate American history to better connect and understand them.
2. Challenge underlying assumptions that friends or colleagues of color are special or different compared to other people of color. Seeing them as outliers can be linked to stereotypes about how you think those in that group behave, speak, or achieve, implying the reason they're your friend or colleague is because of this perceived exceptionalism difference.
3. Advocate for diversity, inclusion, and anti-racism when people of color are not in the room. This promotes seeing diversity and representation as a philosophy and policy and not a checklist. In the workplace, this includes sponsoring more people of color as decision-makers, team leaders, and managers with budget oversight.
4. Resist impulses to view perspectives of specific people of color as representing their entire race, which treats them not as individuals but monoliths. This includes overburdening them to speak on behalf of their race.
5. Avoid thinking the achievement and success of a person of color indicates discrimination and racism have been solved, including for your friends or colleagues of color, no matter how wealthy, educated, or successful they are.

6. Understand that diversity isn't inclusion and mere numbers don't mean there's a sense of belonging or feeling included, deep friendship, or equitable pathways to achievement.

7. Be brutally honest about whether you're creating space for transparent friendships with room for candor. It's tokenization if they're a badge of honor yet you get defensive and feel threatened, challenged, or triggered when highlighting racism close to home—at your workplace, in your community, or through your behavior and choices. This is especially relevant if truthfulness about you causing harm or being offensive prompts you to distance yourself or sabotage their career. If you do this, act immediately to adjust your thinking and implement corrective steps to repair relationships and professional damage.

Without these additional steps, whites often end up with superficial relationships devoid of genuine cross-racial understanding. This knowledge and self-awareness are foundational to caring and connecting authentically and shifting away from tokenization.

You also need to keep a keen eye out for a trap that comes with having genuine friends of color—getting too comfortable. Whites can be lulled into a false sense of familiarity with friends of color where they push boundaries best left untouched. For some classic examples, look to comedian Bill Maher or filmmaker Quentin Tarantino, who both think they're "invited to the cookout" and thus take racist license with the N-word. This also happens if you touch a Black person's hair without consent, make fried chicken and watermelon references, or say they "don't talk like they're Black."

AVOIDING CORPORATE TOKENISM

Corporate tokenism encompasses symbolic gestures or perfunctory efforts to seem racially inclusive, especially by recruiting and hiring people of color to prevent scrutiny and backlash, using diversity smokescreens to imply employees of color are treated fairly, and giving the appearance of racial equality to neutralize accusations of discrimination and lower the risk exposure to litigation. For those in power, tokenism seeks to imply they're not racist or are diversity champions since they recruit people of color or otherwise use them as racialized props.

Hiring people of color to merely check a box is racist, and people can clearly see when it's just "exclusion inclusion" (i.e., hiring props of color while simultaneously not giving them the organizational support and opportunities for career success).

You might be wondering what's the difference between tokenizing people of color and representation—especially if you're trying to diversify your organization, have only one candidate of color on your interview roster, or are at the beginning of your diversity journey.

To weed out tokenism from representation requires evaluating critical factors: *intent* and what *other steps* your organization undertakes to drive diversity and actively support employees of color by creating a *legitimate* culture of inclusion. This includes actively ensuring employees of color aren't lonely onlies. Tokenization ceases when you move beyond lip service and parading around staff of color to give the illusion of diversity—when you have multiple people of color, *including* in leadership, management, and board positions with decision-making authority controlling budgets and overseeing teams.

It's also very telling and important what institutions proactively do to support the *specific person* being strutted about.

The person is a workplace prop if they're used for photo ops while not getting tangible leadership support to advance—to gain skills, get client exposure, handle big projects, manage teams and budgets, and be groomed for leadership roles and opportunities. Anything short of this is token zone.

Here are some examples of corporate and public tokenism:

- **Props**—Putting the sole Black or brown person (or one of a few) in a position voluntarily or involuntarily to speak on behalf or be the face of all Black or brown people in the diaspora.
- **Exclusion inclusion**—Recruiting and hiring people of color for leadership positions but keeping all the power and critical decision-making authority, often paired with creating and maintaining organizational cultures promoting white dominance and not supporting the professional success of people of color.
- **Showboating**—Convening "diversity councils" and "affinity" or "employee resource" groups but failing to build leadership of color on corporate boards and executive leadership teams, including burdening volunteers already with day jobs with unrewarded work without

creating full-time paid diversity officer positions with impactful budgets and headcounts to support these groups and authority to systematize measurable accountability.

- **Trojan horses and bobbleheads**—Weaponizing people of color as mouthpieces and shields against other people of color (e.g., using them to (1) "keep management informed" of another employee of color's work; (2) endorse and perpetuate white-centered status quo strategies and workplace cultures, including diversity officers; (3) discipline other people of color; and (4) rubber-stamp white colleagues, policies, initiatives, products, and marketing campaigns as not racist or otherwise validate work products or decision-making as racially appropriate to deflect criticism and backlash from stakeholders of color).
- **Public enemies**—Leveraging dissent from political or ideological outliers from a community of color as a strategic, pernicious tool to thwart progress for people of color and holding the nonrepresentational voice out as the mouthpiece or emissary of or expert from that community to advance racist or white-centered policy goals, legislation, litigation stances, and company initiatives. This is taking advantage of how not all skinfolk are kinfolk.
- **Ghettoizing**—Hiring people of color only for "minority stuff."
- **Potemkin workplace**—Using people of color in images, online content, social media campaigns, advertising, marketing, annual reports, and other front-facing visualizations to give the impression of diversity when that's not representational of daily life inside the company.
- **Lip service**—Having a section on the company website about diversity plastered with a collage of Black and brown-faced and AAPI-member images when it's not a real corporate value as evidenced by low diversity employee statistics, few people of color in leadership, or discrimination lawsuits.
- **Parachuting**—Corporate executives, community leaders, and politicians strategically positioning people of color directly in the camera shot behind the speaker at public events, including at press conferences in response to public scandals. Poof—there for a second, irrelevant for a lifetime.
- **POC puppetry**—Sending people of color to accept corporate awards or purchasing honorary acknowledgments from organizations of

color through strategic sponsorships to appear supportive of communities of color when it's antithetical to the organizational culture or corporate lobbying and business practices.

- **Monetary magic tricks**—Using white staff or outside consultants or vendors to develop, design, and implement messaging but using people of color as storytellers and poster faces to appear diverse.
- **Funding BS**—Paying white-led vendors and consultants more than what's typically paid to counterparts of color doing similar or equally important work (which also applies to pay and year-end bonus equity for employees).
- **Smoke and mirrors**—CEOs and other employees volunteering in underserved communities, especially after a scandal or to pander to consumers of color to get positive press, particularly when this community engagement isn't standard to business operations, customer relations, or philanthropic giving.
- **Performative box checking**—Developing diversity strategies, hiring diversity consultants and staff of color, or issuing statements (including in support of Black Lives Matter) but never making the requisite organizational change, driving critical internal support, or allocating adequate funds to create a diverse talent pipeline and welcoming workplace for employees of color.

It's folly for people and companies to assume blanket immunity from being a bigot or protection from being labeled a white supremist through mere associations with people from other races.

People of color tend to recognize these optical illusions and not get bamboozled by and fall for the token okey doke.

> To know what is right and not to do it is the worst cowardice.
>
> —Confucius, philosopher

End Jackie Robinson Syndrome

One person plus one typewriter constitutes a movement.

—*Pauli Murray, civil rights activist and legal scholar*

RULE SUMMARY

Stop the "lonely only" status quo. It's a form of tokenism advancing de facto quotas putting ceilings on collective achievement for people of color. Stop appointing role models, spokespeople, and trailblazers. It's conscription for roles people may not want and is often accompanied by simultaneously closing the door to others, rendering them tokenized blockers.

We sure love to celebrate trailblazing firsts—Jackie Robinson breaking baseball's color line and Barack Obama as our first Black president. Pioneers bring pride to their communities and *every* American, giving children hopes and dreams as embodiments of what's attainable.

Having "firsts" makes us feel like we're making racial progress when we can point to the exceptions to the only-whites-succeed rule. It makes us feel warm and fuzzy inside, as if we're moving the needle.

The difficulty? Not everyone *wants* to be Jackie Robinson! No one should *have to be* Jackie Robinson! Often, having "firsts" doesn't go far enough to have a lasting impact and creates a false sense of progress that can encourage inertia and apathy.

Avoid Jackie Robinson Syndrome. It's when people and companies appoint people of color as *solitary* trailblazing "firsts" for their race—effectively making them role models for an *entire* people, which is often racist since whites aren't seen as spokespeople for their entire race but as individuals who represent only themselves. This is often paired with believing that the hard work is now done. Jackie Robinson Syndrome typically includes having just one person break the color line as the lonely only.

HOW TO AVOID THE
LONELY ONLY CONSTRUCT

Being a trailblazer is a lonesome road. It takes courage, but the journey is too damn hard to be a solo flyer. It breaks people down and is exhausting. This is why when people of color notice that a company has virtually no employees of color through its ranks, they get ghost and say, "No thank you." Not everyone is interested in fighting that daily racist battle.

What do people of color want? Company! They want and need workplace compatriots with whom to weather the storm—you know, folks to commiserate with when getting their tenth racist microaggression of the day. They need someone who gets it when they exchange glances and others to share the emotional burden and anxiety of heightened scrutiny functioning under a microscope. They require more people who look like them at the top so they know there's a chance they're welcome and included at organizations. They need lunchtime buddies more likely to be workplace friends and inviting faces to have drinks with to strategize how to bypass bigoted colleagues and share experiences to improve their collective shot at getting promoted.

Organizations need to add company since people of color don't enjoy going it alone and plenty are allergic to pioneering.

Companies need to hire people of color in a group to avoid forcing employees of color into burdensome and fatiguing trailblazer Jackie Robinson roles—especially if the company's racial diversity numbers are low or it's about to make someone a first. Having solo flyers isn't the optimal goal and won't significantly advance racial equality. It's easier charting a course as a cohort and less mentally taxing. It increases the chance they won't flee at the first sign of opportunities elsewhere. Baby-stepping it isn't sustainable.

Jackie Robinson Syndrome gives whites an excuse to sit back, relax, stop pushing for improvements, and rest on the laurels of the few who managed to climb through shut doors. Just aiming for the lonely only promotes laziness and slipping into status quo, white supremacist, barred-access-to-opportunity models.

TIPS AND ADVICE

Avoid forcing employees and coworkers to be ambassadors of color, which relegates them to representing their entire race. Here are some important guidelines:

- **Appointing spokespeople**—It's racist tokenization to think of people of color as public relations reps for all their people. Even if volunteering to be a luminary, you still can't assume they speak for *all* Black and brown people. Each solely speaks for their opinion alone.

If everything Barack Obama said represented all Blacks, then I guess we can assume Adolf Hitler spoke for all whites, right? Or President 45? Because they're white guys saying white people oppression crap, and whites as a group are in the oppressor and privilege camp. By that logic, Hitler and 45 must speak for you too. If you find this comparison perverse, then don't put that same absurd burden on people of color. It's advancing white supremacist ideologies about people of color being monolithic while whites have the freedom of individuality. It's an unfair double standard that's marginalizing.

- **Electing role models**—Voicing opinions and being exemplars should involve consent. When wanting someone to speak on issues of diversity or topics impacting Black and brown people or those from the AAPI community, ask if they willingly signed up for the job. Make sure they weren't hoodwinked or ambushed into vocalizing views they prefer to keep private or into being the face of their race. Too often whites glom onto random people of color or any brown body with a pulse to represent "the minority perspective." Leave the nonvolunteers alone until they signal consent. Let them focus on their daily grind and surviving in a white-dominant society.

- **Unjustly burdening trailblazers**—Stop, hesitate, and listen. Be mindful of the challenges and emotional toll of functioning in an organization suffering from Jackie Robinson Syndrome. Don't unjustly burden and fatigue people of color. Give them a network of key leaders so they can thrive.

- **Assuming racial progress**—Just because you see a person of color who's well educated, has a good job, drives a nice car, has an amazing home, or isn't very dark skinned, don't assume they and their family haven't experienced racism and don't *currently* face bigotry. Imagine what greater heights they could have achieved without discrimination and systemic racism. More importantly, don't presume we've solved racism since there are clear success stories. What you can safely assume is *every* person of color you see walking down the street, in a meeting, at your workplace, or lying in bed next to you has suffered and is suffering through some form of white supremacy. That's a certified given.

Won't it be nice when we don't have "firsts" anymore? The fastest way to get there is to stop clinging to singular beacons of hope. Double down on diversifying with larger numbers. Provide greater access to more people. Create environments for people of color to be individuals, not entire-race emissaries.

> If you don't like affirmative action, what is your plan to guarantee a level playing field of opportunity?
>
> —Maynard Jackson, former mayor of Atlanta

PART 5

Scale Back Your Casual Racism, Deflection Tactics, and Tone Policing

PART 5 focuses on offensive behaviors that invalidate, gaslight, and seek to regulate how and what people of color should think, feel, and believe. It flags how interactions aren't just hurtful and insulting (which shapes negative views of you) but add to the level of collective racial trauma from white people.

If you're struggling with this book's forthright tone or you feel guilty, crave forgiveness, or feel battered by detailing how your behaviors and actions uphold white supremacy, remember your purpose. Saying the quiet part out loud challenges your sense of self. How effective have past efforts that tiptoe around white fragility been? How has circumventing emotional labor and accountability helped the country or led you to understand what's taboo?

Caring about ourselves and others isn't two separate exercises. Caring involves how we treat people and communities. Doing the work is an investment in yourself—your evolution into being a better friend, colleague, family member, spouse, and citizen.

You're here to gain a new perspective. Race Rules lift the veil for a strategic purpose—to change and improve how you think and behave. That can't happen in a nirvana bubble but through rolling up your sleeves and pushing through the tough parts. This book is about reparative reading.

The goal isn't white forgiveness but limiting the volume of discrimination and racism expressed through your actions and inaction. Through behavioral and mindset modifications, you can form stronger friendships. It's acceptable to take breaks. Just come back. Doing the work is the assignment.

Stop Saying You're Colorblind Because It's Racist

The only thing worse than being blind
is having sight but no vision.

—*Helen Keller, political activist*

RULE SUMMARY

Racial colorblindness doesn't exist! Stop leaning into colorblind thinking and saying you don't see color. Mentioning colorblindness is annoying, dismissive of reality, and deeply invalidating.

Colorblindness is an inherently racist ideology that advances the belief that discrimination could end if we treat people equally—without regard to race, culture, or ethnicity. Colorblind statements and philosophies are a common response to racism. More specifically, they're a customary reaction from white people attempting to reject racism.

They're also a clever tool for attacking policies addressing systemic racism, like affirmative action and diversity initiatives. It provides fodder and cover to claim reverse discrimination and seek race-neutral policies that strategically uphold the status quo and protect White Welfare.

Pretending colorblindness is real and achievable today means we cannot address or recognize structural racial inequities and injustice in our own communities.

Colorblindness views people through a white lens and suppresses important narratives of oppression. It assumes everyone in society has the same experience.

People saying they're colorblind are really saying *they* don't experience many negative impacts of *their* race, while simultaneously signaling—intentionally or not—that the experiences of people of color carry marginal value and consideration. "Don't see color" verbiage negates truths that people are treated differently due to skin color.

Instead, be *color aware*. Admit you see color and open your eyes to how people who don't look like you live a different experience that may involve persistent discrimination because the world *does* see color. Once you do this and stop denying race is relevant, you can become a better advocate for equality and disrupt racism.

HOW COLORBLINDNESS HARMS

Supporting colorblindness stops you from having an honest, open, and sometimes uncomfortable dialogue about our different experiences because of our color—allowing white people to pretend we live in a fairytale world of racial equality and post-racialism. It promotes disconnection, limits our ability to identify with different people, and equates color with something negative. Also, it allows you to ignore discrimination and invalidates people's identities and experiences with racism. It's degrading.

Colorblind principles are racist because it means that racist impacts and outcomes won't be addressed. Thus, it supports the *status quo*, which is anchored to white supremacy.

Here are many ways colorblindness shows up in conversations:

- "I don't see color. Green, Black, white—it's all the same to me."
- "I'm colorblind. I don't care if people are green, purple, rainbow, or polka dot."
- "I wasn't raised to see color. I just see people. I raised my son to not see color, and I've never heard him refer to the skin color of his minority friends. He's grown up colorblind."
- "Color shouldn't matter. We're all one race—the human race."
- "Why do you keep using the term *people of color*? Doesn't that term just divide us?"
- "Character, not color, is what matters to me. Just like Dr. King."
  - Word salad "character-not-color" statements show how Martin Luther King's statements are frequently manipulated, hijacked, and strategically used as false-narrative weapons to silence voices of color and demands for equality and restorative justice. Dr. King never advocated for colorblindness. He believed in affirmative action, reparations, and race-based solutions to systemic racism.
  - He was assassinated as his calls for economic justice and race-conscious restitution were increasing and as his demands for full rights, economic solutions, and an end to poverty were sounding increasingly aligned with those of Malcolm X (i.e., convergent visions to address racial oppression). The pathway to

his dream for equality and increased Black wealth runs directly through consciously seeing race.

- "I don't even see you as [insert race/ethnicity here]. I just see you as [insert person's name]."
- "Why does it matter if we hire people with diverse backgrounds? I'll admit that we don't have much racial diversity in our company—okay, maybe virtually no diversity—but shouldn't we focus on skills and qualifications?"
- "Why are we talking about '*Black* lives matter' instead of '*All* lives matter'?"

For more information and to see a Colorblindness Microaggression Translator chart breaking down how statements can be heard and received by people of color, visit FatimahGilliam.com/RaceRulesDownloads.

DEADLY DOWNSIDE OF COLORBLINDNESS

If we don't see the role race plays, then we must assume the deaths of George Floyd, Breonna Taylor, Ahmaud Arbery, Michael Brown, Renisha McBride, Philando Castile, Eric Garner, Natasha McKenna, Trayvon Martin, Atatiana Jefferson, Jordan Neely, Tamir Rice, and Elijah McClain had nothing to do with race, that a white person would have been similarly shot, killed, suffocated, chokeholded, or tased to death.

The impact is we fail to admit being Black or brown results in unwarranted deaths. We can't properly analyze what went wrong and how to prevent the use of excessive force or future senseless killings by the police or supposed law-abiding citizens.

As rogue wannabe cops, domestic terrorists, and so-called vigilantes hunt down people of color like prey and carry out modern-day lynchings (often using baseless self-defense and stand-your-ground claims), colorblind ideologies block us from evaluating how to end these murders. Colorblindness obstructs seeing these as racially motivated murders or continual society-sanctioned devaluations of Black and brown lives.

KEY STATISTICS

- Black Americans are 2.9 times more likely to be killed by the police than whites.[1]
- Ninety-nine percent of all police officers involved in killings had no criminal charges pressed against them, with only the small handful of those who were charged actually being convicted of a crime.[2]
- The government doesn't track deaths caused by the police nationwide.
- It does track the number of cops killed in the line of duty. We count what we value. We see what we want to see.

You probably didn't mean any harm when saying you're colorblind or talked about "green people." If you're white, maybe you're just trying to be an ally to people of color. But pretending we live in an alternate reality is nonsensical, harmful, and dangerous. These statements reveal you *do not care* about injustices faced by people of color.

While you may be trying to demonstrate you're without biases and are coming from a seemingly positive place, you end up ignoring the other person's reality. The result is people of color feel disregarded. Due to willful blindness, a myopic societal view, pure ignorance, or fake wokeism, these blinders render you incapable of seeing the legitimacy of their life experiences.

Maybe you've convinced yourself you really don't see race. But clearly, you see color enough to say to a person of color that you don't see color because—going on a hunch here—you probably don't make these statements as often to your white friends. And if you do say it to fellow whites, you're probably not saying it *about* them but rather *to* them.

Whenever we say we're colorblind, we're typically referring exclusively to non-whites. *Colorblind* is code for negating and invalidating people of color. Colorblindness imposes whiteness on everyone and says that you view everyone as if they're white since the default color for sameness is white and the default lens through which we see society is white. It promotes the superiority of whites and the inferiority of non-whites.

No matter how much the truth is avoided, society's color vision negatively impacts life outcomes (e.g., whether you get a job interview or home mortgage, if you're racially profiled by the police or issued a summons, how much intergenerational wealth your family has accumulated, the likelihood you have equitable access to quality schools and educational opportunities, whether your doctor takes you seriously when you're explaining medical conditions and symptoms, if you're offered a better interest rate when you finance a car purchase, and the underlying reason behind why a shop owner made you check your bag before entering or followed you around the store). We notice race and skin color—culminating in the discriminatory experiences of people of color and the positive advantages benefiting whites. Color does matter even though it shouldn't.

Colorblindness ideologies turn color and diversity into negatives. Colorblindness is codependent on racism and enables it to exist. What's better for society is to be *color aware*—not just recognizing differences but how to be diversity champions and Racism Disruptors by advancing solutions that aren't race neutral (e.g., affirmative action). We must admit the relevance of race to facilitate progress.

Noticing color isn't intrinsically bad. It's *how you react* to color that's important. Not all conversations about color or race are racist.
Color consciousness ≠ racism
You can't disrupt structural racism in an insular bubble detached from reality that is blind to race.

BLURRING COLORBLINDNESS, MERITOCRACIES, AND RESISTANCE TO AFFIRMATIVE ACTION

Colorblind ideologies creep into policies and are at the epicenter of resistance to programs designed to address structural racism like affirmative action. Colorblindness becomes a tool for blocking racial progress. This frequently emerges when people insist on "not considering color" when discussing equal access to opportunities. Suddenly, people start talking about skills, qualifications, and merit as their crutch for opposition.

The assumptions embedded in obstructionist statements are (1) it's difficult to find qualified people of color to hire (i.e., the pipeline excuse) or candidates of color are inherently inexperienced and unskilled (i.e., deficient compared to whites) and (2) the white employees are inherently qualified, not merely average or mediocre, and were hired purely on their own merits. Thus, the narrative often disproportionately centers around qualifications when discussing candidates and employees of color and false notions of a meritocracy.

This same prejudiced mindset applies to college admissions, which has de facto affirmative action for white people (e.g., legacy college admissions, spots held for high-ticket donors, or reliance on standardized tests that have been statistically proven to be racially biased and poor predictors of college success relative to grades).

When people say factoring in race means we're not selecting for excellence, they're blind to seeing how society is *already* factoring in race—the white race. And this is what's constraining the selection of excellence by foreclosing equitable access to opportunities.

TIPS AND ADVICE

The advice below will help you transition away from amplifying troublesome colorblindness ideologies. Also, it provides guidance on what to say when you witness someone claiming they "don't see color" to support and help you develop your racism disruption skills.

YOU—CLAIMING COLORBLINDNESS

If and when you're tempted to claim that you don't see color, this advice can guide you away from racist behaviors:

- Please stop saying you're "colorblind" and "don't see color," and please stop referring to green people and other random nonhuman mutant colors. It's make-believe rambling. Unless you're legally blind, we know you stop at red traffic lights. Admit that you notice race and skin color.
- Instead, consider saying you "recognize your privilege," "have different life experiences," "are doing your best to understand people with different backgrounds," or "welcome help on how to address and discuss the impact of racial differences felt by others."

- If you're a white liberal, as hard as this is, admit adopting color-blind ideologies is *not anti-racist*. Thus, you too are prejudiced and racist. After swallowing this reality pill, focus on your personal growth to truly be the equality advocate you think you are but aren't quite yet.
- When describing someone, sometimes it's acceptable to identify and acknowledge their race if it's relevant or helpful. There's no need to go through verbal Hula-Hoops to describe everything else about someone except their race—especially when it's useful information. Just don't overly emphasize it. It's all in the delivery of what you say and about the underlying reason. For example, there's a crowded room of people all wearing similar attire with few distinguishing characteristics, but the glaring differentiating factor for the person you're trying to point out happens to be that they're South Asian.
- It's not a good look to mention race when it's totally irrelevant. For example, you're recounting a story about someone who kindly let you go ahead of them at the supermarket checkout line and you mention or highlight their race. This is totally immaterial to the story and comes off as racist.

SELF-REFLECTIVE QUESTIONS

When you're about to mention being colorblind, ask yourself these questions:

- Would you say to a man or woman, "I don't see gender"? If we were gender-blind, then we'd be incapable of addressing systemic sexism and misogyny that leads to impacts like women being paid less for the same or higher-quality work. Also, it would mean we're unable to accept transgender people in whichever categories they feel best applies to them—or the very low-bar hurdle of accepting that gender even exists and there are different genders.
- Would you rather someone felt *seen* by you instead of rendered *invisible*?
- Are you saying you're colorblind only to make yourself feel better or to not appear racist or prejudiced?
- Would you say this to your white friend?

- Do you genuinely want to improve how we discuss race, or are you more preoccupied with avoiding acknowledging that race plays a role in people's lives and is a critical determining factor in society?
- What are some of the underlying reasons behind *why* it's so important to you to focus on being allegedly colorblind?
- What are you gaining by denying color exists? What are you afraid of losing if you stop professing you're colorblind? Are you doing this to protect your own privilege? Are you motivated by fear? Is this about trying to hold onto power and not admitting truths about yourself and the cards dealt to you at birth? What harm are you causing to others by supporting colorblind ideologies?

YOU—WHEN YOU HEAR IT

Here are a few ways to respond when someone says they're colorblind:

- With a touch of humor, ask the person saying they're colorblind, "What do you do at a traffic light? Don't you stop?" Or you could say, "Well somehow you managed to color-match your clothes. How did that happen?" Then you can continue with the next point below.
- Acknowledge that we all see color, which is acceptable to admit and discuss—especially when it's helpful information and germane.
- You could say, "I'd like to understand how you came to that worldview."
- Another phrase to use is "Not 'seeing race or color' implies you don't think about race or you don't see a need to consider race. This means race doesn't shape your life and *your race* isn't a burden to you or doesn't hinder your success."
- If the person mentions green people or other random colors, consider saying, "Why don't we stick to discussing actual humans and not mutants and aliens."
- After observing how others react, decide if you should then add, "I wouldn't want to invalidate or negate the importance of recognizing that people from different backgrounds have experiences directly linked to their skin color. I wouldn't want to offend anyone by trivializing what they go through or by equating real discrimination with some imaginary world where we don't see color."

- Highlight that the issue is *how we interact* with people from different backgrounds so they feel included and can form connections with us. Trying to be as nonpreachy as possible, explain that claiming to be colorblind allows people to ignore discrimination, stifles dialogue, and implies race has no impact on people's daily lives (i.e., post-racialism doesn't exist).
- When someone jumps through hoops to not mention someone's race and it's actually relevant, you may want to ask them *why* it was so challenging for them to just state an obvious characteristic.
- If someone says that affirmative action is discriminatory, policies must be race-neutral or race-blind, or the US Supreme Court decided correctly in 2023 to upend race-based college admissions practices, you could say, "Not all court decisions are right. Let's not forget the Supreme Court also ruled slavery and segregation were legal and constitutional. If we can't consider race, what's your solution for addressing anti-Black systemic racism and decades of discrimination?" You could follow this up with "Society already factors in race. It's how dim-witted rich white kids get into elite colleges. If white affirmative action doesn't already exist, then why are so many CEOs white? Because they don't have a monopoly on intelligence and skill."

WHEN COLORBLINDNESS COMES TO CHILDREN

Be mindful of whether the content you're providing to children keeps racist colorblind ideologies alive and contemporary for new generations. It's important to evaluate books, films, videos, social media, and television shows shared with children. Don't assume that just because the person who's producing the information has a reputation of trying to be helpful to people of color that they can't misstep and develop material that's racist and harmful.

For example, in June 2020, actress Kristen Bell released a children's book entitled *The World Needs More Purple People*. Presumably, she thought she was positively participating in advancing anti-racism and diversity. Unfortunately, she achieved the opposite with her book about being a purple person who "looks for similarities before differences." There was immediate public backlash for promoting colorblind ideologies. She was severely roasted on social media, including these gems:

- "You guys will do everything but teach your kids about racism against actual Black and brown people, because reality makes you 'uncomfortable.'"
- "Just . . . use actual races instead???"
- "The world does not need more fictional purple characters. We already have Barney and Tinky Winky."
- "Kristen Bell has written 'all lives matter: the children's book.'"[3]

Through this status quo book and dehumanizing purple imagery, the seeds of racist ideologies and a refusal to address racism are planted early in the hearts and minds of children. It reinforces parents' worldview—teaching toddlers and kids to extend the life of racism for yet another generation. This harmful colorblind book is an intergenerational vector for stunting the country's progress and perpetuating racism.

In your journey to stop saying colorblind statements, understand when and where you're indoctrinating children through beloved family story-time traditions and watching programming together. The goal is to break the cycle of racism and white supremacy from infecting the next generation. Raise children to be Racism Disruptors instead of baby white supremacists.

> The very serious function of racism . . . is distraction. It keeps you from doing your work. It keeps you explaining, over and over again, your reason for being. . . . None of that is necessary.
>
> —Toni Morrison, author and academic

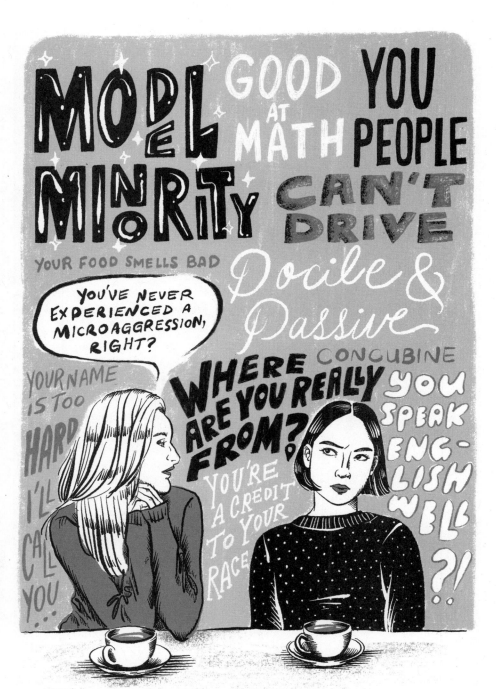

Microaggressions Are Racism

It is never too late to give up our prejudices.

—*Henry David Thoreau, essayist and philosopher*

RULE SUMMARY

Microaggressions are everyday subtle intentional or unintentional verbal, nonverbal, and environmental slights, snubs, insults, indignities, behaviors, or interactions that communicate prejudiced attitudes and hostile, derogatory, or negative messages toward people of color. The difference between microaggressions and overt racism (i.e., macroaggressions) is perpetrators are typically unaware they're engaging in bigotry due to their unconscious biases.

Microaggressions are a form of racism. Just because they're often subtle and done unknowingly doesn't mean they hurt any less, don't cause people of color significant pain, and aren't advancing white supremacy and racist tropes.

They're commonplace, subtle, frequent, brief, cumulative, and repetitive actions of marginalization and stereotyping that mentally break down people of color—gratuitous and never-ending racial assaults on dignity and hope. They can be disguised as compliments or what microaggressors think is offering praise but instead unknowingly amplify racist stereotypes that don't feel good. Nearly all interracial interactions are prone to microaggressions.

They are not limited to human encounters alone but may also be environmental (e.g., when people of color are exposed to an office setting that unintentionally attacks their racial identity).

Microaggressions are subtle acts of exclusion.[1]

THE NATURE OF MICROAGGRESSIONS

Microaggressions primarily appear in three forms—microassaults, microinsults, and microinvalidations:[2]

- **Microassaults**—Microassaults are explicit racial derogations where people engage in deliberate discriminatory behaviors intending to hurt others (e.g., calling someone a name, using hate speech, seating white diners ahead of patrons of color). They're old-fashioned racism conducted on an individual level.

- **Microinsults**—Microinsults are communications that convey rudeness and insensitivity and demean someone's racial heritage or identity, often including subtle snubs with hidden insulting messages (e.g., employer telling job candidates of color the "most qualified person should be hired regardless of race" with the undercurrent being people of color aren't qualified, or they were hired due only to affirmative action goals or racial quotas and not ability).
- **Microinvalidations**—Microinvalidations are verbal statements that exclude, negate, undermine, or nullify thoughts, feelings, or experiential realities of people of color (e.g., complimenting US-born or raised Asian Americans on "speaking English well" or asking where they were born, which negates their American heritage and conveys perpetual foreigner status in their homeland, or telling Black people, "I don't see color" or racism "doesn't exist," which negates their life experiences and discrimination faced due to color).

Downplaying how impactful "dinner-table racism" is on people of color underestimates microaggressions' toxicity and power. They're both symptoms and causes of systemic racism and how deeply embedded prejudicial thoughts are in people's minds—bringing beliefs to the surface and giving them eternal life. They help normalize racism in our daily lives and workplaces.

Microaggressions are dangerous and weathering. They're not innocuous, unnoticed slights. They attack the mental, emotional, and physical health of people of color and their ability to succeed. They cause real trauma. People fed a regular diet of microaggressions can suffer from depression and lack confidence, fail to thrive, and have feelings of anger, helplessness, and hopelessness—all of which can promote suicidal tendencies, erode physical well-being, and cause lower life expectancy. It's death by a thousand racist paper cuts.

Given their subtle nature, they can create attributional ambiguity (i.e., trigger a sense of uncertainty about whether an encounter or event experienced is related to someone's race or other unrelated factors)—making people of color continually second-guess, lose confidence, feel stressed, and get successfully gaslit. These distractions take away from the ability to focus on work or live a satisfying life. See table 19.1 to compare your actions to how they are perceived.[3]

TABLE 19.1 Microaggression translator

What you say or do	What they hear or think
Intelligence	
"You're a credit to your race." "You're articulate." You ask an Asian American to help with a math, science, or computer problem.	"You aren't as intelligent as whites; it's unusual to encounter smart Black or brown people." You assume all Asians are intelligent and skilled in STEM (i.e., model minority trope).
Criminality	
You clutch your purse as a Black person approaches.	"You're a criminal and dangerous."
Denying individual racism	
"I'm not racist. I have lots of Hispanic friends!" "As a woman, I know what you go through as a minority."	"I'm immune to racism since I know brown people." "I can't be racist. I'm like you. Racism is the same as gender oppression."
Colorblindness	
"When I see you, I don't see color." "America is a melting pot."	You deny a person's racial experiences. You tell them to assimilate to the dominant culture.
Meritocracy myth	
"Everyone can succeed if they work hard enough."	"People of color are lazy or incompetent and need to work harder."
Second-class citizen	
You mistake a patron for an employee or service worker.	"People of color are servants to whites and couldn't possibly have high-level jobs."

TABLE 19.1 (*continued*)

What you say or do	What they hear or think
Alien in own land	
"Where were you born?" You ask Asian Americans or Latinos to teach them words in their "original" language.	"You're not American." "You're a foreigner."
Pathologizing cultural values and communication styles	
"Why do you have to be so animated and loud?" (to Blacks) "Why are you so quiet? You need to speak up!" (to Asian Americans or Latinos) You dismiss someone who brings up race or racism at work or in society.	"I'm threatened or irritated by you being you." "Assimilate to the dominant culture." "Leave your insignificant, nonexistent cultural baggage at the door."
Environmental microaggressions	
Schools in communities of color are overcrowded. Films and television shows feature mostly white actors and few actors of color. Neighborhoods of color have an overabundance of liquor stores.	"People of color shouldn't value education." "You're an outsider, don't exist in America, and it's a white world so get used to it." "People of color are deviant or all have substance abuse issues."

Think before you act to avoid offending. Pause and reflect so you don't discourage and demoralize—making people of color feel like outsiders with less value. Before speaking or acting, consider the impact of your words or actions and how they'll be perceived by people of color.

You want your *intentions* to align with your *impact* and how others *experience* what you do and say and how they *feel* after spending time with you. Match your hopes with what actually happens. Impact matters more than intent!

If someone says you offended them or did something racist, don't double down by denying it. This behavior is also a microaggression (i.e., racist). Don't get defensive or flippant because you don't see it, don't want to accept it, or didn't mean to offend. Your intent is irrelevant. Instead, apologize. Learn from the experience so you don't repeat it and inflict microaggressions on the next person.

TIPS AND ADVICE

The advice below will help you not just transition away from engaging in microaggressive behavior but know how to recover when you offend others. It will also demonstrate ways to proactively support people of color when witnessing racist behavior to foster the development of your racism disruption skills.

SAVING FACE AND RECOVERING FROM ENGAGING IN MICROAGGRESSIONS

Given how prevalent and daily microaggressions are, it's wise to have some responses ready when your actions cause pain and you get called out. The shame is less about being wrong but more about refusing to learn and grow. After using one of these talking points, follow your words up with action to learn from mistakes and avoid engaging in empty lip service:

- "Thanks for correcting me. I didn't realize that. I will work on not repeating this mistake in the future."
- "I hadn't thought of it like that. But I understand now. I see how what I thought I said actually meant something else. I'm sorry I was offensive."
- "I should have done more research before arguing this point."
- "Okay, clearly, I have some work to do on educating myself about racism and what's offensive. And I plan to do this work." (Only say this if you're going to self-educate. No one wants to hear empty words. Given how you're a microaggressor, you need to take proactive steps to improve.)

SEEKING TO DISRUPT RACISM WHEN WITNESSING MICROAGGRESSIONS

Microaggressions involve the perpetrator, hurt party, and bystanders. Onlookers are also participants and witnesses. When you see something, say something. Call out people engaging in microaggressive actions to deter this behavior from repeatedly happening. For example, you could take these steps:

- Mention how you used to say similar statements but then learned XYZ information or XYZ about yourself that helped shift your outlook and perspective (e.g., from ABC book, film, podcast, conference, or workshop).
- Ask probing, open-ended questions, forcing them to clarify their meaning (e.g., "What do you mean by that? Can you explain?").
- Point out how what they said was inconsistent with something they care about and their known values (e.g., respect, equality, empathy, making people feel valued and heard).
- Make it more personal and engage their emotional state by asking how they'd feel if someone said something similar to them or their spouse, parent, child, or friend.
- When diplomacy isn't your concern, say what they did was racially offensive or flat-out racist.

Don't leave it solely up to people of color to fight these tiresome battles alone. To curb racism, everyone must play their part, or else we're stuck on this perpetual no-progress hamster wheel going nowhere. Try to turn the encounter into a teachable moment translating how the offender's words or actions landed and what they implied. Since microaggressions are relentless for people of color, you don't want to contribute to their cumulative daily trauma nor be complicit by being silent when you recognize microaggressions are happening. This will help your Racism Disruptor competency skills and ability to navigate racist incidents.

> Fools multiply when wise men are silent.
>
> —Nelson Mandela, first president of South Africa

When POCs Say It's Racist, Believe Them

I am invisible . . . because people refuse to see me. . . .
They see only my surroundings, themselves or figments of their
imagination, indeed, everything and anything except me.

—*Ralph Ellison, novelist,* Invisible Man

RULE SUMMARY

When a person of color says your behavior is racist or an experience was offensively racist, accept it! This is *not* debatable. Your opinion is *not* on the table.

It's not about your perspective but how the person of color sees and experiences encounters. People of color are authorities on their own views and feelings when subjected to racism.

Your primary role in this scenario is to listen and believe them and to not judge, relate it back to your experiences and infuse that into the conversation, nor pepper them with questions signaling you're rejecting their reality. This makes people of color feel ignored and invisible. It's hurtful and disrespectful. And frankly, it's racist.

The conveyed undercurrent is you refuse to accept racism exists. This is a defense mechanism to thwart acknowledging and seeing legitimate racism—possibly because it forces you to admit hard truths about yourself and how society props up your privilege to advantage you.

Their conclusion is you're a bigot gaslighting and invalidating them. You're inflicting emotional abuse. Even if you aren't called out, they've got your number. They know it's just another chapter in the white supremacy tone-deaf chronicles.

Equally important, if you have to ask if it's racist, defend it as not being racist, or feel compelled to say "I'm not racist, but . . ." then it's racist. Boom! Drop the mic. End of story.

Did someone really need to tell you? Be honest. Deep down you already knew it was wrong. That's why you qualified your statement or were trying to justify the indefensible.

Instead of rationalizing something that's offensive, start asking why others see it as racist.

Rather than focusing energy on getting defensive and feeling personally attacked when called out or someone throws you some shade, redirect your attention toward understanding.

I f your goal is to project the best version of yourself, exert more self-restraint. This will limit how much you (1) engage in racist speech and offensive behavior, (2) say things that cause others pain, and (3) reinforce conscious and unconscious beliefs rooted in prejudicial ideologies, stereotypes, and tropes.

A special note: Declarative statements that something "isn't racist" doesn't make it "not racist." You're in a losing battle when proclaiming things contrary to objective facts and a person of color's belief that the behavior was racially offensive. You're just engaging in revisionist history so you don't look bad.

SELF-REFLECTIVE QUESTIONS

Ask yourself these key questions when you start to doubt or ignore the feelngs of people of color:

1. When have you felt excluded or dismissed, and what did it feel like? Do you want to replicate that feeling for someone else?
2. What makes you an authority on how someone else feels? Their experiences and lived truth? Their life journey?
3. What makes you an expert on identifying racism?
4. What in your life makes your racism radar more reliable than theirs?
5. Why are you centering how *they* feel around *your* opinions?
6. How is your view relevant? Do they really want to hear it?
7. Why is it so important for you to reject what they're saying?
8. How would you feel if the tables were turned?

Focus on understanding why a person of color sees the racism and you don't. Your starting point should be to immediately apologize and own your actions. First be mindful of frustrating them. Then you could ask them to point out *how* it was racist so you can understand better while *not* questioning it was racist. But accept it if they don't want to explain. Experiencing your offensive behavior could mean they're done with you.

Under no circumstances should you rope in another person of color coaxing them to validate your view. Even if your conversation pawn claims to agree with you, it's irrelevant. They're not your tokenized trump card and may feign agreement.

It takes courage to step out of your comfort zone and reject defensive instincts. It takes bravery to accept you're wrong. It takes humility to claim ownership over your actions and discover the root cause behind your behavior.

A CLASSIC AND REAL-WORLD EXAMPLE OF GASLIGHTING RACISM

Meghan Markle said her experiences with the British royal family and press were racist, which resulted in countless whites rejecting this as improbable lies. Instead, they should accept her experiences and perceptions as fact and true.

It's racist to tell a person of color what they felt wasn't racist. You're relying on an imperialistic colonizer mentality. The other person's view of their lived experience governs. All that matters is *their* assessment. Defer to them!

I believe much trouble and blood would be saved
if we opened our hearts more.

—Chief Joseph (aka Hinmatóowyalahtq'it),
leader of the Wal'wáama Band of the Nez Perce Tribe

POCs Are Justified in Expressing Anger and Rage

If you are silent about your pain,
they will kill you and say you enjoyed it.

—*Zora Neale Hurston, author*

RULE SUMMARY

People of color are entitled to feel anger and rage. It's dehumanizing to demand expressions of fake joy and swallowed pain. Being angry doesn't mean someone is violent or their behavior is bad. Get over needing to sanitize justified outrage and discomfort with natural emotions.

Why do *you* get to be angry, but *they* can't? Living through discrimination and trauma, their job isn't to make whites feel better about prejudice, convenient complicity, or poorly navigated feelings. When they're expressing legitimate rage, their emotions shouldn't be weaponized to control and maintain white privilege, white supremacy, and the status quo or coddle white feelings and tears.

Anger ≠ Aggression

Vibrant human beings have a wide range of feelings. By denying equal emotional rights, wanting only Pollyanna pleasantries, and framing genuine emotions as misplaced and unnecessary rage, you're stealing the self-worth and humanity from people of color.

People of color are tired of society encouraging them to smile, use their nice voices, and be docile. They're emotionally exhausted from sublimating feelings in deference to the comfort of others—forced to choke on repressed, diverted, and ignored anger and outrage.

Asking people to suppress their feelings is toxic. It's mentally and psychologically taxing. People need free agency.

They're asked to quiet their strength to avoid the angry minority stereotype—tiptoeing on eggshells. Not being allowed to be proud, confident, and human feels like no one has their back. They're alone in a fight for individuality and equality.

People of color have a lot to be angry about. Many have lost their lives and livelihoods for expressing a hint of frustration or disgust.

When your people are killed, attacked, imprisoned, racially profiled, and passed over for promotions; when your ideas and inventions are stolen; when your vote is suppressed; and when people live in engineered poverty, how excited are you supposed to be when encountering racism?

THE ANGER PEOPLE OF COLOR CARRY

Anger is a critically useful and positive emotion. It's not a socially constructed feeling but a primal warning that something is wrong and must change. It's the human response to being threatened with indignity, physical harm, humiliation, unfairness, and injustice—driving us to demand accountability and form politically engaged communities.

People of color have a well-stocked arsenal of legitimate and useful anger. It's a valuable and potent political force that could advance racial equality and catalyze change. This is why there's fear of Black and brown anger—fear of group and individual rage. Whites fear restitution and dismantling the status quo.

Using the angry racialized trope is rooted in whites being afraid of losing power and control. It's not just that Black and brown people are threatening to the social order *when* they're angry but are *always* threatening to the status quo. Beliefs contrary to the social order are typically framed as dangerous or deviant and enforced through social norms, stereotypes, taboos, ostracization, rules, law enforcement, and death.

The core belief that's troublesome for society is racial equality.

The angry-Black-man or angry-Black-woman stereotype is propaganda casting Blacks not only as a threat based on behavior but as a different category of people incapable of reason, logic, self-control, common decency, and social graces. Attaching anger to color is intentional with historic ties. It's about an *institutional structure* that criminalizes Black and brown people no matter how they act or react, which requires the accompanying anger trope as its tool.

This trope is about delegitimizing the issues fueling outrage that started during slavery and when we took Indigenous and Mexican lands. If you can delegitimize the anger, then you can invalidate the issues. Once neutralized, you can trivialize justified anger and rage to rationalize any form of mistreatment to maintain power structures—whipping, raping, amputation, torture, land grabs, and mineral rights seizures.

Today's white entitlement versions of maltreatment (aka oppression) are police brutality, misplaced white rage, voter suppression, microaggressions, and the act of stealing credit for workplace contributions from people of color—all leveraging the angry stereotype as justification to marginalize valid feelings of rage in response to subjugation, discrimination, harassment, and theft.

These instruments of control and racial domination force people of color to modulate themselves and code switch. They're in an unwinnable position. If they're quiet, they signal their approval of being oppressed. If they speak up, then they're angry and menacing. And what accompanies being tagged with a menacing moniker is a license to kill and neutralize that threat.

The undercurrent is the feelings of Black and brown people don't matter and they were happier with slavery and oppression—you know, when things were "great." It's weaponizing color against them to keep their submission in check and penalize them when they "get out of line"—to protect fragile whites from having to confront the realities of racism or their microaggressions and let whites believe their actions are acceptable. Essentially, people of color live in a system that doesn't agree with their very existence.

ANGER IN THE COMMUNITY AND AT WORK

In the community, this trope has fatal consequences. A traffic stop can turn deadly when a Black man questions why he's even pulled over in the first place while whites can get downright indignant with the police without fear of death. Simple inquiries from people of color are an affront to mainstream norms and morph into claims of resisting arrest.

In the workplace, the angry stereotype becomes having an attitude or an aggressive personality; being hostile to others, a bad culture fit, or too confrontational; or not being a team player. It sidelines careers when someone is asking legitimate questions, has an opinion, wants fair credit or pay for their work, and doesn't want to denigrate themselves by rolling over when racist colleagues engage in bigoted behavior and flex their white supremacy.

Using attitude as an excuse is a dog whistle and euphemism to silence and shackle people of color when they're frustrated, requiring them to ingest justified rage so others feel more comfortable. This is destructive since it then plays mind games on people of color—internalizing the negative feedback to second-guess themselves and chip away at self-confidence. They're positioned as weak with their anger, and then they become professionally vulnerable by being emotionally ground down.

Tone policing is a common workplace microaggression. It's a conversational tactic dismissing communicated ideas when perceived to be delivered in an angry, frustrated, sad, fearful, or emotionally charged manner. Managers who value equitable and inclusive workplaces must understand how tone policing silences members of marginalized groups and allows discrimination to persist. It stifles staff and kills creativity. Unable to bring their whole selves to work, they know they're not valued contributors and feel invisible and unwelcome. They're keenly aware it's due to racism.

Employees of color who are unapologetic about being smart and top performers often scare whites. Professional threats disrupting the social order can mentally transform into misguided subconscious perceptions of menacing personalities. This fear of Black and brown excellence translates into white subordinates unwilling to take direction from bosses of color. Feeling the pressure to dim their own light or repress themselves, staff of color become disinterested in and fearful of speaking up in meetings since the consequences are too high. Behind the scenes, professional success turns into negative chatter that someone isn't deserving of promotions and raises—slanderous backstabbing and character assassination since accomplished people of color are intimidating.

WHITE MALE HYPOCRISY—JOHN MCENROE VERSUS SERENA WILLIAMS

White male anger is acceptable and earns a reputation as being passionate and driving results—yelling, screaming, slamming doors, and bullying their way to the top. This is why John McEnroe, with each childish tantrum on the tennis court, didn't hurt his reputation but emboldened it. Whereas Serena Williams faced backlash when justifiably upset when chair umpires disproportionately enforced discretionary penalties against her and let similar behavior slide with white athletes. She's seen as the angry Black woman—a tool to shame her into silence.

Serena isn't an angry Black woman but a Black woman who happened to get angry when bad calls were made, costing her a match. A Black woman's anger responding to societal injustice is dangerous to the status quo.

What's socially allowed is white fury, violence, and poor coping skills. Society brushes off menacing whites as enforcing freedoms or misdirected responses to economic difficulty. Whites can stand proud on public steps with rifles and instigate armed standoffs when illegally occupying federal lands. This doesn't provoke the same public backlash as people of color marching in the streets for BLM. We justify actual violence and proven threats from whites—legitimizing their outrage without accountability and enabling them to direct their dysfunctional anger at marginalized groups. White rage is status quo privilege.

Meanwhile, when people of color want justice for police brutality, hate crimes, and workplace discrimination, their emotions are mischaracterized as too explosive or somehow crazed. They must be their own anger translator and are socially precluded from having feelings and emotions—forced to swallow hurt and injustices. They're deprived of expressing the full spectrum of human emotions. The world beyond their homes isn't a safe space for legitimate public outcry. Black anger is criminalized and deemed monstrous. People of color are not allowed to protest or object to racism. This is dehumanizing.

When anger is weaponized by ideological opponents of Black and brown progress, people learn to suppress emotions to function, live, and stay employed.

Compartmentalization. Self-censorship.
Not thriving but surviving.

Not having an equal right to free expression is a debilitating form of racist erasure. Despair and hopelessness are the opposite of anger.

TIPS AND ADVICE

The advice below will support your ability to avoid stifling people of color's free emotional expression and create space to expand your capacity to humanize them. By learning strategies to sidestep falling into trope pitfalls and invite honest feelings, you'll become increasingly more respectful. The advice also forces you to look within and challenge your thinking to curtail natural tendencies to silence voices of color.

TIPS TO AVOID ADVANCING THE RACIST ANGRY TROPE

When you notice people of color expressing their anger, rage, or animated feelings, or seeing their emotions makes you uncomfortable, take these steps to avoid perpetuating the angry POC trope or any Black-person stereotype:

1. Accept that everyone gets angry and has a right to natural, human emotions—especially Black and brown rage to racism.
2. Don't invalidate feelings. Normalize emotions and anger.
3. To reject tools of control, encourage speaking up.
4. Believe people of color when they say something feels racialized.
5. When someone expresses anger and frustration, admit it's not an excuse to feel threatened (i.e., it's *not* an aggressive attack).

SELF-REFLECTIVE QUESTIONS

Ask yourself the following questions to avoid perpetuating the racist angry trope:

1. Why is anger acceptable for you and not them?
2. Is their anger justified? Is your reaction a knee-jerk response advancing tropes?
3. Do you see Black women as pit bulls and white men as brave?
4. Did you not like how they looked at you? Did they look violent?
5. Were they unprofessional? Raising their voice? Using profanity?
6. Is it that you just can't handle their directness and fair honesty?
7. Are you tone policing?
8. Do you feel attacked since you're too fragile when people of color speak?
9. Would you feel the same if a white man did it? A white woman?
10. Are you quieting their emotions since you don't want to hear *why* they're mad and upset (i.e., a strategy to shut folks down)?

> A riot is the language of the unheard.
>
> —Dr. Martin Luther King, Jr., civil rights activist

Improve Daily Interactions— Communicating, Self-Educating, and Repairing Relationships

PART 6 provides advice on navigating daily conversations and encounters. It offers guardrails for determining acceptable and inappropriate behavior. By understanding how to converse, when to leave people of color in peace, and how to be accountable, you become equipped with tools to develop healthy, supportive friendships. The priority is your impact over intent.

Bluntness is a virtue. Through discomfort, this book protects people of color by candidly sharing perspectives on their behalf to safeguard relationships. You will improve your interactions without asking them to experience racial pain.

Filling knowledge gaps and sensing when to have conversations or zip it won't come without trial and error. Trust that you'll expand your "read-the-room" capabilities over time. You may get burned, but you'll learn from mistakes. The Race Rules limit how much heat and embarrassment you feel and how much pain you inflict on others when moving up the learning curve.

Approach this journey open to continually learning. Dust yourself off, apologize when you offend, tackle information gaps when revealed, and force yourself to keep going. Don't succumb to shame. Charge through trepidation. Don't retreat. The goal is to open your eyes and limit harming people of color by disrupting the racism lurking within you.

When you feel judged for flubbing, resist any urges to become combative. Avoid fleeing if a person of color is open to talking. Just know judgment is part of your learning process. See it as lessons exposing topics where you need to self-educate for future encounters.

It's Not Personal When POCs Don't Want to Discuss Race

You share your story with those who have earned the right to hear your story. . . . It is a privilege to hear. . . . Vulnerability minus boundaries is not vulnerability.

—*Brené Brown, academic and author*

RULE SUMMARY

Don't take it personally if people of color don't want to educate you about racism, discuss race, or share their lived experiences. Your teachable moment is another's lifelong tenure-track professorship in coping with structural racism and navigating people showing up uninvited to the seminar of their life. Maybe they're tired since they live it daily. Be ready to stand in line and take a number because you're not the only one asking. Don't be surprised if they decide to permanently foreclose discussing this with you. Just accept it and move on. Don't force it.

People of color are weary of the endless offensive and unenlightened questions they receive from whites. They're peppered with relentless inquiries from countless people who've failed to adequately educate themselves or create environments for them to safely share their journey and perspective—discussions forced on them while also living in a racist country. Most are exhausted from Groundhog Day conversations.

Are you the only white person they know? Doubtful. It's more likely they're one of a handful of people of color *you* know. And they're fielding outreach from people with whom they have some pathetically tangential and extremely weak connections.

Do not start discussions on race with a random person of color you vaguely happen to know. And a work colleague, neighbor, or someone you pay for a service isn't necessarily a "friend."

You may claim *them*, but do they really claim *you*? Do you know their kids' names? Birthday? Have you been to their house? Invited them over? Gone to dinner? Attended their wedding? Been given their personal number? Attended their relative's funeral? Gotten them a job? Had their back during a tough time?

If the answers are no, then you're not friends. You're acquaintances or merely just fellow global citizens. Best case scenario, you're friend adjacent (i.e., still not a friend).

Have you even *earned* the right to explore something so deeply intimate as race with someone? What gives you the right to get personal with them? Feel a sense of entitlement? They owe you nothing. With race, people feel entitled to take liberties and cross boundaries. Even with genuine friends, you must still tread lightly.

Out of curiosity and to understand sexual violence, would you ask a neighbor if they were ever raped and what that was like? No! Because that's *extremely* private and traumatic. Living under a repressive regime of incessant structural racism and daily microaggressions is also traumatic—especially when you pile on discrimination, stolen wealth, police brutality, racial profiling, and historic intergenerational legacies of racial violence and using sexual terror as a strategy for oppression.

Asking people of color to discuss race is asking them to *relive past moments of pain and trauma*. You're asking them to reexperience all that baggage—along with whatever ignorant, prejudicial, and microaggressive things you say—all for *your benefit*. This is what you're actually asking of them. Can you understand why they don't want to talk to you? Why they don't want your questions?

Plus, it's frustrating to explain discrimination, racism, white supremacy, and subtle racism to people in the dominant culture who've benefited from White Welfare, are blind to the realities of racism and privilege, and exhibit casual and overt racism during that discussion.

It's not a welcomed conversation if you do any of the following:

- Don't believe people of color or gaslight—challenging or debating when told something is racist.
- Get defensive or think it's others who are racist but not you—being blind to racism right before you.
- Are ignorant and ill informed due to your own laziness.
- Come ill-prepared to navigate your own feelings and those of people of color.
- Play the victim and tearful sympathy card.

To learn more about race, start by educating yourself on your own. Read books and articles. Watch documentaries, but avoid feature films advancing the White Savior or Magical Negro tropes. Listen to podcasts. Attend community meetings and open discussions, starting with your listening rather than speaking tour. Volunteer with a social justice organization. If you were truly interested, you'd take responsibility for your educational journey without burdening exhausted people of color. This may include not asking others to curate your anti-racist curriculum. Instead, proactively use the internet.

But if this sounds like too much effort, then you aren't serious. If you still want to discuss race with a person of color after self-educating, wait until they freely bring it up unprompted. If waiting for an invitation yields nothing, let it go. But once in a discussion, be mindful of your words, tone, facial expressions, body language, microaggressions, culturesplaining, and white centering and whether you're making the discussion about you and your feelings.

Follow their lead. Don't push too hard. Filter your words. Pay attention to their emotions. Focus on the encounter's impact on them, not your intentions. And do *not* cry! White tears equals white centering. This also applies to ally tears. People of color are fatigued by white performance art, white victimhood, and white feelings hijacking the focus away from their trauma to what feels like trivializing and co-opting the realities of living under racism. This makes you the center of attention, distracting from the necessary, critical analysis of racism and offensive behavior.

SELF-REFLECTIVE QUESTIONS

These questions will help you see your impact on people of color when you ask them about race-based topics:

1. How many Black friends do you have? Native American? Latino? Arab? People in the AAPI community? While you consider them to be your friends, do you think they all consider you to be their friend (i.e., not an acquaintance but a close friend)? What makes you think so?
2. Do you see asking people of color about race and their experiences as personal questions? If not, why?
3. Do you have a right to discuss race with and ask unprompted questions of the people of color in your private or professional life? If so, under what circumstances? What makes you think that's okay?

4. When discussing race, do you pay attention to nonverbal cues to see if the person of color is uncomfortable? When you observe discomfort, do you keep the conversation going? If so, is that okay?

5. When you're discussing race-based topics with people of color, do you accept what they say when they express an opinion you disagree with (including when they say something was or someone is racist)? Or do you give pushback? How about when they challenge your behavior?

6. When you're curious to understand race, racism, or an incident or situation, do you typically start with research and trying to understand the issue on your own first? Or do you instinctively reach out to a person of color you know?

7. If you normally reach out before self-educating and problem-solving, how do you think this impacts them or makes them feel? Could it cause them pain? Could this strain your relationship with them? What do you think is their takeaway impression of you and the encounter?

CORONAVIRUS ANALOGY—WHAT IT'S LIKE TALKING TO YOU ABOUT RACE

Let's put this in perspective, recall life living in the COVID-19 pandemic. Do you remember that haunting feeling you felt that never went away— that the virus was lurking at every corner? You couldn't escape it because there were reminders everywhere—on the news, online, in social media, and when you saw your neighbors or people on the street. You felt a sense of omnipresence as you walked around—always on high alert, looking at others to see if they wore masks, looked ill, or coughed. You noticed them and observed how they reacted to you. You were in constant fear of your death. Loved ones may die or did die, and you felt perpetual anxiety.

Your mental health was impacted along with your physical health from the stress. You had trouble sleeping. You weren't even safe in your own home because the virus could come to your door. You didn't know if you could trust the government or if officials had your best interest at heart— unsure if they would do something to kill you. You felt powerless, as if there were nothing you could do to change things, to make your life better since you weren't in control. You had to resign yourself to your circumstance, but you didn't want to accept your reality. You wanted to resist and somehow make things better. When you tried, you didn't succeed.

That's what it's like living under racism every day—24/7/365. Racism is a pervasive, invisible force, just like COVID. There's no escape. It's constant, never a break or reprieve. It's isolating and marginalizing. It attacks your life, bank account, livelihood, housing, healthcare, schools, and dinner table and separates your family. You want the government to do something about it, but politicians want you to laissez-faire your way to nonsolutions—absolving themselves of responsibility, willfully blind to its impact. *You* suck it up. *You* deal with big-picture systemic issues. Pull yourself up by your bootstraps. Heal yourself. Pave your destiny. Avoid your own death or murder.

Welcome to living like a Black or brown person in America. But with racism, there's no vaccine coming—no magic pill to inoculate society. This is what it's been like since the 1500s. It isn't getting better. There are new strains, new waves, and invisible resurgences. Mutating. Reinventing itself. Seemingly dormant but always there stalking, ready to strike and viciously kill. This is the reality. It's bleak.

When you want to discuss racism, sometimes people of color want to discuss it only with those who understand what they've gone through—not white folks who will trivialize things, which is akin to speaking to an antimasker who berates innocent and defenseless store clerks. That's *you* questioning racism and their experiences. *You're* the antimasker antivaxxer in the conversation when you come with covert microaggressions, overt aggression, a lack of knowledge, and rejection of facts. Now can you understand why no one wants to talk to you? They're already too busy trying to literally survive!

> It doesn't require many words to speak the truth.
>
> —Chief Joseph (aka Hinmatóowyalahtq'it),
> leader of the Wal'wáama Band of the Nez Perce Tribe

Stop Asking POCs to Explain Racism— Educate Yourself

I hope you do the research before you
come to me because I'm exhausted.

—*Issa Rae, actress*

RULE SUMMARY

Turning to Blacks and people of color as your *go-to source* for information, knowledge, and understanding of race and racism is pure laziness. It demonstrates an absence of genuinely caring and possessing the requisite interest in the topic. *If* the topic were truly important to you, you'd take the time to educate and prepare yourself for a substantive exploration of difficult issues. And you'd recognize *you are* the one responsible for your own awareness, ignorance, and ability or deficiency to drive solutions.

Stop fatiguing and ambushing already depleted people of color! They're not walking Encyclopedias Negrannica[1] ready to data dump their pain and experiences on a whim because you're ready to parachute into the topic for a hot minute and helicopter right out. They're not at your beck and call to verbally live stream their lived oppression and explain history that you should have learned in school but actively failed to supplement as a self-determining adult. They're not information vessels on speed dial who should have to simultaneously navigate ignorant questions, offensive commentary, your hurt feelings, and often inevitable white guilt and white tears.

Frankly, having to do your work for you feels like déjà vu oppression. Learning and self-educating is *your* modern-day White Man's Burden, not theirs. Bridging information gaps is your job.

But you were just asking for ideas on how to solve racism, actionable steps, books to read, and films to watch, right? Wrong! You were asking people carrying the daily anvil of toxic discrimination and bigotry on their backs, who live through the trauma and downside of the nations's history, to do your homework. They already feel cheated, but now you're asking them to usher you through a one-hour certificate course on racism when you need to commence your doctorate program on understanding the country.

The most perfunctory internet search can answer basic questions. Those interested in only rudimentary exposure seek the lazy route—dumping emotional labor and handholding on marginalized groups.

Don't expect nor require people of color to participate in your educational journey if that's what they elect to do. It's not their responsibility to be your pro bono instructor in your quest for an honorary degree at Race-Awareness University. It's your duty as a citizen and functioning adult to fill your own knowledge gaps. Part of learning to unlearn includes purging yourself of bad habits on how you gain knowledge, behave, and act.

TIPS AND ADVICE

Here's what to do before rolling up with questions:

1. Come correct by having done legitimate recon. This doesn't mean you watched an online video clip, skimmed an article, or read a poem. It means you invested substantial time (many hours over an extended period of time) and effort into understanding America's history as it relates to people of color—Blacks, First Nation peoples, Latinos, Asian Americans and Pacific Islanders, Indian Americans, and Middle Easterners—by reading books (plural), taking a seminar, attending numerous cultural events and workshops, listening to multiple in-depth discussions, and immersing yourself in cross-racial learning.
2. Arrive prepared to manage your own emotions—especially after dredging up others' distressing historic hurt committed by whites against people of color or pain caused by your past behavior.
3. Be capable of experiencing their pain and anger without running away from truths and getting defensive. Part of the preparation work is being comfortable with legitimate rage and coping when they express frustrations with you and personally about you.
4. Understand how you and your family personally benefited from privilege and White Welfare.
5. Don't make discussions about you (i.e., white centering) other than how you can support society's racial progress or to explore studied topics that still confuse you. You're not the victim. They are.
6. Show up prepared to express thoughtful, strategic, and impactful actionable steps you will take to make a difference at your job, in your community, within your family, and in driving helpful policies that atone for and correct the past and address the present.

Anything short of these steps implies you were just topic dabbling for the day, which won't go over well. No one wants to rip off their painful racism band-aid for sport—to make you feel better and appease your instant-gratification need for momentary or situational knowledge. They want to see positive and tangible results from you and society so sharing their traumatic pain was worth it for them.

If this sounds like too much work, then it's obvious your interest isn't legit. You just wanted to virtue signal and feign caring.

WHEN IS IT OKAY TO ASK FOR BOOK AND FILM SUGGESTIONS?

You can ask for guidance *after* completing steps 1 through 6 above *and* you're looking to supplement the self-educating in which you're already engaged. Your purpose should be to learn something more poignant or nuanced beyond the scope of your due diligence and not to bypass doing homework.

Note this is an *and* guideline and not an *or* statement. If you haven't already spent hours researching, reading, and viewing films and video content on your own and undertaken advance emotional preparation, then it's premature to ask people of color in your orbit for help. You haven't done enough individualized work to justify inquiring about triggering topics like racism and racial awareness.

Also, it's important to read the room. You need to wisely select *whom* to ask. It's best if this is a *genuine* friend or someone with whom you already discuss topics like politics or current events.

We have become focused on the transactional rather than the transformational.

—Ken Burns, documentary filmmaker

Culturesplaining—
Stop Telling Me about Me

Race Rule #24 applies not only to race but also to ethnicity, heritage, culture, one's given name, national origin, religion, citizenship, immigrant status, and so on. A subset of culturesplaining is *whitesplaining*, but people of color are also guilty of culturesplaining to other groups and people of color.

The answer to injustice is not to silence the critic,
but to end the injustice.

—*Paul Robeson, activist, actor, and athlete*

RULE SUMMARY

Don't culturesplain someone's race, culture, background, or name to them, especially when you're not a member of that group (i.e., not a card-carrying member).

Accept the stated facts as the truth when a person of color tells you something they experienced, felt, or witnessed was racist. Avoid giving pushback and proposing alternative reasons why an experience was anything other than racist when told it was.

Being dismissive or otherwise centering on white viewpoints that contradict or refute Black, brown, and AAPI lived experiences is based in white supremacy. Your personal experience isn't the benchmark. *Theirs* is.

Culturesplaining is annoying, offensive, and condescending. Most importantly, it's patronizingly racist. This behavior definitely warrants an eyeroll and a "talk to the hand."

WHAT EXACTLY IS CULTURESPLAINING?

To culturesplain is to give a paternalistic, condescending, arrogant, unsolicited, and unwelcomed lecture given by a non-card-carrying member of a group. This person may do any of the following:

- Explain something regarding race relations, people of color's behavior, or sociopolitical issues related to that group, presuming the listener's inferior understanding of the topic even though the listener (i.e., culturesplainee) is a card-carrying member of that group.
- Enlighten and "educate" on topics or historical context related to race, ethnicity, heritage, culture, one's given name, national origin, religion, citizenship, immigrant status, and so on, presuming the culturesplainee isn't already knowledgeable; is unable to speak for themselves or defend their view; doesn't have their own opinions, experiences, and feelings on the topic; or generally isn't an expert on their own background and experience.
- Define what should and shouldn't be considered racist or prejudiced against that group while most likely exhibiting their own racism— including explaining away perceived racist incidents as not that bad

or saying they should otherwise be given the benefit of the doubt when such incidents would never happen to the person giving the uninvited sermon (i.e., culturesplainer).

In essence, it's the race, culture, and ethnic heritage and background version of *mansplaining*.

HOW IT SHOWS UP IN CONVERSATIONS AND CORPORATE AMERICA

Culturesplaining appears casually in everyday conversations with friends and coworkers. It also emerges on a grander scale when companies, news outlets, colleagues, and friends engage in denialism, gaslighting, erasure, and revisionist history to negate the validity and reality of the experiences and truths of people of color living in a country where racism touches every aspect of society and life.

These instances can include the following methods:

- **Invalidation**—Explaining to a card-carrying member why an experience isn't racist when the person feels it's racist or said it's racist or had a racial undercurrent (e.g., rebuffing the reasons for being mistaken for a receptionist or support staff).
- **Steamrolling**—Interrupting and speaking over a person of color who is sharing their perspective or experience only so you can tell them how they should think or feel about it or otherwise correct or explain something to them about themselves (e.g., rudely "educating" them that never being invited to client dinners has nothing to do with being the only team member of color—aka racist mental manipulation and mind tricks).
- **Fact policing**—Speaking up when you think someone got a fact wrong when recounting a prejudicial experience they lived through and trying to correct it—implying the other person doesn't understand what happened to them (e.g., telling a patron of color that the clerk wasn't following them around the store but probably checking on something in another department or saying they track everyone when only the movements of non-whites are monitored; telling an Arab American stopped at the airport that the bag search was part of the random security selection process).

- **Insensitivity training**—Indicating you think the other person's feelings are wrong—that they're overly sensitive when it comes to race or prejudicial incidents (e.g., a manager being dismissive of discriminatory behavior by telling someone to toughen up or develop thick skin around specific people who "mean no harm" and don't have a "racist bone in their body" or saying they must have misread the situation since what they're hearing "doesn't sound right").

- **Unsolicited schooling**—Meeting someone with a supposed ethnic, unusual, so different, unique, nontraditional, exotic, and "un-American" name and then giving them an unsolicited lecture—Name Origin History Lesson 101—when you're not an expert in anthroponymy or an etymologist. This same analogy applies to unprompted lectures and history lessons about someone's background, lineage, race, religion, ethnicity, national origin, and so on (e.g., telling someone of East Asian descent about the origins of Lunar New Year).

TYPICAL SENTENCE STARTERS
WHEN CULTURESPLAINING

If you hear or find yourself inclined to say the following, your radar should start going off. Here are sentence starters frequently used when about to engage in racist culturesplaining:

- "I think what you mean is . . ."
- "I heard another [insert race] person say . . ."
- "That's not racist. Racism is when . . ."
- "I know [insert name], and he's never treated me that way. He doesn't have a racist or prejudiced bone in his body."
- "That's never happened to me when I've gone there. Something sounds off. When I went there . . ."
- "Did you know [insert previously known information] about your [race/name/heritage/religion]?"
- "I read [obvious detail] about your [race/name/religion]. Did you know that?"

A CLASSIC WATERCOOLER EXAMPLE
OF CULTURESPLAINING

Here's a classic example: A white person begins to tell a Black colleague what it's like to grow up as a Black person in America or what it means to be Black. The offense is especially amplified when coming from someone with a comfortable upbringing or who has never had immediate family members harassed by the police, been negatively racially profiled, had to wait hours in line to vote because the polling station was relocated across town and understaffed or equipped with broken machines, or been turned down for a job because they "just don't seem like the right fit" for the company's culture and workplace environment.

MASS MEDIA CULTURESPLAINING

Culturesplaining also happens through corporate messaging that subliminally reinforces racialized stereotypes, predominantly told through the eyes of whites to shape society's mainstream view of cultural identities and the journeys of people of color. For example, companies in the entertainment industry often have a myopic and warped view of what constitutes the "Black experience" or "Latino experience." This is evidenced in what news stories are highlighted by predominantly white producers (e.g., poor, inner-city, downtrodden people of color in crime-filled communities), ads and commercials are produced (e.g., Blacks dancing, playing sports, or eating soul food), and films are greenlit reinforcing tropes (e.g., gangbangers and families in the projects).

This also happens when white writers are hired to write from the lens of the "Asian experience" in lieu of hiring a scriptwriter of East Asian descent to write from their own voice. These are instances of mass-market culturesplaining. These practices push the white-gaze view on the public to tell people of color what it means to be from their communities instead of promoting opportunities for them to tell their own stories. This robs voices of color of influencing the public's understanding of their communities, culture, views, and heritage.

WHY CULTURESPLAINING IS RACIST

Culturesplaining belittles and invalidates people of color's expertise, feelings, and truths. This practice centers on white perspectives, placing white views and experiences at the epicenter of what's considered factual even when predicated on misguided, racist notions. This condescending pontification is offensive.

By culturesplaining, you're making a paternalistic assumption that the other person lacks the knowledge and ability to accurately articulate their own experience. You're operating under the false belief that you're more qualified to speak about a marginalized group than the individual belonging to that group.

When you culturesplain about race, be prepared for people to openly or quietly think that you're racist—that you're probably someone who's trying your best not to appear racist or who thinks you're not racist but is ipso facto racist as evidenced by your race-based culturesplaining. You're not engaging in intellectually post-racial behavior, just good ole racist conduct. By the way, it's impossible to claim we're in a post-racial society when racism still exists.

You might think you're harmlessly just trying to be a part of the conversation and share your view on race. It's acceptable to engage in dialogues about race with people from different backgrounds (when they signal they're open to it). But in this case, you're informing someone and telling them about their own experience or people. No matter how harmless you think you are or what your perceived low stature on the jackass meter is, you've gone too far and are now getting under the listener's skin in a very racist way.

The problem with culturesplaining is it's not just innocently discussing topics like racism or other forms of prejudice when chiming in. In reality, it's dismissive and implicitly acting on racist ideas that, at their core, have an undercurrent that people of color are wrong—including being ignorant about their own life experiences, that whites are enlightened and people of color are misguided.

CORE PROBLEM WITH CULTURESPLAINING

Maybe you're thinking this isn't fair. Maybe you feel like people of other races explain things to you all the time about race. Maybe you're even tired of hearing them speak about being discriminated against or you think they're just pulling the race card. Besides, isn't it the same thing when they explain things to you? Why can't you also explain things?

Here is why it's critically different. You're not a subject-matter expert. You flat-out lack the knowledge and life experiences to opine in the same way as a person of color talking about what happened to them or their life journey. Sometimes you just lack basic street cred to share an opinion or try to school someone. Given your lack of lived experiences limiting your ability to identify with the other person's plight or understand their perspective, you should be quiet. Censor yourself, listen, and accept what they say as facts.

White people have been conditioned to speak up all the time. That's the benefit of privilege. Often, it results in *speaking over* others and dominating conversations. Whites are accustomed to sharing their thoughts and being affirmed by society when volunteering opinions—even when clueless about the topic and they can't relate.

Think of it like this: if it's your first day on the job, you'd be a fool to advise senior staff on how they could do things better because the newbie lacks knowledge and needs to sit back and learn before sharing opinions. When it comes to race, whether you're twenty-five years old or fifty-five years old, consider yourself a newbie and filter your words.

By all means, participate in the conversation! No one is saying you must remain mute. Just look out for *when* you should remain silent. Notice when it's appropriate and beneficial to listen and truly hear what the other person is sharing. Maybe through patience you'll learn something new or see things through a new lens when you filter what you share.

A better way to connect and empathize with others is to understand *why* you'd experience things differently because of your own race, background, and life experiences.

A note on tokenization: If you have relatives of color, a Black boyfriend, or a South Asian adopted child, this doesn't mean your level of understanding has risen to having the requisite knowledge, lived experience, or right to culturesplain. That's just living in white privilege and thinking you have a free pass with racial license to engage in bigotry due to your affiliations. When you walk into a store or get pulled over by the cops, the color of your skin is your real freedom card with the complexion for protection.

A note on reverse splaining: While there's *whitesplaining* (a subset of culturesplaining), where whites speak with their presumed knowledge of non-white groups and racism and belief that they're more qualified on these topics, there isn't an equivalent *blacksplaining*. When a person of color talks about race with a white person, they don't have the same institutional power as whites belonging to the dominant culture. This may sound unfair if you're white, but it's all about underlying societal power dynamics.

TIPS AND ADVICE

Knowing when it's safe to speak up is difficult to maneuver. You're probably wondering how to discuss race without telling a person of color how to feel, point out something you think is racist, ask questions without offending, or disagree when you don't feel something was racist (note that you should keep your thoughts to yourself with this last one). Maybe you're so fearful of saying something racist or hurtful that the anxiety of getting it wrong will render you voiceless—thinking it's better to just remain silent than culturesplain. In all honesty, there are times you should self-censor, listen, and defer to others. The tips in the following section will help you determine when to hold back and when to speak up.

WHEN YOU'RE TEMPTED TO BE A RACE RULE BREAKER

When someone shares their experience, instead of culturesplaining, do the following:

- If you hear a person of color complain about racist behavior, resist the urge to interrupt with something like "[Name] is the least bigoted person I know! He volunteers at his local Boys Club."
- Instead of speaking up, listen and learn. Silence can be a great tool in advancing cross-racial understanding. But after someone shares a painful story, you could add, "I feel bad you had to experience that. How can I best support you and help limit this from happening again?" This question is appropriate to ask a peer, whereas a manager is now on notice. Bosses must act to prevent racist behavior from creating hostile and toxic workplaces, which rightfully attract litigation.
- Accept the other person's truth. Avoid giving pushback or trying to reshape facts since this will offend and anger the culturesplainee (e.g., "We don't engage in discriminatory lending practices. I reject

that. We just issued a mortgage to a Latino family last week. There are other reasons explaining why we haven't underwritten loans to more people of color.")

- Stop yourself before shifting the conversation to being all about you and your worldview by saying, for example, "I find it hard to believe [teacher] is biased. In my class, I call on the Black and brown students. And I don't discipline them more than whites."
- When you hear someone recount an incident they feel is racist and you don't see it, ask them, "I want to understand better. Forgive me for not seeing it, but can you explain *how* or *why* this is racist so I can identify it better on my own in the future?" This situation is different from previous guidance advising against asking people of color questions about race. Here, the person opened the door to discussing race by sharing a story, providing an opportunity to seek understanding.

Before you educate someone, cut them off in conversation, talk over them, question them about the facts when they already told you what happened, give them a history lesson about themselves, or explain to them how they should feel about something they already categorized as racist, hurtful, and offensive, ask yourself if you are culturesplaining or if chiming in does any of the following:

- Negates how the other person feels about something that happened to them or their people (i.e., unsympathetically gaslighting to control the narrative and manipulate the conversation).
- Serves to protect you from being perceived as racist or supports your thinking you're beyond racism.
- Quenches your insatiable thirst to engage in discussions on race even when lacking personal knowledge.
- Shows that you're an informed and woke ally or a self-perceived ride-or-die white liberal who is down for the cause after recently reading a book, seeing a documentary, downloading a podcast, signing a petition, feeling the weight and shame of white guilt, or wanting to distance yourself from white privilege as you enjoy the benefits of White Welfare—basically just making yourself feel good, virtue signaling, and patting yourself on the back, feeling entitled and justified to talk to others about themselves.

- Enables the person to feel listened to, heard, and seen (i.e., validated with humanity and dignity).
- Creates space where the person would feel comfortable in the future sharing personal experiences or information about their background with you.
- Facilitates your ability to learn about other races and cultures in ways celebrating their heritage without unwillingly placing them in a position of being your teacher.

TREAD LIGHTLY WITH SOMEONE'S GIVEN NAME

You might think that it's safer to ask about someone's name origin because you're not lecturing on what you perceive as their background, but you still may be skating on thin ice.

What you may really be asking is "Where are you *really* from?"

The true implication of your inquiry is that the person is less American than you—that they're an other, an outsider, or not part of the mainstream.

You can ask about someone's name, but it's all about the *how*— the word choice, delivery, and underlying motivations.

A simple way to open the discussion door is to say, "Your name is lovely."

This supports their ability to have agency with their identity and how open they want to be. They may volunteer personal details. If not or they just say "Thanks," then consider the subject closed.

WHEN YOU SEE OR HEAR IT

If you witness someone else culturesplaining, step in and use one of these tricks:

- If the culturesplainer is interrupting a card-carrying member to shift the focus on themselves, say, "Wait, I'd like to hear what [insert name] has to say about this" or "I'm interested in hearing the story and what happened to them."

- When the culturesplainer is in a position of power—your boss, a big client, store manager, or community leader—you have difficult decisions to make. In the workplace, assess the blowback you'll suffer by raising the issue or reporting the conduct. Weigh the magnitude of the harm, behavior patterns, impact on the company culture and brand, and your risk and trauma tolerance level. Explore if you can report anonymously or to the government. If you decide to do nothing, have the conscious realization that you made a trade-off to advance your own interests—you opted to protect yourself instead of calling out racism. While your behavior is logical, seeing risks in acting isn't a free pass letting you off the hook. It's important to have self-awareness about your choices. In a community context, you won't be immune from backlash but should feel freer to root out racism and speak up. This is what being a Racism Disruptor looks like—moving from bystander to action.

- Under no circumstances should you then tell the culturesplainer that they're culturesplaining *in front of* the person of color. That's you culturesplaining. Let the culturesplainee speak for themselves in that moment. Maybe you don't need to rescue them. Yes, you can help create space for them to speak by saying you'd like to hear what they're saying, but don't appoint yourself as their white savior. You can always have a sidebar conversation with the culturesplainer another time providing feedback on what you witnessed and how they took over and dominated through culturesplaining behavior. While it's fine to try to limit how much someone interrupts and talks over someone else, don't use it as an opportunity for a teachable moment right then and there with the card-carrying member present unless they signal they welcome real-time backup. #Doubling-Down-on-Paternalistic-Behavior

Depending on the circumstance, how direct you feel you can be, and your confidence in your room-reading skills, you could use these additional talking points as needed:

- "While you may not have intended this, the impact of your words signaled you don't accept someone's experiences are true and their perspective valid."

- "When people tell others about how they should feel about something that happened to them as a person of color, that's engaging in white-centering and racist behavior."
- "As a company and team, we really shouldn't be in the business of defining what's the experience or story of people of color. That's just leaning into the status quo or advancing stereotypes. Instead, we should be more inclusive by providing a platform for diverse groups to tell their stories as part of our standard business practice. Also, we should remain alert to when we're disseminating tropes."
- "I'm curious to understand what experiences you've lived through that enabled you to become an authority on [race/name]?"
- "Why can't we just accept what was said as fact? What message do you believe you're sending when rejecting what you were told and giving pushback? Why do you feel that's a necessary response?"
- "I know you care about [e.g., people feeling valued and heard]. What I just heard doesn't align with that."
- "What you did really felt like virtue signaling and patronizing culturesplaining. I know that's a frank statement, but I feel the need to be candid. I have a hard time witnessing this when I know you might not intend to send certain messages to others and know you have the capacity to receive constructive feedback."

> People won't remember what you said or did, they will remember how you made them feel.
>
> —Maya Angelou, poet and civil rights advocate

Don't Ask about Someone's Name, Ethnicity, or Race

You can't understand how powerfully racist that question is, can you? ... Even the inquiry comes from a position of being in the center.

—*Toni Morrison, author and academic*

RULE SUMMARY

The safest route is not to ask someone about their race or lineage, even indirectly.

Presume people of color will be offended if you comment on their racialized appearance or racial identity. Always assume there's more to their story than what you see.

Looks can be deceiving and identities richly complex.

Don't put people of color in the position of having to decide if they want to make the situation less awkward for you or let you flounder. Don't force them to help you through your discomfort when you engineered a microaggressive conversation. It's not their job to hold your hand through your racism, especially when you're not the hurt party but the perpetrator advancing white supremacy.

Tread lightly when curious about someone's name, ethnicity, race, or background. Think about your word choices, if you should even ask, and if you're crossing a line. Less is more.

There's an art to asking people of color about their heritage—it requires cultural sensitivity to avoid othering and making people of color feel unwelcome in their homeland.

When in doubt, stay in your own lane and keep your mouth shut. You don't have a right to know people's private information.

Often when meeting someone new, we naturally ask questions to get to know them better. Small talk and discovering what we have in common feels normal. Maybe we're curious or confused about a person's background, wanting to know more about *who* and *what* they are. We start asking questions.

There's no perfect way nor magic formula to inquire into someone's lineage. Names, races, ethnicities, and group affiliations are very personal to those getting the questions—taking direct aim at individual identities and how they see themselves fitting into the world. No two people will respond the same way. Without the appropriate level of sensitivity, finesse, racial emotional intelligence, and self-awareness, prying could rapidly spiral into racist microaggressions and offensive probing—making people of color feel like perpetual foreigners in their own land.

What's complicated about microaggressions is they're mostly unconscious biases, which makes being mindful of when, where, and how you're inquiring into someone's background critically important.[1] You probably think you're just genuinely curious with well-intentioned desires to understand other cultures. But when your seemingly innocent inquiry results in feeling you're asking loaded questions and conjuring up negative connotations, they might believe your questions aren't merely ignorant but backed by racist malintent. The impact is you're inflicting racial harm.

WHY THE RACE RULE MATTERS

Background questions set the tone for relationship development—leaving lasting first impressions and irreparably destroying existing friendships. This conduct impacts your ability to genuinely connect. Moderating your behavior isn't about censoring yourself but filtering. It's about creating a cross-racial dialogue that doesn't force people of color to feel *they* must self-censor or feel compartmentalized. Exercise caution. Which questions would bother you isn't your benchmark. When in doubt, keep your curiosities to yourself. Beware of questions translating into "You don't *seem* like you *already* belong here."[2]

TYPICAL OFFENSIVE GETTING-TO-KNOW-YOU QUESTIONS

Do not ask any of the following offensive questions:

- "Where are you from?"
- "Where's your family from originally?"
- "Where did your family immigrate from?"
- "What's your ethnic background?"
- "What race are you?"
- "You don't look [race/ethnicity], what are you?"
- "What kind of name is that?"
- "I haven't heard that name before. Very exotic/different/unique. Where is it from?"

Seemingly innocuous conversation starters can trigger feelings of alienation. These microaggressions reinforce and magnify unequal power structures. They amplify racial marginalization and differences, especially since many whites never have their membership in the American mainstream challenged.

Whether your family fought in the Revolutionary War or your passport's immigration stamp is brand new, when you're white, the assumption is you belong and everyone else is an other. You're the archetypal default American—fitting the classic narrative of what an American is supposed to visually look like and be. Othering behavior signals that those with a white-European external appearance are the true people from here who rightfully own this country.

Identity questions are frequently rooted in an underlying white supremacist belief that the "exotic," "different," "ethnic," or non-white person doesn't really *belong* here—that they're not equally American. Poorly phrased and prying questions validate patronizing existing beliefs about social identities, implying their level of un-Americanism while reinforcing your Americanism. Basically, you're asking, "Where did this FOB (or fresh-off-the-boat) person immigrate from?" even if they speak perfect English with an obvious American accent.

The "immigrant identity" isn't universal. To deter perpetuating and fueling personal prejudices that marginalize people of color, avoid these racist assumptions:

- **FOBing Chinese Americans**—Chinese people started coming to America in the 1800s. There are sixth-generation Chinese Americans who don't speak Mandarin or Cantonese. Assuming they and other ethnicities are newly minted Americans is rooted in xenophobia.

- **Denaturalizing Natives and nonimmigrants**—If the person's family was here before the United States became a country, you're othering *original* peoples and nonimmigrants. Borders were drawn and nationhood was forced on them. This applies to Native Americans, Alaskan Natives, Native Hawaiians, Puerto Ricans, and Californios, Tejanos, and Hispanos (i.e., Mexican Americans, many who mixed with Indigenous peoples, whose families descend from non-Indigenous Spanish-speaking colonizers and conquistadors who were in California, "Tejas" or Mexican Texas, New Mexico, and other formerly Mexican territories before the United States violently annexed parts of Mexico and claimed them during the Mexican-American War and solidified its conquest through the Treaty of Guadalupe Hidalgo in 1848).

- **Invalidating enslavement legacies**—The descendants of American slaves never immigrated. As Malcolm X famously said, "We didn't land on Plymouth Rock . . . Plymouth Rock landed on us." Asking origin questions implies second-class status, when everything about their heritage is quintessentially American and woven into our historical origin story. It reminds Foundational Black Americans no matter how long they've been here—hundreds of years later—they're never accepted in the eyes of white America. Coerced sacrifices are meritless for citizenship and freedom. Asking from what specific African country their family originated heightens the offense. Most Black Americans with slave lineage can't trace their heritage to any specific country or tribe. They're forced to accept their ancestors were from the vast African continent. Genealogy is a painful, empty void filled with racial grief and outrage.

Origin questions strike directly at America's deficiency in teaching American history and most whites' inadequacy in proactive self-learning. The failure of most whites to educate themselves to better understand their own country beyond a white lens perpetuates an inexcusable lack of basic knowledge.

THANKS FOR ASKING— IT'S A DAMN SLAVE NAME!

When whites ask about Blacks' last names, this can be very irritating and impertinent—especially if it exposes your ignorance and promulgates microaggressions (i.e., racism).

Black Americans whose ancestors were enslaved typically have last names given to them by enslavers. Names were detached from their Black bloodline and then intertwined with the enslaver's, who erased their identities by imposing the enslaver's family name. European last names simultaneously represent the names of brutal whites who raped, tortured, trafficked, and killed their enslaved relatives.

The confusion on white faces asking unanswerable questions reveals the level of white ignorance. The inquiry could prompt a clap-back about rapists, slavery, or the slave trade. But if retorts result in feeling white discomfort and jaw-dropping shock from frank replies about America's dirty past, reject your urge to express feeling uncomfortable. Don't become the victim. Their response was fair and honest. Your question came from a place of racial obliviousness wearing historical blinders. They shouldn't have to dance around fragile feelings when they're offended or candid.

When inquiring, accept you may never get satisfactory answers. Maybe they don't feel like sharing nor trust you. They could perceive you as a nosey line-crosser failing at empathetic question phraseology. Or maybe they avoid single-identity labels as complex human beings—feeling that box-checking negates the nuances of their individuality. Asking a mixed-race person to classify according to the dominant culture's worldview could imply their existence is peripheral to one of their identities, making them feel stuck between two worlds yet part of neither. And ethnically ambiguous people are often fed up with a lifetime of fatiguing, intrusive, marginalizing questions that dispute their identity's authenticity.

Before embarking on a risky journey of alienating people of color and making them feel othered, first determine if you should even be asking *any* questions. If you decide to pose very personal background questions, approach this with as much diplomacy as you can muster up. Know you may not get what you want. You may need to quickly pivot by letting it go. Remember, you're not entitled to this information. People reveal what they want to reveal. It's their choice.

WHAT THEY MAY THINK BUT NOT SAY TO YOUR FACE

Figure 25.1 shows an example of conversations that happen daily. This example isn't hypothetical for shock value but demonstrates how many interactions unfold, the result being what a person of color may think

"So where are you from?"

"California."

"But where are your parents from?" (doubling down)

"California."

"Where are you *really* from? What *are* you?" (tripling down)

Internal thoughts: "Where am I from? My mother's womb, dipstick! Asked and answered. What's up with the microaggression rinse and repeat? I'm from here! What racist and rude place are *you* from? Wait, let me guess, White-Centered-Ville—a place where whites feel entitled to ask any and every thought bubble without consideration for alienating people of color. Thanks for making me feel like an outsider in my own country. I'm so tired of this crap. And FYI, I find it particularly rich that you're asking me this through *your* thick accent."

FIGURE 25.1. What POCs may think but not say to your face

internally about you. It isn't merely to illustrate someone getting upset. Their inside voice at the end reflects the negative impact your inquiry has on relationships, with them walking away with a tarnished impression of you as a racist.

What isn't said to your face reveals whites have encounters that they think are relatively normal or not a big deal but people of color view as utterly offensive. Clueless, you walk away believing you have a decent relationship, while they conclude that they can't stand you, want nothing to do with you, or dread the next time they must interact with you, see your face, or work alongside you. Too often, whites and people of color have drastically divergent assessments of whether they're even friends or if encounters are benign.

LEXICON SHIFTING

Terminology is constantly evolving. Is It *Black* or *African American*? *Latino* or *Latinx*? *Indian* or *Native American*? *POC* or *BIPOC*? It can be confusing to know what the most up-to-date terms are. Meanwhile, jargon is very personal. One person might prefer *Black* while another *African American*. And while *Latinx* is growing in popularity at companies, at schools, and in the media, it currently isn't universally used, accepted, or even known by those of Latin American descent. This implies that *Latinx* is being imposed on them. Since people have individual preferences, there's no singular vocabulary. You can't rely on one person's terminology as the gold standard for an entire race or ethnicity. It invites an awkward exchange with them checking you or secretly feeling annoyed.

Instead of coming out of the gates with questions that could backfire like "Do you prefer *Latino* or *Latinx*?" ask, "How do you *self-identify*?" There are countless ways to self-identify. But no matter the various nomenclature options, start with open-ended questions over picking specific terms for them. This approach creates space for them to self-determine their preference. It gives them control and free agency. The strategy also enables them to respond without saying anything about race or ethnicity, which is a signal to shut down the inquiry into their background.

If and only if the person has been more open about discussing race and their background, you could consider this alternative phrasing: "I don't want to assume, but I'm curious if you're open to telling me how you racially identify."

The advice above is about everyday interactions. However, there's nuance with governmental reporting rubrics. There's a difference between casual encounters in conversations and categories used by companies for compliance purposes. It's different when human resources asks, tasked with collecting demographic data and following the racial categories described by the government. They should request it in company-wide, anonymous surveys giving people the option to opt out.

SAY MY NAME, SAY MY NAME

As a rule, fully skip asking personal questions that link to someone's identity beyond how to properly pronounce their name. Steer clear of asking *what kind* of name they have. In your private friend-zone life compared to the workplace, there's more leeway, but the runway is still short. Follow cues and check your tone to help preserve professional relationships, friendships, and family ties.

Under no circumstances should you *ever* assign a nickname to someone whose name is challenging for you to properly pronounce without them volunteering one. It's rude. Nicknames require consent and being cool with each other. And note that "being cool" doesn't mean *you* think you're friends. It means *they* feel you're cool enough to call them anything other than what's on their driver's license. This guideline applies even if you hear *someone else* calling them a nickname. Without them giving you a green light, you must call them by their given name and learn how to say their name correctly.

Also, don't assume someone's name has something to do with their race, ethnicity, national origin, or religion. Sometimes names are just names. If you potentially know something about the origins of their name, stop yourself. Resist the urge to culturesplain by telling them about the history of their name, asking how or why they got this name, saying it's not an American name, or saying it's from XYZ country, like first names are exclusive to any specific nation.

TIPS AND ADVICE

Before peppering people with personal questions tied to their heritage, focus on getting to know them as a person. Ask questions about interests, values, character, and hobbies. Share information about yourself so it's mutual and not an interrogation. However, determining if you should skip asking about someone's background or proceed boils down to these key considerations:

- The motivations behind the inquiry.
- The context and place.
- What you're asking.
- How you're asking.
- If the topic surfaces organically.
- How the person responds.
- How you adapt, pivot, and respond based on their reaction to your questions (i.e., how you read the room).
- If and how you genuinely and properly apologize when your words offend and cause pain.

Successful navigation requires good judgment, self-awareness, and keen perception skills. See table 25.1 for more examples of how your questions can be perceived.

ON-THE-JOB INQUISITION—ASKING QUESTIONS AT WORK

Thinking about asking colleagues about their heritage and background? Skip it! Don't make colleagues feel uncomfortable. This hinders your ability to foster mutual trust and respect. You could lose all credibility, with them concluding you aren't someone to trust nor befriend since you alienated them with your inquiry. If the questions aren't directly related to a project, company goals, or diversity initiatives, focus on your work and lighter topics like hobbies.

Racist conversation starters can plant the seed for a toxic, microaggressive workplace.

They will dread being around you and coming to work, and they might start looking for a new job.

If and when it's germane to company work, it's best to let the person have the conversation on their own terms by using open-ended and broad questions so it doesn't feel invasive or othering.

TABLE 25.1 Racist taboo translator for loaded questions

What you said	What they heard or thought
"What are you?" "Your name is so ethnic/exotic/ unusual/different/multicultural/ woke." **Alternative**—"Where did you grow up? East Coast, West Coast, or the Heartland or South?" Or "What's your home state?"	"There's no way you can ever be a part of America's mainstream. Let me other and marginalize you. I'm prone to reducing people to their skin color, a category, or type. I'm itching to know so I can neatly shove you into my myopic world-view. By the way, your feelings are secondary to knowing what's not my business."
"Where are your ancestors/ people/peeps from?" **Alternative**—"What is it you'd like me to know about you?"	"Hey, why aren't you white?"
"Where's your accent from?" **Alternative**—"What kind of music do you like? Or what's your favorite book or film? My favorite music/book/film is . . ."	"Hey, foreigner! How come you speak English so well?"
"Oh, you were born in Dallas. I've always believed it's important for us to embrace and learn about other cultures and visit each other's countries. So, was it hard learning English?" **Alternative**—Listen to what people are saying!	"Yes, I'm patronizing. My brain couldn't process your being born here. Why would I think you could speak English even as a native-born American since that doesn't align with your physical appearance? Besides, your being American never registered since I ignored the words you said."
"I'm sorry, I don't mean to pry, but . . ." **Alternative**—Say nothing. Wait to see what they volunteer. White privilege is thinking you have a right to other people's personal information.	"FYI, I'm about to ask some inap-propriate bigoted bullshit. Ignore my sentence qualifier. Prying is exactly what I'm about and intend to do."

(continued)

TABLE 25.1 Racist taboo translator for loaded questions (*continued*)

What you said	What they heard or thought
"What kind of Asian/Hispanic/Arab are you?" "So are you an immigrant Black, or did your family pick cotton here?" "What's that dot/turban/headwrap/scarf on your head for? What's that about?" "Are you Mexican or something, or do you live on a reservation?" **Alternative**—Shh. Turn around. Go home and watch *Roots* from start to finish along with the sequel! And find some nontropey material to learn about other groups. You have a lot of unlearning and self-work to do even before someone consents to discussing race.	"I leave a trail of flabbergasted people of color wherever I go. Racist collateral damage is how I roll."

Also, intrusions place them in a precarious professional position if they mention feeling offended. Often, the person of color is sidelined and ostracized when they're the victim, not the perpetrator.

WHEN YOU HEAR IT

To help pump the brakes when witnessing these racist microaggressions, you could question the inquisitor. But be careful of culturesplaining in front of people of color. When speaking up, you could ask them, "What's the reason *why* you're asking about race/ethnicity/box checking?" The strategy of asking why can be effective in getting people to see through their own biases.[3] You could keep asking why questions until they see the hypocrisy of their white centering. Or you could keep asking why until you make them as intentionally uncomfortable as you want them to be.

There are times when whites need to feel that lesson with all its gut-wrenching discomfort. It's a fair strategy for repeat offenders used to alienating people of color, reducing them to boxes, and failing to see their individuality and humanity. Some lessons are tough to experience yet need to happen so people learn and grow. This could help them diplomatically navigate future discussions about race and identity. At the very least, they'll learn if they can't stand the heat, they better stay out of the othering kitchen. Next time, they'll think twice before channeling their privilege and snooping into people's provenance instead of minding their own business.

> It is not our differences that divide us. It is our inability to recognize, accept, and celebrate those differences.
>
> —Audre Lorde, poet and civil rights activist

Prioritize POCs' Views and Feelings When Discussing Race

Prejudice is an emotional commitment to ignorance.

—*Nathan Rutstein, journalist and author*

RULE SUMMARY

Whether the topics of race and prejudice float into conversations casually or they're addressed intentionally at work, consider how words will land and who's the priority during these discussions. These conversations must prioritize people of color above whites. Focusing on their real-time experience minimizes racial tensions and promotes positive interactions. Your goal is to limit any pain, offense, and trauma inflicted on people of color by regulating what you say, your tone and demeanor, and how you respond.

Too often, conversations that should focus on real, quantifiable, and legitimate harms to people of color become hijacked and engulfed in discussions about whites' feelings, expectations, and needs. White participants arrive deciding what will be discussed, what they'll hear, and what they'll learn—effectively making it just a white space.[1] White centering is antithetical to progress. It reinforces existing power dynamics. As Ijeoma Oluo, author of *So You Want to Talk about Race*, said, "If your anti-racism work prioritizes the 'growth' and 'enlightenment' of white America over the safety, dignity, and humanity of people of color—it's not anti-racism work. *It's white supremacy.*"

As a white person, you need to show up knowing the assignment, that it's not about you but *people of color* and what they feel.

Arrive knowing you're there because *you're part of the problem*. Come prepared to appreciate deconstructing White Welfare and supremacy is your duty. Any other agenda is just circling the drain.

If you can't do this, you're just virtue signaling, engaging in performative acts, and showboating—pretending you're really trying to change or learn. While you might think you're doing something impactful or transformational, you're just dancing in the status quo. There's no point replicating what doesn't work and involving people of color in useless conversations. If this is what you're doing, then please spare people of color from these talks until you're ready to come correct. You'll cause more harm to them and society than good—inflicting toxic trauma and engaging in psychological warfare and racialized verbal abuse.

START WITH R-E-S-P-E-C-T
TO CHANNEL YOUR BEST SELF

Respect is the critical starting, middle, and end point in cross-racial under-standing and interactions essential for developing and maintaining positive and lasting relationships with people of color. If you can't be respectful and empathetic when discussing race or speaking with people of color, then you'll undoubtedly hurt them and cause pain. If you can't modulate your behavior and self-censor to avoid subjecting people of color to verbal trauma, microaggressions, and demoralizing overt racism, then you're not ready to have substantive and meaningful interactions. Given the realities of white privilege and structural racism, you need to be more careful than them in causing injury. While this might feel unfair, it's a reality and your obligation given societal power dynamics and which group historically bears the brunt of oppression. Being respectful will limit the chance of acting like and being an oppressor.

When discussing race with people of color, keep the following steps and best practices in mind:

- Bring kindness, compassion, empathy, patience, and civility.
- Arrive ready, willing, and able to prioritize the views and feelings of people of color above your own.
- Insist on race-centered conversations, avoiding distractions discuss-ing gender, sexuality, class, and other isms. Focus strategically on racism, even if exploring intersectionality with race.
  - While other groups are also important, talking about them often cannibalizes topic space. Others become included at the expense and in lieu of people of color. Thus, people of color become vehi-cles for other marginalized groups' progress, and understanding people of color and solving the negative impacts of racism remain ignored.
  - For more information on the importance of race-centered con-versations, visit FatimahGilliam.com/RaceRulesDownloads.
- Be willing and able to demonstrate understanding by showing gen-uine interest in the person and topic and that you're thinking about them so people of color feel seen, heard, valued, and respected.

- Come willing to trust by demonstrating belief in what you're being told by people of color, which you can show by accepting what they say is racist as a fact instead of questioning or pushing back.
- Follow their lead. When they indicate wanting to explore a topic more or move on, defer to them even if this makes you feel uncomfortable, personally targeted, or ignored.
- Be an active listener to encourage sharing.
- Don't interrupt someone speaking, even when excited or wanting to support an idea. Don't steamroll by talking over others and hogging up all the space, especially if you're not allowing people of color enough airtime. No one wants to speak with people seeking to hear their own voice.
- Leave your debate skills at the door. It's a conversation, not a moot court competition. People of color shouldn't feel attacked, challenged, worn out, and depleted from spending time with you.
- Create space for people of color to share their views and feelings. If you notice others being dismissive of the people of color present or fellow whites engaging in offensive or microaggressive behavior, strategically shift the discussion to limit the negative impact of other whites on participants of color. Establish opportunities for people of color wanting to share their opinions. This supports voices of color.

If you're having a planned discussion (e.g., at work, on campus, with friends, in a book club, after viewing a movie as a family), it's helpful to have conversation guidelines to create a safer space and set the tone. This could include guidelines allowing leeway for participants to ask "dumb questions" and openly reveal knowledge gaps. But permit this only if (1) this comes from a spirit of learning versus unfettered license to unapologetically vomit trauma on others and (2) participants willingly consent to a discussion format where people can learn and fail in the open. This buy-in for candid ignorance is particularly vital from participants of color. Without their uncoerced, non-peer-pressured consent, skip it. Establishing parameters promotes respect and sets expectations, shepherding participants toward positive, productive dialogue.

TIPS AND ADVICE

Here's what to avoid when discussing race:

- **Unrealistic expectations**—Don't expect to solve racism or repair relationships in one discussion or marginalized groups to be devoid of emotions, anger, and resentment. The goal isn't to create false unity or reconciliation. This is usually just code for wanting to sweep racism under the rug, let whites off the hook, and make them feel better without atoning and taking responsibility.
- **Forgiveness**—Don't anticipate exoneration from or reconciliation with people of color for your past behavior or real-time offensive behavior. Don't manipulate forgiveness when it's not yours to give.
- **Entitlement and hostages**—Avoid forcing people of color into discussions on racism when they're not interested, expecting them to reveal intimate, personal stories, or prying into topics that are too invasive when you have no right to this information.
- **Inquisition**—Avoid asking questions about unimportant details or focusing too much on information that misses the big picture.
- **Comedy central**—Don't tell jokes. While you may want to cut the tension or mask anxiety or discomfort, joking can backfire when people feel raw and vulnerable. It can trivialize their feelings.
- **Defensiveness**—When your behavior is called out as being prejudiced or topics hit home, don't get defensive. The only preemptive move is not to offend in the first place. Own your behavior, and don't double down by expressing hostility, shutting down, making excuses, or engaging in other reactionary tactics.
- **Mission creep and trauma porn**—Avoid equating racism with other forms of discrimination, shifting the focus to other marginalized groups beyond race, or talking about your own personal struggles (i.e., white victimhood). They're avoidance strategies to evade tackling racism, which is invalidating and negates the specific relevance of race. People of color don't want to hear about comparisons, who else had a difficult road, or what hardships you've overcome, making them feel ignored and relegated to the service road.
- **White tears and fragility**—Avoid crying or becoming overly emotional when struggling to cope with mirrors held to your face or

confronting racism. People of color do *not* appreciate discussions being commandeered by white tears and white feelings. It's coddling and prioritizes your emotional needs at the expense of people of color. If you need to temporarily excuse yourself to control your emotions, do it respectfully. Otherwise, suck it up. While you're important, too, the larger issue is you're *always* important and they're not. You must "take one for the white team" to create space for them to speak and you to learn and develop better coping skills.

- **White centering and narcissism**—Don't make this about you! While you're also a valued participant, and collective white behavior can be at the epicenter of the discussion, don't pivot toward placing whiteness and white values at the center. This succeeds only in marginalizing the marginalized.

- **White grievance**—Don't take up discussion time to raise gripes about perceived wrongs to whites when whites are privileged and collectively oppress people of color. Nor should you bring up feeling you're a new white minority or invisible in America. Whites still hold most of the political and societal power as the dominant group. While some may feel this way, it's not grounded in the realities of American society. It's offensive. If you feel maligned as a white person, it's time to recalibrate your outlook. This thinking shows you're not getting it and there's a vast sea of misunderstanding between you and them.

TRIGGERING THE WHITE VICTIMHOOD MENTALITY

The truth is triggering. It requires self-analysis of complicity and an internal evaluation of proactive personal malfeasance. Since most people don't want to take themselves on as a project,[2] they reject facts, statements, and experiences requiring hard admissions and self-reflection. Many whites will do anything to avoid being uncomfortable and honest, including irrational behavior. Otherwise, they're confronted with having to change and do something with new understandings. They reject facing their white supremacy. This is too frightening. As a result, many opt for racist distractions, defense mechanisms, emotional outbursts, hostility, tears, and narcissism and undermine productive conversations.

Equating your life challenges to systemic racism is textbook white victimhood, albeit more subtle than getting emotional or overtly hostile. If your words make you the victim, you're distracted from seeing what people of color experience. Even when trying to identify with them, be mindful of comparing a difficult childhood, personal tragedies, or European atrocities to slavery, extermination, racial violence, and intergenerational discrimination and poverty caused by White Welfare. People of color find this infuriating and disrespectful.

Don't fall for or into others' white victimhood traps nor allow them to hijack talking about race. If it's someone else doing this, show them the door when necessary. Prioritize the emotional safety of participants of color.

If this is you, remove yourself from the conversation. Work on yourself. Focus on shifting your mentality away from victimhood. Prepare yourself for the next discussion.

Here are some phrases to skip when discussing race:[3]

- "You're taking it the wrong way."
- "Don't play the race card."
- "I'm not racist."
- "Race has nothing to do with it."
- "I have Black friends."
- "I'm colorblind."
- "You're racist!" which derails discussions particularly if saying this to a person of color.
- "That reminds me of the time . . ." to top off someone else's story, especially when it demotes the significance of their racist experience or segues into a story about you.

NAVIGATING CONFLICT AND POWDER KEGS

When encounters blow up and angers flare, don't panic. Stay present. Try to understand what's motivating feelings and responses. If it's someone else, don't write them off or check out. If it's you, calm down and reflect. Understanding the whys could illuminate the pathway forward.

But pay attention to whether understanding emotional outbursts and underlying motivations is cannibalizing the conversation and harming the psychological safety of the participants of color.

EXIT STRATEGIES

When conversations get too heated and people of color hit their tolerance limit with inevitable microaggressions that surface, be ready, willing, and able to end them. Also, if some whites drive an abusive racist verbal truck over people of color, participants of color are justified in abruptly exiting stage left and walking away.

But if people of color present still want to keep discussing, then whites must harness thick skin and stay. Whites should hear what they want to say. It's part of the assignment. Far too often, whites are quick to flee when uncomfortable, even if they initiate conversations. When whites prematurely end dialogue, check out, shut down, or melt down, they're just leveraging their privilege. People of color never have the luxury of retreating from being discriminated against, oppressed, uncomfortable, and traumatized. You must quickly get comfortable with discomfort and candor. Come prepared to hear what people of color want to share, no matter how stressful, difficult, or directed at you their truth might be.

Establishing ground rules increases the likelihood that conversations will be productive. Once participants get going, however, often it's inevitable for tempers to flare or even tears to flow. But people of color have negligible bandwidth for white tears and white drama. During these moments, increase your sensitivity to whether people of color feel ignored, invisible, and mistreated as a byproduct of conversations with whites and you.

With structured discussions at work, companies should delicately give employees of color the choice of attending or opting out. Yes, white employees may also want to opt out, except they're the demographic needing to do the hard work. Requiring participation from people of color can be inappropriate, especially since what usually happens is whites expect the attendees of color to take responsibility for the whole conversation. It's a fatiguing, unwelcomed role. The emotional burden and job of carrying the dialogue and sharing is unfairly dumped on them, along with psychologically navigating colleagues' overt white supremacy.

FIGHT-OR-FLIGHT RESPONSE

If someone deeply offends you or you want to discuss their racist behavior one on one, consider saying, "I'd like to discuss this interaction with you at a later time."

This creates space to process your thoughts and response. You don't always have to navigate in real-time. This applies to speaking to a white person whose offensive behavior bothered you. If a person of color offended you, you may need to forgo having that conversation.

For whites to evolve beyond just being more skilled at discussing race but toward successfully getting along and living and working side by side with people of color (i.e., improve race relations), whites need to develop deeper respect for people with dissimilar backgrounds. The way to nurture and grow this foundational respect is through cross-racial *personal contact*.

The more you interact with people of color, the less you'll require special, planned, and intentional discussions and trainings on race and culture that educate you and help you become less ignorant. Over time, you will evolve, especially if you anchor your approach to prioritizing the feelings, views, and experiences of people of color.

> To not have the conversations because they make you uncomfortable is the definition of privilege.
> Your comfort is not at the center of this discussion. . . .
> You have to choose courage over comfort.
>
> —Brené Brown, academic and author

Be Accountable—
Apologize and
Make Amends

Success is not final. Failure is not fatal.
It is the courage to continue that counts.

—*Winston Churchill, prime minister of the United Kingdom*

RULE SUMMARY

Whether you're ashamed, embarrassed, or fearful of confrontation or exposing yourself to honest criticism and judgment, it's imperative to apologize when you've hurt someone, caused them pain, and were offensive. Apologizing can repair, restore, and maintain relationships. They help build trust *if and when* you own up to your mistakes. Admitting wrongdoing can open up a dialogue with others, possibly even allowing a stronger personal connection.

Apologies can restore your integrity in the eyes of those you hurt. They allow you and hurt parties to discuss what's acceptable and outside the scope of appropriate behavior. They also give injured parties a platform to explain how deeply you hurt them and why, presuming they open up. It's a good idea to follow best practices for conversations on race when embarking on an apology tour.

Apologies provide opportunities for people of color to process their feelings and restore their dignity. More importantly, they give you a chance to make restitution. Apologies without restitution and genuine sincerity are hollow and meaningless. The point is for you to act better in the future to maintain self-respect and minimize inflicting trauma. If you're just going through the motions, then you're multiplying the level of offense and harm.

Apologies should be given freely and without the expectation of receiving anything in return. While they may make you feel relieved by confessing wrongdoing, apologies don't entitle you to receiving forgiveness, making amends, or repairing relationships. You shouldn't pressure anyone into saying they forgive you because this negates your entire apology. They may need time to heal and process, and they may conclude you're not someone they want in their friendship circle. If that's their decision, you must accept it because actions have consequences. Being accountable means accepting what's difficult and respecting others' decisions.

ANATOMY OF APOLOGIES

Your apologies should include *each* of these fundamental components to be valid:

1. **Express remorse**—Your objective should be to express genuine regret for the harm caused to the other person, acknowledging your impact on their feelings and pain. Don't apologize if you don't mean it and have an ulterior motive (e.g., repair a relationship, save your reputation, not look racist). Focus on the collateral damage and impact of your actions on others above the intent of your behavior.

2. **Admit responsibility**—Own your actions and be accountable. Empathize with the person of color you wronged. Articulating exactly what you did signals you understand how you were wrong and your impact. Far too often people toss out empty apologies without appreciating the role of specific behavior choices. Say something like, "I recognize that I hurt your feelings when I did [bad thing] and know it was wrong to treat you like that."

   You should include awareness of engaging in microaggressive behavior as well. For example, if you assumed a colleague of East Asian descent wasn't born in the United States or wouldn't speak English well, you could say, "I apologize. It was out of line and based on the false assumption you weren't born in America. My apologies. I need to work on jumping to conclusions about fellow Americans and making you feel like this isn't your country just as much as mine. I plan to work on prejudging others and brush up on American history to avoid repeating this behavior."

3. **Make amends**—Take action to make the situation right. You could add to the statement above by saying, "I don't want my apology to lack meaning. I plan to [action steps] so I don't repeat this again." The action steps depend on the situation but could include volunteering with a community organization to increase your exposure to people of color, reading books, watching documentaries, taking a workshop, or attending cultural events. If you cut down a colleague or negatively impacted their career, create an opportunity to restore the damage to their career or reputation, even if it means

stepping aside. Cleaning up your mess is a critical component of contrition.

4. **Promise learning**—Explain that you won't repeat the action to reassure them and others you're changing your behavior. This rebuilds trust. If you're apologizing after time has passed, articulate exactly what you've implemented since causing harm to educate yourself (e.g., reading a book, volunteering). But during real-time apologies, tell them you're going to reflect on your actions to develop a proactive plan to improve, and then take action so your initial words don't ring hollow. Invite them to unabashedly call you out if you do it again.

5. **Act**—Whatever you promised when making amends, honor your commitments to break the cycle and not repeat mistakes.[1]

HOW GENUINE APOLOGIES FACILITATE HEALING

A genuine and effective apology can yield the following results:

- Restores the harmed person's dignity and sense of control.
- Communicates the offender's empathy.
- Relieves the person of color's sense of responsibility for experiencing harm and trauma.
- Allows people of color to express feelings and ask questions.
- Creates space to understand others while defining boundaries and improving communication pathways.

Benjamin Franklin put it best when he said, "Never ruin an apology with an excuse."

TIPS AND ADVICE

Follow this guidance to avoid ruining or failing to make a legitimate apology. These tips will help you bypass sinking into doomed relationship quicksand where recovery and repair are increasingly insurmountable:

- **Tick tock**—While it's never too late to apologize, sooner is better. Don't assume the incident will just blow over. Letting more time pass allows the wound to deepen by ignoring the harm you caused. With racism and microaggressions, often offensive behavior isn't forgotten but banked in people's memories, along with that missing apology.
- **Great expectations**—Apologies don't require forgiveness. If you apologize with the goal of being forgiven, then it's not a real apology. Also, they don't always restore friendships and professional relationships. Sometimes there's no turning back, but that shouldn't stop you from doing the right thing. You still owe an apology for causing pain. It might just be a learning experience that promotes positive future interactions with other people of color.
- **Blame shifting**—Don't say, "I'm sorry you felt upset" or similar statements. This transfers blame from you to them. It sidesteps taking responsibility for the offense. Instead, take greater ownership by saying, "I'm sorry my actions were hurtful."
- **Confession booths**—Don't apologize and verbally vomit your guilt on others hoping for absolution if you're just doing this to release your feelings of shame and embarrassment. If you don't understand what you did was wrong, take action to make amends, and commit to never repeating those behaviors again, then you're motivated by selfish interests. When the apology is just about you, you're not taking responsibility for injuring others.
- **Verbal hot air**—Apologies need to include action to show they're genuine. This isn't the same as apologizing for spilling wine on someone's shirt. You caused racial harm, which cuts very deep and is compounded by historic trauma. Treat offenses with greater care since they're not simple slights, no matter how minor you think they were. Racism doesn't happen in a bubble of isolated events for people of color. The effects are cumulative with the white supremacy of other whites. You can't view your behavior as individual or isolated but must see it as collective racist action.
- **Outsourcing**—Don't have someone else apologize for you, especially by using another person of color, if you lack the courage to do it yourself (i.e., tokens).

- **Financial performance art**—While making donations to social justice causes and community organizations is encouraged, you can't check-write or mobile-deposit your way out of remorse. Supporting organizations is useful. It's an important step in making amends and a critical piece of restitution, damages, and reparations. But you can't use it as your *primary* method of reaching for absolution. It's not a substitution for understanding *what* you did wrong and being regretful and penitent. This is just you self-pardoning.

- **Pulling teeth**—Don't make people feel the need to force an apology out of you or that getting one is like a tooth extraction. You need to voluntarily offer apologies that go beyond the superficial or placating. Acknowledge the hurt you caused by doing more than the bare minimum since that's *not* enough (i.e., merely saying you're sorry and moving on). And if you're forced to work for your apology (e.g., groveling or other required steps due to the other person's anger or profound sorrow), suck it up. You're the bad actor in the equation who marginalized a person of color.

- **Bobbing and weaving**—Never make excuses when apologizing. It negates the value of the apology.

- **Half stepping and justifications**—Apologies need to be whole and complete. Partial apologies don't count. Don't say it was not your intent since what matters isn't what you meant but how your words or actions landed. Be mindful of diminishing apologies by trying to explain them away or imply what you did was less than how it felt to the other person. Offering justifications nullifies your apology.

- **Rationing and shrugging it off**—If you're told you injured someone, which naturally invites an apology, then give one. Don't rebuff someone revealing you caused them racial pain. This only pours salt on the wound. Don't hold back, even if you don't understand in the moment. If you don't fully know *how* or *why* you hurt someone, ask them if they're open to explaining while simultaneously expressing genuine remorse that your words or actions caused pain. While initiating discussions on race with people of color is generally discouraged, this is different. It's obvious you just hurt someone since you were told, giving you leeway to ask questions. But avoid becoming defensive. Listen and validate them. You may need to think about what they shared afterward to reflect and return with a more poignant apology expressing how you understand better, that you reflected more, and what you did since then to expand your enlightenment.

- **Weak whatevers**—Never say it was a joke since that's probably untrue. There's often a tinge of truth in jokes, offering insight into what you really think. Conjuring up the joke excuse is disrespectful. Is the offended person of color genuinely laughing? Doubtful. So don't go there.

For additional talking points when apologizing, see the section "Talking Points for When You Offend and Try to Recover" in Race Rule #10 and the section "Saving Face and Recovering from Engaging in Microaggressions" in Race Rule #19.

COLLECTIVE APOLOGIES AND REPARATIONS

We can never have healing without reparations to address systemic and foundational American issues. For whites to truly own their privilege, take responsibility for White Welfare, and take real steps toward a racial reckoning and improved race relations, communities need to make amends. People need to apologize and atone even for systems put in place before they were born. These structures still exist, and whites benefit from them today through White Welfare. Companies need to atone for unjust enrichment and benefiting from prosperity paving their growth, especially old American institutions since they definitely created our current system of oppression.

However, don't personally make general apologies to people of color for all whites. Not only are these awkward, but they're often motivated by white guilt. This is just about you feeling better about your shame and wanting to feel like you're doing something to advance society. These apologies are empty. They don't mean anything to people of color unless you're apologizing for your specific family's actions or something you've personally done with macroimpact to advance White Welfare. Apologizing broadly for white privilege, racism, or oppression is useless—especially if you're doing nothing to solve these things. If you were serious about America's white supremacist culture, then you'd couple that blanket apology with reparations and pushing for real atonement and damages.

When it comes to people whose ancestors were enslaved and exterminated and still living the downside of that legacy, before they hear apologies, they want restitution. Calls for unity, healing, understanding, and an end to divisions don't mean a damn thing without taking significant action to correct for past and present wrongs. Machiavellian kumbaya maneuvers skip critical steps by invalidating the impact and reality of racial harms. You can't have truth without elevating reconciliation. Reconciliation requires atonement. Atonement requires repair. Reparations are the gateway to repair and amends.

There's no greater sign showing self-accountability in how whites treat people of color than to acknowledge wrongs were committed and link that to solutions addressing White Welfare. Until then, hold the broad apologies and verbal ambush for slavery or the Trail of Tears. People can't take that to the bank to close wealth gaps caused by systemic racism and subjugation.

> Vulnerability is not winning or losing; it's having the courage to show up and be seen when we have no control over the outcome.
>
> —Brené Brown, academic and author

PART 7

Take Action—Move beyond Complicity and Graduate to Racism Disruptor

PART 7 details actions for transitioning into a Racism Disruptor. Learning and self-analysis are helpful in advancing anti-racism, but then what? Things shift into performative virtue signaling if learning doesn't lead to better choices and behavioral change. Unlearning racism isn't just about changing your thinking but driving results to positively impact lives of color. Accompany a growth mindset with proactive action for tangible impact. This section provides pathways to jump-start combatting White Welfare and minimizing harming people of color.

White people are on a spectrum. Some are more racist than others. But the existence of a sliding white supremacy scale shouldn't negate doing the work. Don't assume personal work isn't required. These Race Rules' action steps support your ability to exit the Denial Lane and get on a path toward progress through acts and deeds.

Along this journey, you may not have understood everything. Maybe you felt challenged, didn't always agree with the advice, and found it jarring. You were uncomfortable and maybe even offended. This book provides a new worldview with information to help you adjust behaviors. It shares how many people of color perceive things, including believing that if you're not a part of the solution, you're unequivocally the problem.

If you feel tapped out from anti-racism learning and reflecting, remember that sins aren't acceptable, but sinners are redeemable. You've been learning how past choices were offensive and upheld racism. The road to redemption begins with action. Everything beforehand helped prepare you for taking action to disrupt racism.

Take Action to Move from Ally and Bystander to Racism Disruptor

A man who stands for nothing will fall for anything.

—*Malcolm X, civil rights activist*

RULE SUMMARY

Awareness or good thoughts alone aren't enough to dismantle systems of oppression and structural racism. Effective anti-racism requires not just noticing injustice but also taking action to bring attention to the injustice and seeking to correct it. This involves moving from being just an ally or a bystander to a Racism Disruptor.

Ally or Bystander ≠ Racism Disruptor
Racism Disruptors take action!

Allies can be passive bystanders since allyship doesn't require action steps. They can complicitly rely on hearts-and-minds ideologies, falsely thinking simply disagreeing with bigotry or empathizing with marginalized groups is sufficient. This mindset nurtures laziness and discourages speaking up or moving beyond perfunctory, performative steps. Racism Disruptors are proactive, action-oriented anti-racism advocates who express support for anti-racism through behaviors and choices that *positively impact* people and communities of color. Greater than allies, they aim to align their thoughts and intent with helpful external action to uplift people of color and limit racial trauma.

While allies sometimes act, allyship is also different from advocacy and activism. When coupled with action, it's focused on the individual level (e.g., individual steps and education to support causes and people we know). Conversely, advocacy and activism focus on collaborating with others to challenge and change systems.

The shortcomings of overvaluing the impact of allyship are underscored by Deloitte's 2019 State of Inclusion Survey. It found that while 92 percent see themselves as allies at work, only 29 percent actually speak up when they perceive bias, and nearly one-third ignore it.[1]

Allies swimming in inactive inertia are delusional if they think they're part of the solution, anti-racists, or true friends to people of color.

Be a stronger supporter of anti-racism and people of color. Transition from a woke cerebral ally and passive spectator or bystander to Racism Disruptor. Intervene early and often.

THE SPECTRUM FROM ALLY
TO RACISM DISRUPTOR

In order to understand what it means to be a Racism Disruptor, it's important to understand basic nomenclature. A Racism Disruptor isn't the same as an ally. There are important distinctions, and there are also wolves in sheep's clothing posing as anti-racists who improperly claim allyship—performative, cookie-seeking, virtue-signaling people who aren't really down for the cause but are up for the status quo.

Use the following definitions as a barometer to discover if you engage in genuine, meaningful, impactful behaviors supporting people of color, or if you're giving yourself a pass to not act. The assignment for whites is to disrupt racism, not placate or enable it by your choices.

Ally—An ally is a nonmarginalized person making a concerted effort to understand the challenges faced by people of color through impediments like racism, discrimination, and racial violence who *may* stand up for them, use their privilege, recognize privilege exists in society, and proactively advocate on behalf of or in alliance with those lacking that same privilege. Allegiance could be limited to awareness—people who ideologically support the struggle for equality but may fail to act.

Performative ally—A performative ally is someone who positions themselves as an ally by sharing trending information, throwing out popular slogans, or saying the right things often without the necessary research or self-reflection to deservedly self-identify as an ally. This includes doing or saying things to earn ally cookies and street cred. They're virtue-signaling ally imposters.

Fair-weather ally—A fair-weather ally is someone whose support of anti-racism is a temporal fad and who isn't truly committed to equality in the long run and may slip back into the convenient comfort of their privilege and white supremacy. Classic examples include in-the-moment clicktivists, those who say they support the goal but not the methods, and people who claimed to support Black Lives Matter shortly after George Floyd was murdered but whose support waned months later when the issues, deaths by cops, and the urgency hadn't changed. These individuals are not real allies.

Bystander—A bystander is a witness to racist behavior and microaggressions who may or may not consider themselves an ally but does nothing to limit discriminatory or bigoted behavior other than to possibly disagree with it in their head. They elect to do nothing to disrupt problematic behavior. #SilentComplicity

Bystander effect—This phenomenon occurs when a group of witnesses silently watch racist action and are less likely to intervene when more people are present since being a part of a crowd makes it so no single person has to take responsibility for an action. Diffusing responsibility makes well-intentioned people complicit in whatever acts of violence or discrimination they silently witness.

Racism Disruptor—A Racism Disruptor is an ally who proactively and consistently speaks or acts in support of an individual or cause, particularly someone who intervenes on behalf of a person being verbally or physically attacked or bullied or is the target of racism and microaggressive behavior (i.e., intentionally using their voice and influence to act in solidarity with and as an accomplice for marginalized groups and individuals). They work to create cultures actively rejecting harmful or discriminatory behavior through targeted interventions. When they see bad things happen, they make intentional choices to respond to the concerning behavior (e.g., recording suspected police brutality or challenging microaggressions and casual racism like dinner-table racism). Acting on beliefs in equality and justice, they support or advocate for policies and initiatives that challenge the status quo (e.g., civic engagement, workplace leadership, and voting). They outwardly express support for anti-racism through choices and behaviors that align intentions with impact and action.

MOVING FROM ALLY AND BYSTANDER TO RACISM DISRUPTOR

The bottom line is you need to be more proactive in your daily life and community activism to curtail racism. Nothing will change if people wait on the sidelines. Passively sitting around for others to solve racism has brought us to where we are today. We've barely progressed since the civil rights movement. But you have an opportunity to be a force for positive change by being accountable, accepting your responsibility, and responding to this call to action.

Moving from allyship to racism disruption at the individual level does require some trial and error because it's hard to always know when is the right time to jump in and when to temporarily sit back to avoid culturesplaining. But this shouldn't deter you from acting. The point is sitting by the wayside and leaving people of color to do all the emotional work and activism to attack racism is sidestepping our collective obligation to help society evolve.

There isn't a balancing act when deciding to drive initiatives in your community and workplace or when witnessing crimes, egregious behavior, and casual racism when no people of color are in the room. The finessing and judgment calls come into play *when people of color are present*. The tips below will help you better assess when to table the issue and revisit it later and when to act in real time. When you're on the fence, act! It's how you will learn over time and do your part in attacking white supremacy. As politician Stacey Abrams said, "You are not guaranteed victory, but you are guaranteed failure if you don't try."

Frankly, if your motivations are tainted by being a performative ally, that's better than being complacent and complicit. What this means is you need to work on yourself to get your thought process and mental framework in the right place. While it isn't ideal and is still problematic, acting for the wrong reasons is better than doing nothing so long as the impact and the outcome have a positive effect. But this doesn't fully get you off the hook since this does little to help you personally deprogram and unlearn your own internal racism since your objectives are disingenuous.

Take the following steps to move from being an ally or bystander to a Racism Disruptor:

- **Mental shift**—Shift your philosophy from being theoretically down for the cause to action and proactive support for people of color so they're not pushing against racism alone. Moving from bystander or inactive ally or bystander to Racism Disruptor is how to effectively support people of color. This is you recognizing your responsibility in moving society from white supremacy.
- **Performative allyship and the white savior complex**—Genuine anti-racism is *not* about one-time badges or ego strokes. Mere

ideological support from the sidelines is not sufficient. Demonstrate effective allyship through ongoing, consistent action (i.e., not performative). Taking proactive steps through behavioral change and action is how you transition from ally to Racism Disruptor.

- **Motivation check**—Ask yourself if you are seeking a gold star or diversity champion halo. Who is being centered in your actions? Are you aiding people of color to be seen as the good guy? If you're doing it to look good, then work on unpacking this and releasing yourself from self-serving objectives to shift to wanting to improve society and conditions for people in your life and community.
- **Accomplice**—It's a tough balancing act, but moving from silence to action in individual settings (i.e., not activism but more applicable to settings like workplace meetings or a potluck) first requires determining if being silent means you'll be a complicit accomplice.

SELF-REFLECTIVE QUESTIONS

These prompts aren't intended to cosign on inaction nor endorse free passes but facilitate understanding when real-time inaction is acceptable. Inaction can only be temporary and must be followed by action to avoid complicity.

1. If you do nothing, what's the downside and the harm? How will it impact the person of color? Relationships? Their job? Their mental health? Their personal safety? Systemic racism?
2. Are you remaining silent out of fear of doing or saying the wrong thing? Fear shouldn't be about stopping you, but fear could help your understanding and learning.
3. Are you assuming all people of color cope with trauma in the same way, and thus might you be misreading the need to stand in solidarity?
4. How can you best support them in *this* moment? You could even ask the target of racism, "How can I support you right now? What's most helpful in this moment? I'm more than happy to speak, I just don't want to step on your toes."
5. Should you act now or address this one on one privately? If you wait, then you must follow up. Otherwise, you're in the complicit accomplice zone. With waiting, consider the immediate impact on

people of color and the message accompanying real-time inaction or delay.

6. Is your motivation for potential inaction due to the fact that stepping up feels uncomfortable or rocks the boat? Are you making action contingent on yourself and your needs at the expense of prioritizing people and communities of color and disrupting racism?

7. Are you waiting for others to act for you? Are you leaning into the situation or racism being an intractable problem as an excuse to avoid getting involved in solutions?

Remember, internal headspace work to unlearn racist beliefs is helpful, but unless you take action, you're not doing nearly enough. Keep taking action even when you're tired since racism is never on vacation. This is what transitioning to being a Racism Disruptor and dismantling the status quo looks like.

Being an effective Racism Disruptor isn't a thing to be but rather a way to live.

> We cannot hold a torch to light another's
> path without brightening our own.
>
> —Dr. Martin Luther King, Jr., civil rights activist

Your Choices about Housing and Schools Are Drivers for Racial Inequality

White Americans and other people with socio-economic
status have to be willing to give up something to
have a more just and equitable society.

—*Matthew Delmont, historian and academic*

RULE SUMMARY

Each of us can and should take action to minimize racism through the personal choices we make. If you're trying to disrupt racism, don't do it just with how you engage on an interpersonal level but also with your life choices. This includes where you live and educate your kids, what you do with your money, and how you shape your workplace. It's about your daily decisions impacting communities—whether your actions disrupt racism or instead entrench it by supporting segregation, opportunity hoarding, White Welfare, and tiered outcomes. Your daily decisions have a macroimpact on a broader racialized caste system. Consciously counter the status quo even if this seems against your immediate selfish self-interest to avoid advancing white supremacy.

We won't put a sizable dent in racial equality and fair access to opportunities until whites make policy and personal decisions impacting where they sleep and send their children to school. Schools and housing are ground zero in the struggle to curtail White Welfare, white privilege, and white supremacy. These should be your starting points in incorporating anti-racist choices beyond individual interactions.

School and neighborhood desegregation are the ultimate test of how committed white people are to equality and removing racist structures in society. It's your white supremacy litmus test.

What typically happens is whites want all the change to happen *over there* in someone else's community. Progress is all well and good until NIMBY comes knocking where you educate your kids and call home. This is when whites begin derailing change and sounding like Alabama's Bull Connor. These roadblocking good white people are motivated by unconscious racism and the seductive comforts of white privilege and unfair advantage. Often, they vote for Democrats and identify as liberal yet have a diametrically different perspective about their own backyards. #NIMBY-Runs-Deep

We will know evolution is real and not symbolic when whites change what's in their own communities—supporting affordable housing in their neighborhoods and school integration programs. Most whites aren't willing to take this critical step. We can't have seismic and real change until you're willing to relinquish some power and resources where you live and educate your children and your life choices aim to disrupt racism.

Desegregation is critical to leveling the playing field for people of color and decreasing white prejudices and racism.

MODERN-DAY SEGREGATION METHODS AND NEO–WHITE FLIGHT

According to the Economic Policy Institute's 2020 report, sixty years after *Brown v. Board of Education* declared school segregation illegal, less than 13 percent of white students attend predominantly Black schools, while nearly 70 percent of Black children do. Black children are still relegated to separate and unequal schools.[1]

Communities nationwide are creating new, whiter school districts and pushing for regulations that maintain white neighborhoods. The following modern-day segregation strategies illustrate how your individual choices to protect where you sleep and learn can impact communities and support a racialized caste system.

SECESSION[2]

Secession is where communities splinter off from larger school districts to create their own districts. It's typically done by seceding from integrated districts to create affluent white enclaves using neutral-sounding causes like *local control*. It occurs in school systems where whites are the minority and public-school enrollment is increasingly students of color. This practice sorts students into separate districts by race. It's *segregation by another name*.

A 2019 study found school district boundaries accounted for roughly 60 percent of the school segregation of Black and white students in 2000. By 2015, this increased to 70 percent, with the remaining 30 percent attributed to school segregation within a district.

Secession is a new twist on white flight. Instead of packing up and moving, people redraw district lines to create "better schools" (i.e., whiter, more affluent, better funded). This drives up white property values and triggers home depreciation or slower price growth in the left-behind school districts of color. As property values fall and schools become less attractive, capital and investment flows out and into the wealthier, white communities. It's a rinse and repeat of the suburbanization white flight and subsequent urban blight of the 1950s.

MAGNET AND SPECIALIZED SCHOOLS

Another new form of white flight that's more subtle is where whites skip out on their neighborhood school and apply for magnet or specialized schools within the public school district where white kids can congregate and be separated from children of color. They're still in the district but don't have to racially mix. And when officials try to integrate these schools or tweak biased policies that favor white admission, white parents show up with their picket signs and time-warp us back to the 1950s with racist rhetoric.

PRIVATE AND RELIGIOUS SCHOOLS

Private, parochial, and religious schools are used as a strategy to segregate white kids from children of color in public schools. In *Carson v. Makin* (2022), the Supreme Court kicked open the door to using public monies for religious schools, undoubtedly promoting more segregation.

RACIAL TIPPING POINT

When redrawing lines and creating white school bubbles within districts don't work, there's always the racial tipping point. Many whites are accepting of people of color in their neighborhoods so long as they don't feel it's becoming a thing. When too many people of color move in, old-school white flight kicks into high gear, and whites flee for other towns. This further exacerbates housing and school segregation since they'll move to racially segregated communities inaccessible to many people of color due to the high cost of entry into that community thanks to White Welfare.

ZONING LAWS

Zoning laws have always been a tool for racial segregation. Community leaders can still prevent people of color from moving into white neighborhoods by using exclusionary zoning laws blocking the construction of low-income and affordable housing.

While people of color are no longer legally barred from moving into any area since racial restrictive covenants are illegal, it's functionally and practically impossible for many people of color to move due to lower incomes, assets, and wealth that preclude migration. The system feeds on itself to promote conditions where segregation is inevitable and multiplies.

PROPERTY TAX POLICY[3]

To fund public schools, most local governments rely on property taxes that are based on property values and assessments. A higher tax base in wealthier neighborhoods translates into higher tax revenues to fund schools, libraries, roads, parks, and other public services that make those predominantly white communities more desirable. Neighborhood attractiveness fuels wealth-gap cycles that worsen as homes appreciate, making those communities increasingly unaffordable to many people of color.

Linking education funding to property taxes strategically supports racial disparities in access to opportunity and achievement by providing grossly divergent qualities of education—schools that are separate and not equal. This tax model shields wealthier whites from funding services for people of color in their own town, county, or state. Not pooling tax dollars into a general state fund for equitable per-child appropriations serves to handicap universal access to education, preparation for the workforce and adulthood, and economic growth. These policies fuel modern-day segregation.

Property taxes are regressive (i.e., a flat tax pegged to a home's value and not income), which disproportionately hurts homeowners of color given their typically lower incomes and wealth. They pay higher property taxes relative to their home's market value. Also, their properties tend to be overvalued for tax assessment purposes, while whites' homes tend to be undervalued, resulting in people of color unfairly paying higher taxes when considering equitable tax burdens.

Federal tax policy supports de facto subsidies through tax deductions, rebates, and credits exclusively for homeowners, who get to deduct mortgage interest, property taxes, and home improvements, thereby getting a preferential financial windfall unavailable to renters (i.e., White Welfare), with tenants shouldering tax burdens for the wealthy. States also offer tax breaks available only to homeowners. Meanwhile, predominantly Black and brown renters are precluded from buying homes due to educational debt, low wealth, and negligible savings. Many communities with well-funded schools and tax-subsidized homeowners have limited affordable rental units, making these schools inaccessible and segregated.

LIFE CHOICES DISADVANTAGE KIDS AND UNDERMINE RACIAL PROGRESS

Housing policy is ground zero for racial equity since it impacts where you can send your children to school, which prepares them for college and the job market. In turn, this impacts wealth and access to opportunities and life's possibilities. White parents are poorly preparing their children to function as adults in a modern 21st-century America, with its diversifying demographic, if their progeny don't experience integration before entering the workforce. Not only will they be a new generation of racists, but they will also have failed to develop interracial interpersonal skills essential for our browning future.

Without housing and school integration, the country can never have a true racial awakening. To achieve this, it's not just about policies. Yes, we need to alter how we fund schools with property taxes, allow parents to secede from districts siphoning off resources, and develop specialized schools with inequitable admission policies. And we need to take direct aim at zoning laws and build affordable housing. But it's equally about the choices you make each day that back these policies and shape your community. It's about the personal decisions you make in your own life that support privilege, segregation, and White Welfare.

Remember, racism isn't about attitudes as much as it is about actions. Choosing to support segregated educational systems and neighborhoods through your decisions is acting to maintain anti-integration policies due to racial motivations. When you support magnet programs that siphon off resources for mostly white kids, enabling your child to grab a leg up, you've decided to personally leverage white privilege to maintain an engineered unfair advantage. You're choosing white supremacy, opportunity hoarding, and White Welfare for your family. When you lean into NIMBYism to block changes to zoning laws that would produce more housing for people of color, you're making a selfish individual choice with status quo impacts along typical racial lines.

Instead, work to create an equal playing field so everyone has the same start and people aren't blocked because their zip code determines their life's outcomes. If you truly believe in racial equality, it's time to align your actions and philosophy and prove it. Integrate *your* local schools and *your* neighborhood. If that's an emotional challenge for you and you start spewing excuses, then you're not serious about racial equality. You never were and were just showboating and virtue signaling. You were just playing games to look and sound good. Legitimate anti-racists and Racism Disruptors directly target racism's ground zero, including when it impacts their neighborhood and their personal lives.

TIPS AND ADVICE

You need to target racism negatively impacting housing and schools on three levels: (1) individually through daily life choices impacting you and your family, (2) at the community level through activism, and (3) politically to facilitate change on a national scale. This will counter trends moving us backward toward racial segregation. Here are key issues to consider when making decisions, which should guide you toward anti-racist choices and outcomes. These can inform your actions and behaviors.

INDIVIDUAL LEVEL

Take any of the following steps to disrupt NIMBYism and segregation at the individual level:

- Consider where you decide to send your children to school and buy a home.
- Don't move out just because more people of color move into your area or attend your local schools.
- Consider which community you decide to spend money in. Do you drive one town over to a fancier shopping district? Do you ever shop in low-income communities to help attract investments, economic development, and business growth there?
- Ask yourself what comes to mind when thinking of a good school, bad school, good neighborhood, and bad neighborhood? Who lives and goes to school there? What do they look like?

COMMUNITY LEVEL

Keep the following steps in mind when trying to disrupt NIMBYism and separate-and-unequal disparities at the community level:

- Become actively involved in decisions shaping your local community.
- Reconsider pushing for the development of magnet schools, specialized programs, and new school districts or laws that allow public funds to be allocated to private schools.
- Support changes to zoning laws and the development of low-income and affordable housing.
- Undertake efforts to support policies and initiatives that diversify and desegregate your local schools and neighborhood—including at your assigned school or on your block or next door.
- Get involved in initiatives curtailing gentrification, and support alternative approaches enabling low-income families to not just remain in their homes but reclaim their community and live in neighborhoods without economic stagnation.[4]

SOCIETAL AND NATIONAL LEVEL

Taking any of the following steps will help in the societal and national fight against segregation:

- Support and advocate for changing laws that stop linking school funding to property taxes (e.g., a system where funding isn't tied to home values but with a fixed appropriation model based on headcount and not neighborhood).
- Endorse policies where *your* tax dollars are reallocated so spending per child becomes equitable.
- Donate to candidates, causes, and organizations that push for policies and legal changes that seek to desegregate housing, schools, and communities, including personal volunteerism to support these efforts. The goal is to create diverse and integrated communities.

The personal choices you make must exceed merely voting for the right people or anti-racist causes. To be a genuine Racism Disruptor positively impacting the lives of people of color and taking direct aim at white supremacy, you must act in ways that impact your personal life and your local community on multiple levels.

> We treat racism . . . like it's a style that America went through. Like flared legs and lava lamps. Oh, that crazy thing we did. . . . We treat it like a fad instead of a disease. . . . You've got to get it at a lab, and study it, and see its origins, and see what it's immune to and what breaks it down.
>
> —Chris Rock, comedian, actor, and producer

It's White People's Job to Dismantle Racism

This country is desperately sick.
And man is on the critical list.

—*Fannie Lou Hamer, voting and civil rights activist*

RULE SUMMARY

Here's the core message for whites above all else. Racism is not your fault, but it's *your* responsibility. It *becomes your fault* when you do little to proactively remove it from society and systems. Racism is a *white* person's problem to solve and dismantle—period!

It's called *white* supremacy for a reason. Whites created, uphold, and perpetuate it. Whites cause it through their actions, cultural influences, and apathy—you're the ones who sustain it and elect not to abolish it since you like the benefits accompanying White Welfare, white privilege, unfair advantage, crippled competition, and power imbalances. Racism is a white invention.

It's unreasonable and unrealistic to assume *anyone other than whites* can give it the ultimate death blow. How can people of color dismantle racism as prey? They can't. They lack the requisite political power to effectively eviscerate it.

Marginalized groups can champion causes but are *not* tasked to demolish systems that oppress them. This is white supremacist thinking and skirting white accountability.

Relying on and expecting people of color to eliminate racism is the epitome of sitting in privilege, and waiting for an invitation for others to upend white constructs perpetuates racism. Let people of color focus on surviving in a caste system built by and for whites. They're not in all-white conversations when racism is discussed. Nor are they leaning into subconscious beliefs of racial superiority. Whites are. This may be hard to swallow but it's true.

You have a duty to reverse the melee of white-made mayhem.[1]

Ask *yourself* how *you* can dismantle racism and implement change. Strategically target and sustain efforts to be a Racism Disruptor.

You're responsible for attacking racism and acting on three levels:

1. Individually in your personal and daily life.
2. In your home, neighborhood, community, and workplace.
3. In society.

White Welfare and privilege are the invisible glue that bond millions of whites together, jointly supporting unearned yet valuable societal structures. Systemic racism will persist if whites have more opportunities and freedoms. Race-based privilege can't disappear until whites divorce themselves from unequal power and manufactured unfair advantages. Both individually and collectively, whites must own transforming minds and developing sustainable solutions to promoting equality.

Bigotry expresses itself through anti-Blackness, microaggressions, prejudice, white privilege, white fragility, white supremacy, political power, and opportunity hoarding. For centuries, these have been instituted and normalized—birthing slavery, Indian removal, Jim Crow laws, mass incarceration, redlining, voter suppression, police brutality, education and wealth gaps, and human rights violations. Whites unconsciously perpetuate racism because it's routine and ingrained, fused with society—like the fish in the ocean that doesn't notice the enveloping water is vital to its present condition unless it evolves.

White supremacy has a multiplier effect, growing from people's personal beliefs and actions as it malignantly manifests into institutionalization through its cumulative effect. This is why your journey toward anti-racism can't just focus on what you're doing to change how you understand and interact with people of color. Your choices must move beyond yourself and your daily life to also include you implementing broader behavioral shifts impacting your community and society in general. You have a three-prong obligation: dismantling racism in yourself, your community, and your country.

TIPS AND ADVICE

Since many of this book's Race Rules focus on your internal work and unlearning racism shaping your individual thinking and behavior (i.e., the first level of white responsibility in disrupting racism), the advice below mainly focuses on ways your personal choices and actions can create a large-scale impact in your community and country (i.e., the second and third levels of your duty in upending bigotry). This guidance includes activism and strategies to advance anti-racism that attack systems and structures.

You can take the following steps in your community to have a meaningful influence on universally limiting racism and white supremacy in our country—moving from individual to societal impacts.

INDIVIDUAL LEVEL

To create a macroimpact at the individual level, take the following actions:

- **Propaganda and tropes**—Leveraging principles of supply and demand, stop consuming news and doomscrolling content from racist sources to better educate yourself, support solutions, and curtail racism. Yes, this specifically includes Fox News and similar media outlets anchored in racism, dishonesty, and misinformation peddling to advance a white-power social order. Rely on news from reputable sources (i.e., not social media or online trolls or right-wing news sources with a reputation of spreading untruthful information but instead media outlets that fact-check and use industry integrity standards like the *New York Times*, the *Washington Post*, BBC, *PBS NewsHour*, and *Democracy Now!*).

  Pay close attention to what messages, language, and imagery are used that perpetuate racism and racial division, which often plant cancerous resistance to integration, amplify racist stereotypes, and encourage discrimination (e.g., stoking white fears and doom-loop false flags about supposed rising crime, drugs, border crises, and alleged socialism, which is code for "lazy Black and brown invaders want handouts, are bringing undesirable integration, and are physically dangerous and will hurt you"; using dog whistles and catchphrases like Black-on-Black crime, cancel culture, critical race theory, identity politics, wokeism, state's rights, local control, reverse discrimination, and law and order; spewing conspiracy theories about stolen elections and voter fraud; routinely showing images and videos of people of color when stories are about crime, poverty, homelessness, immigration, and violence at political protests). This serves to discourage trusting, humanizing, and being comfortable living and working alongside people of color to maintain segregation, discrimination, and White Welfare.

  When you notice racism in the media, be vocal and express concerns to news companies. Also post comments in discussion threads. Be intentional about the language, visual messages, and video content your employer or company uses and speak up to foster positive change. When you hear family, friends, and colleagues fuel misinformation and rely on racist reporting, correct them, don't remain silent, and offer them alternative news sources and information. But to counter actual fake news, you need to stay informed about real news and accurate statistics (e.g., data showing crime is declining, police brutality isn't decreasing, and BLM protests are overwhelming peaceful). You can't combat and correct propaganda and tropes and thwart being manipulated when you're ill-informed and don't know the facts.

COMMUNITY LEVEL

Take action at the community level to create bigger impact and expand the scope of your actions in disrupting racism:

- **Local politics and elections**—Don't miss voting in an election, and know who the candidates are. Many battles are won and lost at the local level. Be vigilant about who represents your voice and which candidates support white supremacy, propose racist policies, and make bigoted comments.
- **Criminal and civil justice**—Show up for jury duty and report racist behavior (e.g., housing and job discrimination, hate crimes). Pay attention to who's running for district attorney and judge seats so you elect those less committed to racism and the prison industrial complex.
- **Desegregation**—Test your true belief in anti-racism. Housing and school policies are central in sustaining racism. Support affordable housing developments in *your* town and neighborhood. Advocate for desegregation in *your* kid's school. Encourage an evaluation of how schools are funded and the racist link to property taxes.
- **Public education and curriculum reform**—Encourage revising school history books to accurately reflect true American history (e.g., not white-centered, whitewashed, white supremacist, nor revisionist). Be unapologetically vocal in response to white nationalism (e.g., slavery was *not* a job training program). Advocate for accurate, year-long history at your kid's and local schools (not just during heritage months) along with diversity with teachers, staff, and administrators

to enrich educational experiences and everyone's exposure for generations. Vehemently oppose book bans, and seek to replace anyone in office, on school boards, and running educational institutions who supports censorship.

- **Reparations and restorative justice**—Encourage your community to identify opportunities to atone for the past, centered not on apologies or unity but financial restorative justice to close wealth gaps and discrimination linked to White Welfare. Apologies mean nothing if action isn't taken to address harms, damages, and restitution to move beyond trauma. Truth and reconciliation are sequential.
- **Local focus**—Start where you are (i.e., your town, not the whole world). Often, people like to save the planet and problems "over there" instead of concentrating on their own backyard where battles can and should be won.
- **Disruption**—Think about what social, political, and cultural constructs act as barriers to progress—then actively oppose them. Determine where and how you can interrupt bias in your community.

SOCIETAL AND NATIONAL LEVEL

Take the following steps at the societal and national level to make the greatest impact with long-term sustainability and to strategically disrupt systemic and institutional racism:

- **Voting rights**—Oppose legal efforts to limit voting rights in your state (i.e., modern-day Jim Crow targeting voters of color). Support reinstating voting rights for former felons. If there is one singular cause you advance, supporting voting rights is the most important thing you can do. Our country requires fair access to voting for people of color if we're to be a legitimate representational democracy.
- **Lobbying**—Call your local, state, and federal representatives to support social justice causes (e.g., voting rights, reparations, BLM, police reform, prison reform, education and housing policy, residency requirements for police and fire departments). They actually listen to constituent interests, especially when voices are numerous and loud.

- **Affirmative action and White Welfare**—Support affirmative action policies and resist the urge to cling to meritocracy or model minority myths, fictitious bootstrapping or reverse discrimination ideologies, and "My family didn't own slaves" or "We just got here" machinations. Pay attention to whether policies, practices, and structures advance White Welfare and opportunity hoarding for whites. When you see engineered and uncompetitive white advantage, disrupt it.
- **Economic justice**—Support living-wage and economic policies benefiting communities of color, including student loan debt relief.
- **Tech companies**—Pressure technology companies to ban racism on their platforms, including fake news entrenched in racism. Do you want to repeat January 6, 2021? Do you want a platform inviting a new civil war?
- **Corporate and institutional accountability**—Attend company shareholder meetings to demand diversity (e.g., employees, senior executives, board members, and external vendors), and push for change (e.g., you only need one stock or shareholder proxy to attend). Hold your alma mater and public employee pension fund (e.g., for teachers, government employees, and first responders) accountable for how they invest and who they invest with to drive diversity and limit predatory practices. Pressure pension funds, foundations, endowments, and governments to invest with diverse fund managers and not support companies that exploit Black and brown communities (e.g., drilling through sacred Native lands, borderline de facto slavery with workers in Africa and Asia, immigrant child labor in domestic food processing plants and farming). Encourage government programs supporting and attracting businesses owned by people of color in your community (e.g., access to capital, loans with favorable terms, small business grants).

In doing this work, resist the urge to become defeated by internalizing personal responsibility for centuries of wrongdoing. Focus on how systems that benefit you need upending. Blow them up. But here's what you should internalize—since unraveling racism is your job, you can't expect a pat on the back for owning your responsibility. Do we praise parents who feed their kids and don't beat them? No, because it's their duty. You don't get a badge of honor for working to dismantle the racist system in which you're complicit and a beneficiary.

What you get is the satisfaction of knowing you're helping to break the cycle of personal and intergenerational racism, creating an environment of mutual respect to build stronger cross-racial relationships, and living your values.

> My theory is, strong people don't need strong leaders.
>
> —Ella Baker, civil rights activist

Implement Your Personal Action Items Today to Disrupt Racism

You don't make progress by standing on the sidelines,
whimpering and complaining.
You make progress by implementing ideas.

— *Congresswoman Shirley Chisholm, politician and educator*

RULE SUMMARY

The only way for society to systemically improve is if *each* of us pro-actively commits to change and action. Often people sit back and wait for someone else to solve society's problems. This is how inertia breeds and stagnation festers. Turning our heads away and expecting someone to lead us or carry the load, searching for the easy path as lazy freeloaders, or resting on the laurels of the over fifty-year-old civil rights movement isn't how great nations flourish. It's not how progress is made but dies.

If not you, then who? If not now, then when?
Don't assume someone else will fix this.
Your credo must be "Choose to disrupt racism every day."

This book explains how white supremacy thrives and operates in plain sight in our communities, companies, and minds and how it and complicity are an existential threat to democracy, freedom, fairness, and racial equality. The goal is to educate and tell you what others won't say for fear of reprisal or because they're not interested in having a transparent discussion with you. Now what? You need to use this knowledge to have more meaningful interracial friendships and connections at work and in your community. You need to keep learning to deprogram white supremacist messaging that's embedded in our society. Armed with more knowledge, you must personally take responsibility for how society is shaped. Work to repair racism's collateral damage on people of color to be a stronger force for good over the status quo.

It's time to personally implement your anti-racism to-do list. Use this book as your guide as you continue your personal development and civic participation journey toward being a Racism Disruptor. Leverage it as a tool as you personally impact change.

As you work to be a better friend to people of color and champion anti-racist causes, balance your enthusiasm to help with evaluating the *impact* of the solutions you support. Sometimes we need to analyze if our actions help or hurt people of color. While this shouldn't stop you from acting, it's a cautionary reminder to align actions with your intentions. A good way to determine this is to research what social justice experts and thought leaders say about proposed solutions to determine the positive or negative impact of initiatives and choices.

For example, we want to live in a world free of racism, but race-neutral policies that don't recognize that race is a factor only have the effect of supporting society's racist status quo.

Disrupting racism through acts and deeds is your desired destination.

Get comfortable with the reality that you can't control change in others and society. You can guide and influence others, but you can't predict every outcome, nor can you promote solutions that seek to eliminate racial barriers yet still cling to privilege. They're mutually exclusive. To eviscerate racism, we must eliminate white privilege and White Welfare. What you can control is what you decide to change in yourself, which includes taking positive action to build momentum to help catalyze change in others.

ANTI-RACISM ACTION PLAN FOR WHITE PEOPLE

As Salma Hayek, actress and film producer, said, "People want to control change. People say they want change so long as they know the result. We have to be okay with the unknown result of the change."

While the Bedrock Race Rule is a learning-and-action tool to help you evaluate specific issues as they arise and provides a universal framework for how to behave, the following action plan supplements it. It can jump-start your anti-racism learning and evolution beyond situation-specific analysis. This action plan helps you further put the Bedrock Race Rule into action and broadly attack racism in phases, which you can follow in order. In providing additional specificity and granular direction, this guides your transition toward being a Racism Disruptor who incorporates anti-racism into your daily life.

Step 1—Learn to unlearn (external education)

1. **Recognition**—Acknowledge and accept there's a problem (i.e., racism, privilege, and White Welfare). This includes admitting *you* too are part of the problem and have an *obligation* to solve this.

2. **Enlightenment**—Educate yourself to better understand how society's systems, institutions, and communities are broken and where solutions are devoid.

Step 2—Reflect to repair (internal evaluation)

3. **Acceptance**—Identify and deconstruct the advantages whites experience. Go beyond thinking of the negative impact of racism on communities of color and individual people of color. Recognize the many ways whites have benefited from years of racism, making life easier and better for themselves (i.e., White Welfare). Make sure this includes seeing the upside of white privilege in *your* life, career, housing, income, intergenerational wealth, job opportunities, education, healthcare, life expectancy, standard of living, quality of life, mental health, personal safety, and police encounters. What's your racialized place and role in society?

   But you can't stop there, even if you're feeling white guilt. Nor can you dwell too long on white confessionals so you don't focus on the confessor instead of the confession. This is where whites tend to check out and thus progress flatlines.

   You can't *just* focus on unearthed racial privilege like it's the final act that will end racism or it's even a *substantial* act of anti-racism. You must tackle systems that commit economic, physical, psychological, and spiritual violence on people of color. Dedicated political, financial, social, and personal action, investment, and sacrifice are necessary for sustainable impact. Stopping here is premature, self-serving, and lazy.

Step 3—Act to address (positive action)

4. **Reconciliation**—Focus on reconciliation. After truth and increased understanding, there must be atonement, restorative justice, and reparations. This isn't about apologies. You can hold onto those unless they're bundled with restitution. Until whites own

their duty to correct what they created and sustain, racism will never be solved, and society can't move forward.

5. **Active dismantling**—Act, implement, dismantle, and deprogram with a focus on systems and structures. A continuation of the reconciliation phase, this is the hardest stage to reach since most whites tap out, throw in the towel, and bounce before repairing. This is where your commitment is tested. But this is the most critical stage.

    To dismantle racism, you have to keep charging ahead to arrive here, proactively taking steps to fix what's broken and deprogram racist thought processes and systemic racism. If you skip this phase and don't get here quickly enough, then nothing will change in your lifetime.

    Don't burn up time on the first three phases dillydallying (i.e., recognition, enlightenment, and acceptance). If so, you're failing with your most important duty as a white person, which is to annihilate what your ancestors created and what you presently support by accepting the benefits of white privilege, power, White Welfare, and a system dedicated to your limitless and unencumbered winning.

Creating a continual learning and improvement cycle

6. **Self-discovery**—Engage in ongoing self-work. Learning is an important phase in the journey. This can be done in tandem with the active dismantling phase, but it's important not to let the personal deprogramming push out the critical work of eradicating systemic and institutional racism.

    Yes, it's important for you to see your own complicity and individual racism, but if we don't tackle power structures that oppress people of color and the dominant culture's stronghold on white privilege and a white supremacist culture, then we won't move the needle far enough.

    This requires a laser focus on macrosolutions, which can't be at the expense of erroneously thinking racism can be solved primarily at an individual level. Focus on your impact in personal encounters at work and in your community, but sustain prioritizing systems and structures as a core focus.

7. **Dedication**—When you get tired or believe you've done your fair part, keep going! People of color can't check out of racism and subjugation. Therefore, whites can't check out of their obligation to end racism since White Welfare and white privilege won't stop when you go on an anti-racism vacation.

   This is the Modernized White Man's Burden 2.0. This is your lifelong duty and emotional work, from the cradle to the grave. If you stop, you cease being a Racism Disruptor.

8. **Legacy and lineage**—Make sure you instill in your children and the next generation a duty to do their part. Share your knowledge and lessons with them. Don't pass on racism as an intergenerational heirloom. Break the cycle with your flawed racialized approaches and thinking.

   Avoid teaching bad habits, a sense of entitlement, ideologies that uphold white privilege, feelings of intellectual superiority, and an expectation of claimed or tacit white power and domination. Teach them *accurate* history so they develop a thirst for truthful knowledge and a rejection of systemic racism. Be selective about the books you read to them starting in infancy. End the legacy of toxic behaviors and mindsets.

DAILY ACTION STEPS

These are action items you can implement on an ongoing basis to expand your understanding of people of color and better connect with them on an individual level. Daily action items can be drawn from a list of overarching activities you've prioritized to pursue on a weekly and monthly basis. This enables having accessible, daily incremental steps that are easier to accomplish and sustain yet are coordinated with longer-term personal goals. These action items support and facilitate ritualizing your daily practice toward disrupting racism. These are aligned with the Bedrock Race Rule.

Step 1—Learn to unlearn (external education)
- **Weekly learning**—Each week, pick a topic that covers a more accurate and inclusive national history to learn something new about people of color in the country. This can be a short article

or podcast. It doesn't have to be arduous but a weekly practice of learning and thirst for multicultural knowledge.

- **Monthly learning**—Monthly, pick a book or film highlighting stories of color to read or see as a family, aiming for ones written or made by people of color to limit the chance of advancing the white savior trope. Then discuss it as a group or with other families.

- **New friendships**—When you meet people of color, try to learn more about them as people and their perspectives to improve your interracial contact. This doesn't mean discussing race but could focus on general topics to get to know others—for example, their favorite film, sports team, or vacation spot. They will reveal what they want about their background, but this helps you to identify with people of color.

- **Heritage months**—Celebrate each heritage month and notable historic event in your home and community (e.g., ritualizing Juneteenth like July 4 but skipping the corporate profiteering and commoditization).

Step 2—Reflect to repair (internal evaluation)

- **Microaggressions**—Acknowledge that your tone may need tweaking and modulate your behavior to quell your microaggressions. Becoming more aware will minimize engaging in subtle racism and help your proficiency and cultural intelligence. This includes the challenging task of consistently working on yourself to move away from buying into white exceptionalism and falsely believing it's other people who are invested in status quo white comfort. Every white person has some conscious or subliminal dedication to white privilege given society's powerful messaging. But by educating yourself and looking in the mirror, you can quiet the messaging and limit stealthy racism.

- **Communication**—Incorporate anti-racist goals into your daily speech (e.g., avoiding colorblind phraseologies or microaggressions but not randomly tossing in woke-esque terminology to sound anti-racist).

- **Intergenerational**—Consciously model and teach the next generation through your behavior and choices to break the cycle.

Step 3—Act to address (positive action)

- **Vocalizing**—When you see racism and discrimination happening in front of you, speak up and stand in solidarity with marginalized groups. Do this in your daily life and community. Silence and inaction are enemies.
- **Workplace**—Push your employer to hire people of color and provide access to opportunities and advancement for coworkers and vendors of color. Encourage inclusion on projects at work, including making sure people of color have a voice in meetings. Stay alert for marketing that promotes tropes, advances tokenism, or amplifies colorism. Bring your energy for anti-racism to the workplace to help remove discriminatory barriers and diversify your workplace. Treat diversity and inclusion as a routinized business practice in *every* department. ·
- **Charities**—Select a charity to support with your money and time.
- **Events**—If hosting a gathering or party, always invite people of color to expand your acquaintance base into friendship circles. And remember, people of color like company, so avoid the lonely only so they don't feel like a token invitee.

TAKE A PERSONAL PLEDGE TODAY

Commit to taking *at least three actions* today and follow through with them.

Pick three actions you will start or complete within the next fifteen days.

Select ones that both focus on your internal work to better understand people of color *and* impact your community or society.

Open your calendar right now and schedule when you will take these next steps. Plan and routinize your personal accountability to maintain a perpetual loop of actions to disrupt racism.

When you get tired of pushing against racism, remember that people of color are required to cope with racial trauma every day, which impacts their mental, physical, and economic health and life expectancy. Truly caring about ending racism means an irrevocable commitment to caring and doing the work.

Personal contact with people of color is critical to your evolution. Increased exposure, prompting learning and unlearning, helps ritualize your transformation into a Racism Disruptor. The more people of color are in your life, community, and workplace, the more being respectful and supportive and less racially harmful toward them becomes natural. Contact and interaction facilitate anti-racist beliefs and actions, becoming a sustainable way of life where you understand, successfully interact, and positively disrupt.

As you expand your cultural intelligence, it invites more people of color to want to be and remain your friend. This further triggers a growth and development cycle. Forming friendships holds open the door to promoting your lifelong learning loop of developing respect, empathy, and racial understanding—with much of this starting and ending with learning how to make better choices and adjusting your behaviors in ways that minimize harming people of color and advancing White Welfare.

> Ours is not the struggle of one day, one week, or one year. Ours is not the struggle of one judicial appointment or presidential term. Ours is the struggle of a lifetime, or maybe even many lifetimes, and each one of us in every generation must do our part.
>
> —Congressman John Lewis, civil rights activist

Glossary of Terminology
and Word Inventions

To convey the message of the book, new terms were created. They're indicated with an asterisk below.

AAPI—People of Asian, Asian American, or Pacific Islander ancestry who trace their origins to the countries or the diasporic communities of these geographic regions (e.g., China, Vietnam, Indonesia, India, Hawaii, Guam, Polynesia). The AAPI community is very broad. This isn't a cultural grouping. This diverse group is a racial classification, with some viewing the collective AAPI community as a political affiliation that isn't monolithic. Most people in this community don't self-identify as "AAPI" per se but rather with their or their ancestors' country of origin (e.g., Filipino American, Japanese American, Sri Lankan American, Native Hawaiian), with each being American.

ally—A white person who is sympathetic to and recognizes the existence of discrimination and racism faced by people of color who tries to understand systemic racism and those in marginalized communities. Support could be limited to aware-ness of inequality and ideological empathy but failimg to act and stand up for them. See Race Rule #28.

ally cookie—The special praise sought by some whites for "not" being racist. See Race Rule #5.

anti-racism—Practice of actively identifying and opposing racism, with the goal of actively changing policies, behaviors, and beliefs perpetuating racist ideas and actions.[1]

authoritarianism—A political system that typically rejects opposing political views, uses strong central power to preserve its political regime, and reduces the rule of law, separation of powers, and democratic voting through strict obedience to authority at the expense of personal freedoms.

bigotry—Believing in, expressing, and/or acting on unfounded prejudices and biases about another group linked to personal characteristics (e.g., race, religion, immigration status), which could advance one's superiority.

BIPOC—Black, Indigenous, and people of color.

blackfishing—A modern form of blackface combined with cultural appro-priation where non-Blacks alter their skin tone, bodies, features, fashion, appear-ance, or speech patterns as they play into racial ambiguity to cosplay stereotypical understandings of Blackness or visually present as Black without fully engaging in racial identity theft and living as a Black person (e.g., Kim Kardashian). See Race Rule #15.

BLM—Black Lives Matter, or the BLM Movement.

blockbusting—Practice of using fear of people of color moving into a neighborhood to encourage whites to sell property at low prices and below market value and then profit by reselling it to newcomers of color at a high price. It both profits from and fuels anti-Black racism.

bystander—A witness to racist behavior and microaggressions who does nothing to limit discriminatory or bigoted behavior other than to possibly disagree with it in their head (i.e., complicit witness). See Race Rule #28.

bystander effect—Phenomenon that occurs when a group of bystanders are less likely to intervene while witnessing racism, discrimination, or racial violence as more people are present since being in a crowd discourages a sense of responsibility to act. See Race Rule #28.

caucasity—Audacity of white people and willingness to take bold risks only whites feel entitled to or safe doing; stereotypical arrogant and entitled whiteness.

clicktivist—Someone who demonstcates support for social or political causes, movements, or campaigns through minimal and perfunctory internet-based actions (e.g., "liking" or sharing social media posts, signing online petitions, emailing form letters to politicians or CEOs), usually in ways involving little effort, commitment, or risk. Activities could be characterized as performative, virtue signaling, superficial, or lazy.

code switching—Modulating and adapting behaviors, speech, dress, mannerisms, and engagement style depending on who the person is speaking to in a way that's different from how they'd speak at home and among their own people to conform to the dominant culture's social norms.

colorblindness—An inherently racist ideology that advances the belief that discrimination could end if we treat people equally, without regard to race, culture, or ethnicity. It's a response to racism and attempts to appear not racist but invalidates people of color. It views them through a white lens, ignores oppression, assumes everyone in society has the same experience, and can be used to attack race-based policies seeking to address discrimination and racism. See Race Rule #18.

colorism—Prejudice and discrimination against darker-skinned people of color (i.e., preferring lighter skinned people).

Columbusing—"Discovering" something that's already in existence and known to certain communities of color. Typically, this "new" discovery merely makes it known for more white people.

contract buying or selling—Predatory homeownership practice available to people of color unable to purchase homes due to redlining and other discriminatory housing practices. Buyers put down a large downpayment, paying price-gouging monthly installments at high interest rates and high purchase prices while accruing no equity. If payments are missed, the buyer is evicted and loses the entire investment. Homeowner is denied full ownership and deed possession until contract is paid in full.

critical race theory—Academic movement seeking to critically examine laws, history, policies, and American society as they intersect with issues of race and to challenge mainstream approaches to racial justice by anchoring our historic record and present-day policies in an inclusive truth. Its central idea is that racism is not merely the product of individual bias or prejudice but something embedded in legal systems, policies, and our telling of American history.

cultural appropriation—Stealing from another's culture or identity, often outside of original cultural contexts, such that traditional significance gets distorted in ways that advance racist tropes and stereotypes, fail to give credit to the original source, or don't adequately share wealth or income flowing from cultural commodification. It's colonization since the taking culture has more societal power than the copied culture, often imitating or grifting against the wishes of people of color. See Race Rule #14.

culturesplaining—Arrogant, condescending, unsolicited commentary from a white person schooling a person of color about something the white person is unqualified or ill-suited to speak on (e.g., what racism is, how the person of color's culture works, how a racist experience isn't racist), typically assuming the person of color doesn't already understand or possess more knowledge. See Race Rule #24 and Race Rule #3.

discrimination—Outward expression of racism in treating others (i.e., oppression).

diversity—Reflecting, representing, and including those from a broad range of backgrounds—race, gender, age, national origin, sexual orientation, disability, etc. (i.e., the mix).

doomscrolling—Excessive scrolling through and reading large amounts of negative online news and social media content (aka doomsurfing). It negatively impacts mental health.

equality—State of being equal, especially in status, rights, and opportunities (i.e., sameness).

equity—Equal access to opportunity (i.e., fairness).

fair-weather ally*—Someone whose support of anti-racism is a temporal fad and who isn't truly committed long-term to equality and easily slips into the convenient comfort of their privilege and white supremacy (i.e., not a real ally). See Race Rule #28.

fascism—A far-right, authoritarian, ultranationalist political ideology and movement that emphasizes extreme nationalism, militarism, and the supremacy of the nation and a single, powerful leader over individual citizens. Often it involves a dictator, centralized autocracy, forcible suppression of opposing voices, belief in a natural social hierarchy, and the subordination of individual interests and freedoms for the perceived betterment of the nation and a specific race.

five-O—The police or police officers.

Forced Founders*—The Native Americans and enslaved Africans who built this country into a superpower at its inception as the victims of forcible theft, violent coercion, and wealth redistribution mechanisms carried out by white American colonizers and settlers to establish White Welfare (i.e., Indigenous land seizures for free land and African enslavement for free labor).

Foundational Black Americans—Black Americans whose ancestors were slaves in the United States and thus descend from people who were at the epicenter of building this country and its wealth as unvoluntary contributors to White Welfare (i.e., at the foundation of having built the country from scratch). Synonyms include Generational Black Americans (or Generational African Americans) and American Descendants of Slavery (ADOS).

gaslighting—Using manipulation, lying, or scapegoating to invalidate facts and lived experiences, trying to get someone else or a group to question their own experiences, reality, memory, perceptions, or powers of reasoning.

hue-jacking*—Offensive and invalidating practice of comparing suntanned or olive-toned skin color to a person of color's skin tone, as if tanned skin were the same as being Black or brown, or bronzing or using bronzer were are all it takes to be a person of color, when lived experiences are very different due to racism. This includes physically putting your arm next to the person of color's arm to compare skin color and skin tones. See Race Rule #15.

inclusion—State of being valued, respected, and supported, and focusing on the needs of every individual or group and ensuring the right conditions are in place for each person or group to achieve full potential (i.e., getting the mix to work well together and/or feel welcome or invited to participate).

individual or internalized racism—See table G.1.

institutional racism—See table G.1.

interpersonal racism—See table G.1.

intersectionality—An analytical framework for understanding the interconnected nature of social categorizations and overlapping identities like race, class, gender, and sexuality and how these characteristics combine to create different modes or systems of discrimination (disadvantage) and privilege (advantage). It involves interlocking systems of power that affect those who are the most marginalized in society and an understanding that oppression doesn't happen in isolation (e.g., discrimination against Black women isn't just a simple combination of misogyny and racism but more complicated). The term was created by legal scholar Kimberlé Crenshaw.

Jackie Robinson Syndrome*—The behavior, pattern, or practice of white people and companies to appoint a person of color—a lonely only, solo-flying trailblazer, spokesperson, or role model—to represent their entire race or ethnic group (or consider them as such). It's a form of tokenism where one person (or a very small number) breaks the color barrier. Their ceiling-breaker presence can be inappropriately used as proof positive that racial progress has been achieved, thereby creating de facto quotas that close doors to future progress, invite coasting and inertia, and render these trailblazers as tokenized blockers. See Race Rule #17.

jungle fever—White person's preference for a sexual or romantic interracial relationship, typically with a fetishized attraction to Black people. The sexual or romantic desire or lust can be less about who the person is (e.g., personality, values, similar interests) and developing a relationship organically and more about what the person is. The initial or underlying desire can be consciously or unconsciously influenced or sparked by the other person's race, with part of the attraction rooted in their Blackness.

Karen, Ken—A *Karen* is an entitled, aggressive, racist white woman who uses her privilege trying to get her way. This can manifest in being a line-crossing, self-appointed conduct monitor who weaponizes her whiteness by illegitimately calling the police on the innocent for "breathing while Black" while spewing racist comments. Male version is sometimes called *Ken*, although the equivalent male term is less settled by the public.

Magical Negro—Trope often in films where a Black character serves as a counselor in the white person's journey to self-actualization.

microaggression—Everyday subtle intentional or unintentional verbal, nonverbal, and environmental insults, indignities, behaviors, or interactions that communicate prejudiced attitudes and hostile, derogatory, or negative messages toward people of color that marginalize them. It's a form of racism. See Race Rule #19.

microassault—Deliberate, explicit discriminatory behavior intending to hurt others (e.g., using hate speech or calling the police without legitimate cause). It's old-fashioned racism conducted on an individual level. See Race Rule #19.

microinsult—Communications that convey rudeness and insensitivity and are racially demeaning of someone's racial heritage or identity. They often include subtle snubs with hidden insulting messages. See Race Rule #19.

microinvalidation—Verbal statements that exclude, negate, undermine, or nullify thoughts, feelings, or experiential realities of people of color. See Race Rule #19.

misogynoir—Discrimination experienced by Black women.

NIMBY, NIMBYism—"Not in my backyard." Opposition to locating undesirable things near or in your neighborhood, community, or town (e.g., affordable housing, powerplant, racially diverse school).

okey doke—Being lied to, tricked, or duped or someone trying to pull the wool over another's eyes.

oppression—Prolonged malicious, systemic, and unjust treatment or exercise of power over less powerful groups through governmental, institutional, or cultural structures to support the sustained societal position or power of the dominant group.

othering—Making someone feel or treating them like they don't belong, are outside the mainstream, or are otherwise outside social norms; marginalizing someone or a group to feel different and inferior to the dominant social group.

Not to be confused with how this book highlights the need to stop othering who's racist. Not othering racists is about whites ceasing to engage in white exceptionalism and not assuming they're not racist. Instead, they should look within to move away from racially offensive behaviors and choices toward anti-racism and disrupting racism.

performative ally—Someone who tries to give the impression of being an ally to people of color through perfunctory and follow-the-bouncing-ball actions, notice-what-I'm-doing behaviors, or strategically saying the right things. They're virtue-signaling imposters who seek to appear anti-racist but aren't and want to earn ally cookies to look or feel good. See Race Rule #28.

POC—Person of color or people of color (i.e., non-white).

po-po—The police or police officers.

prejudice—Preconceived negative views, feelings, opinions, and stereotypes based on someone's perceived group membership that disregard facts. It's not the same as racism. See Race Rule #3.

Pretendian—Person who falsely claims to be Native American but lacks legitimate links to tribes.

props, or racialized props—Person of color used like they're human performance art in tokenized supporting roles as protective deflectors to shield whites from accusations or the appearance of racism (e.g., photo ops, press conferences, potentially when on legal teams defending discrimination claims).

PTSD—Post-traumatic stress disorder. Not to be confused with post-traumatic slave disorder, which is slang for the internalization of oppression by people of color resulting in a colonial mentality or colonized mind such that the oppressor's cultural values become viewed as superior to their own, and as whites' prejudices are internalized, they metastasize into inferiority complexes, undermining their own people's racial progress and equality, or pandering to whites. This slave disorder is not the same as post-traumatic slave syndrome, which isn't viewed as a disorder with simple treatments but a syndrome that requires profound social change. A theory by Joy DeGruy, post-traumatic slave syndrome is the multigenerational psychological trauma, sustained traumatic injury, and injustice experienced by Blacks from slavery to today, including murders and brutality by the police and the incessant onslaught of and weathering by racism, discrimination, and oppression endured daily in America.

racial home training*—Home-taught manners and social etiquette about how to properly behave in cross-racial interactions in ways that avoid being offensive (i.e., home training relating to race and what various Race Rules help teach).

racism—Prejudice and power combined. The marginalization and oppression of people of color based on a socially constructed racial hierarchy that predominantly privileges whites, supporting the superiority of the powerful caste and inferiority of the less powerful (i.e., white supremacy). Racism combines discrimination (an act of oppression) with racial prejudice (a preconceived opinion not based on reason or actual experience). See Race Rule #3.

Racism Disruptor*—A proactive, action-oriented, anti-racism advocate. An ally who proactively and consistently speaks, acts, or intervenes in support of an individual or cause to support anti-racism, stand in solidarity with people of color, and use their voice, societal power, and privilege when witnessing racism and discrimination. They work to create cultures actively rejecting harmful or discriminatory behavior through targeted interventions. They outwardly express support for anti-racism through choices and behaviors that align intentions with impact and action. An advanced-level Racism Disruptor is a lifestyle practitioner who's specifically interested in and dedicated to long-term actions, strategies, and ritualized practices that disrupt and counteract White Welfare and systemic racism not just at the individual level but also at the community and societal levels. See Race Rule #28.

redlining—Government-backed and created policy and practice that established no-lending human topography zones encircling Black communities that denied them mortgages or home insurance, with Black neighborhoods earmarked as high risk. It caused systemic and institutional racial discrimination in housing, excluded Blacks from homeownership, and trapped them from moving out of and ghettoized their neighborhoods. While formally illegal today, it persists informally through discrimination in the housing, mortgage-lending, and home-appraisal markets. See Race Rule #7.

reverse discrimination—Dominant group in power believing they're being discriminated against. Stems from whites feeling they're losing privilege with increased racial equity.

secession—Act whereby communities splinter off from larger school districts to create their own districts, typically in school systems where whites are the minority. It sorts students into separate districts by race and is a modern form of segregation. See Race Rule #29.

status quo-er*—Someone who supports and advances the status quo and is resistant to change and progress either by complicit inaction, sitting on the fence, or actively blocking change and reform. This includes those who claim neutrality, which effectively supports current societal constructs and power structures (i.e., white supremacy).

structural racism—See table G.1.

systemic racism—See table G.1.

token—A person of color included in or held out as an affiliate of a majority-white group to give the false impression of that group's fairness, equal treatment, and racial inclusivity. They're used as superficial markers for diversity and racism shields, often to avoid criticism and appear anti-racist. See Race Rule #16.

tokenism—Believing in and acting on the myth that proximity to Blackness or people of color immunizes whites from having attitudes rooted in racism or engaging in racist behavior. Race Rule #16.

tokenization—Involves how people of color are treated by whites as tokens, used as racialized props, and leveraged to block including additional people of color or to silence them. Race Rule #16.

tone policing—An oppression conversation tactic to diminish or undermine the validity and importance of a person of color's statements by attacking the tone used to express them. This includes focusing on how something is said (or related expressed emotions) to negate the truth and validity of what's said. It seeks to silence people. See Race Rule #21.

whataboutism—An argumentative or debating technique or practice in response to an accusation, difficult question, or topic by leveraging deflection tactics and retorting with a counteraccusation or raising a different issue (e.g., slippery-slope arguments to evade answering or discussing a critical question or argument).

whitesplaining—A subset of culturesplaining, it's culturesplaining by white people. It's the practice of whites speaking with their presumed knowledge of non-white groups and racism, along with their belief that they're more qualified on these topics, who share their unsolicited and unwelcomed supposed knowledge with people of color. It differs from culturesplaining in that whitesplaining involves whites engaged in the "splaining'" behavior. With culturesplaining, people of color can also be guilty of culturesplaining to other people of color. See Race Rule #24.

white centering—Belief that white culture, values, and norms are the normal center of the world, which renders everything outside the white dominant culture as not part of the mainstream.

white entitlement—Belief, social construct, or conscious or unconscious righteous expectation that the world is built for limitless white winning (i.e., mindset and outcomes upholding White Welfare and white privilege).

white exceptionalism—Belief a white person is one of the good ones as an ally or somehow impervious to all the real racism in society (i.e., an exception to the rule). Plays into false notions of inherent goodness instead of focusing on ways people are unaware of how they're causing racial harm and supporting racism.

white fragility—Discomfort whites feel when discussing race, confronted with their prejudices, or experiencing racial stress, which can trigger defensiveness or shifting victimhood to whites.

white fear—An underlying conscious or unconscious fear a white person can have of increased racial diversity in communities and across the country (i.e., a majority-minority nation and "the browning of America"), making them generally afraid of people of color, shifting and shared power structures, and proximity to Blackness and other people of color. This can trigger a toxic rise in white supremacy, white nationalism, segregation, book bans, anti-POC racial violence, hate crimes, and voting restrictions to maintain a white-dominant social order.

white feelings—White-centered feelings, emotions, and views of whites that seek to usurp the emotions, feelings, pain, trauma, perspectives, lived experiences, and concerns of people of color, especially in ways that prioritize the interests and sentiments of whites above disrupting racism.

white guilt—Collective guilt, shame, and sense of responsibility felt by whites for racism, discrimination, White Welfare, unearned and unfair racial privilege, oppression, historic atrocities, societal maltreatment, and past and present racial harms, including guilt and embarrassment for personal prejudices, choices, ignorance, and behaviors.

white nationalism—A type of racial nationalism that seeks to maintain a racial and national identity, with many adherents supporting the concept of a white nation. It's the belief, theory, or doctrine that white people are inherently superior to people of color and non-white ethnic groups, which can include advancing theories of genetic superiority. White nationalists are fanatics and extremists who may resort to violence and domestic terrorism to advance white supremacist ideologies.

white savior—White person rendering aid to people of color in a self-serving or self-affirming manner. By rescuing them from the perils of poverty or negative consequences of racism and discrimination, it enables whites to erroneously believe they can absolve themselves of their privilege or own racism. Playing the hero washes away white guilt and lets whites feel racism is solved or things are getting better because of personal actions. This mindset fuels the white savior trope in the media.

white savior trope (in films)—Story about people of color centering on benevolent actions of a white character, who's often the protagonist or most developed, multidimensional character sidelining the characters of color. Usually, a happy-ending feel-good movie to create a false narrative that we've solved racism by the film's end. Centers on analyzing racism through the eyes of whites. Exploration of race is always on an individual level, never touching on systemic issues or bigger solutions, thus advancing notions that racism and privilege can be fixed merely by caring and empathizing.

Examples include *Green Book, The Help, Django Unchained, The Blind Side, Hidden Figures,* and basically any film with slaves made by whites since there's always at least one good white person aiding subjugated slaves even if that white savior owns slaves.

white supremacy—Beliefs and ideas purporting natural superiority of whites over other racial groups. It doesn't require consciously believing in white nationalism or genetic supremacy. It includes engaging in actions, choices, or complicity supporting the status quo, opportunity hoarding, White Welfare, and whites remaining in a dominant position through a caste system.

white tears—The crying that happens when whites are called out for racism, start to feel white guilt or uncomfortable, or are overwhelmed by emotions involving racism. Tears can flow when discussing race and empathizing with a person of color's pain, trauma, and lived experiences. It hijacks conversations, redirects attention away from people of color and solving racism, and allows the white person to become the victim and center of attention. It requires no malicious intent but is unwelcomed by and fatiguing to many people of color.

white victimhood—A nefarious strategy to undermine discussions or racial progress and a toxic response to racism and feeling uncomfortable that inappropriately seeks to position whites as victims (e.g., due to false beliefs they've been victimized by racialized harms; whites endure more prejudices and attacks on their identity than people of color). It's a racist mindset and seeks to cannibalize attention away from people of color, disrupting racism, and prioritizing legitimate harms committed against people of color. It can include equating life difficulties and struggles due to classism or bad luck with that of systemic racism and white supremacy.

White Welfare*—Society's ultimate entitlement program for whites built on historic oppression, racial discrimination, and white-centered opportunity hoarding that privileges whites at the expense of people of color through theft or unjust wealth transfers to build intergenerational and present-day exclusive white wealth and power that fosters a white-entitlement mentality, unfair competition, and pro-white market conditions. It's the daily power-and-wealth windfall of white privilege and supremacy built on history, policies, and social norms. See Race Rule #7 and introduction.

woke-esque*—Wannabe woke, woke-like, woke, or involving wokeness or perceptions of being woke.

woke, wokeness—Actively alert to and conscious of racial discrimination, oppression, and injustice. See Race Rule #14.

Worldstar—Video foolishness of extreme conduct, including someone going viral in videos posted on social media for ridiculous or combative behavior and causing drama.

wypipo—White people, with a "wypipologist" being someone who "studies" whites, their history, behaviors, choices, culture, political ideology, and social habits.

TABLE G.1 Levels and examples of racism terminology[2]

Definition	Examples
Individual or internalized racism	
Personal beliefs, attitudes, and actions supporting or perpetuating racism.	<ul><li>Stereotypes</li><li>Telling racist jokes</li><li>Believing in superiority of whites</li><li>Denying racism exists</li></ul>
Interpersonal racism	
Discriminatory behavior toward people of color ranging from micro-aggressions to physical violence.	<ul><li>Job discrimination</li><li>Harassment or hate speech</li><li>Touching Black person's hair without consent</li></ul>
Institutional racism	
Unfair and discriminatory policies, practices, or behaviors within an organization or institutional structure resulting in inequitable outcomes benefiting whites that disadvantage people of color, reinforcing racism.	<ul><li>Hiring practices</li><li>Students of color more frequently in overcrowded classes or the lower track</li><li>Farming subsidies disproportionately given to white farmers</li></ul>
Structural racism	
Cultural values so ingrained and normalized in societal daily life that they support white superiority and the subjugation of people of color. Structures (laws, policies, institutional practices, and norms) are systems' scaffolding for maintaining a racialized caste system. **Synonym**—systemic racism.	<ul><li>Voting restrictions</li><li>Property taxes</li><li>Redlining</li><li>Food, transportation, and hospital deserts</li><li>Stereotypes of people of color as criminals in films and the news</li><li>Book bans</li></ul>

(continued)

TABLE G.1 Levels and examples of racism terminology[2] (*continued*)

Definition	Examples
Systemic racism	
Normalized racism embedded in society's policies, practices, institutions, and culture so integrated in systems that it's often assumed to reflect the natural, inevitable order of things. It involves whole systems (political, legal, economic, healthcare, job market, housing, school, criminal justice system, etc.), including the structures upholding the systems, working collectively building on centuries of racism and discrimination. It includes structural racism. **Synonym**—structural racism.	• Present-day segregated schools and neighborhoods • Higher lead levels in water in Black communities • Higher incarceration rates for Black and brown people • Wealth gaps • Different life expectancies • White-centered curricula and textbooks

Notes

Significant diligence, hard work, and good faith went into properly crediting sources. If any sources were missed while eagerly seeking to share this book with the public, the website noted below will be updated to reflect any additional sources as they become known.

For a more complete list of sources that informed, influenced, and helped to shape this book (including historical context and trends, concepts, examples, key points, terminology, and phraseology that were sometimes paraphrased), visit FatimahGilliam.com/RaceRulesBibliography for a comprehensive bibliography. The bibliography is a more thorough list of sources that are also being credited throughout this book. The endnotes below are a significantly reduced list of sources that do not represent the full scope of sources that were used and reviewed.

Thank you to every writer, journalist, scholar, academic, news outlet, thought leader, and source whose interesting analysis and commentary served as a beneficial foundation in writing *Race Rules*, enabling this book's ability to summarize key concepts and broad-ranging topics for readers in one location.

PREFACE

1. This phrase is a household saying attributed to Julia Randall and Tamara Thompson.

RACE RULE #2

1. Kelly M. Hoffman et al., "Racial Bias in Pain Assessment and Treatment Recommendations, and False Beliefs about Biological Differences between Blacks and Whites," ed. Susan T. Fiske, *PNAS* 113, no. 16 (April 4, 2016), pnas.org/content/113/16/4296.full; Janice A. Sabin, "How We Fail Black Patients in Pain," *AAMC*, January 6, 2020, aamc.org/news-insights/how-we-fail-black-patients-pain.

2. Silvia S. Martins et al., "Racial and Ethnic Differences in Cannabis Use Following Legalization in US States with Medical Cannabis Laws," *JAMA Network*, September 27, 2021, jamanetwork.com/journals/jamanetworkopen/fullarticle/2784528.

3. Devan Cole, "Graham Denies Systemic Racism Exists in US and Says 'America's Not a Racist Country,'" CNN, April 25, 2021, cnn.com/2021/04/25/politics/lindsey -graham-systemic-racism-america/index.html.

RACE RULE #5

1. Michael Kaess (@WaluigiSoap), "At the Foodtown site, housing opponents stood in the driveway, trying to spook shoppers that 'low-income housing' is going to be built there," Twitter, June 14, 2022, twitter.com/i/status/1536831921547886593.

2. Associated Press, "From Rep. John Lewis, Quotes in a Long Life of Activism," *Washington Post*, July 18, 2020, washingtonpost.com/national/from-rep-john-lewis -quotes-in-a-long-life-of-activism/2020/07/18/7ee684d8-c8b0-11ea-a825 -8722004e4150_story.html.

3. Layla Saad, *Me and White Supremacy: Combat Racism, Change the World, and Become a Good Ancestor* (Naperville, IL: Sourcebooks, 2020).

4. George Sachs, "10 Ways White Liberals Perpetuate Racism," *HuffPost*, September 1, 2015, www.huffpost.com/entry/10-ways-white-liberals-pe_b_8068136.

RACE RULE #6

1. Adeldayo Akala, "Cost of Racism: U.S. Economy Lost $16 Trillion Because of Discrimination, Bank Says," NPR, September 23, 2020, npr.org/sections/live-updates -protests-for-racial-justice/2020/09/23/916022472/cost-of-racism-u-s-economy -lost-16-trillion-because-of-discrimination-bank-says; Bureau of Economic Analysis, "Gross Domestic Product, Fourth Quarter and Year 2020 (Second Estimate)," news release no. BEA 21-06, February 25, 2021, bea.gov/news/2021/gross-domestic -product-fourth-quarter-and-year-2020-second-estimate; Dana M. Peterson and Catherine L. Mann, "Closing the Racial Inequality Gaps: The Economic Cost of Black Inequality in the U.S.," Citigroup, September 1, 2020, icg.citi.com/icghome /what-we-think/citigps/insights/closing-the-racial-inequality-gaps-20200922.

2. Sundiatu Dixon-Fyle et al., "Diversity Wins: How Inclusion Matters," McKinsey & Company, May 19, 2020, mckinsey.com/featured-insights/diversity-and -inclusion/diversity-wins-how-inclusion-matters#/. The results show the likelihood of financial performance above the national industry median. Analysis is based on composite data for all countries in the data set. Results vary by individual country.

3. "Knight Diversity of Asset Managers Research Series: Industry," Knight Foundation, December 7, 2021, knightfoundation.org/reports/knight-diversity-of -asset-managers-research-series-industry/; Cara Slear and James Munro, "These Hedge Funds Are Rare but They're Starting to Shine," *Bloomberg*, April 2, 2020, bloomberg.com/professional/blog/these-hedge-funds-are-rare-but-theyre-starting -to-shine/.

4. Slear and Munro, "These Hedge Funds Are Rare." The hedge fund data are restricted to Bloomberg clients who completed the Accredited Investor and Qualified Purchaser questionnaire required by Bloomberg Compliance per SEC guidelines.

"Diverse" funds are defined as funds owned (more than 50 percent) or managed (C-suite-level investment role) by a person of color or woman.

5. "Decoding Diversity: The Financial and Economic Returns to Diversity in Tech," Dalberg, June 23, 2016, dalberg.com/our-ideas/decoding-diversity-financial -and-economic-returns-diversity-tech/." Full representation of underrepresented people of color and of females in the tech sector could potentially create $470 to $570 billion in value per year consisting of higher revenues and higher market value— adding 1.2 to 1.6 percent to the national GDP. This study examined 167 technology companies in the United States.

6. "Decoding Diversity."

7. Drew DeSilver, "U.S. Students' Academic Achievement Still Lags That of Their Peers in Many Other Countries," Pew Research Center, February 15, 2017, pewresearch.org/short-reads/2017/02/15/u-s-students-internationally-math-science/.

RACE RULE #7

1. Ijeoma Oluo, "The Pyramid Scheme of White Supremacy," interview by Trevor Noah, *The Daily Show*, December 9, 2020, youtube.com/watch?v=6O4ivGObux4.

2. Holocaust Museum of Houston, "Genocide of Indigenous Peoples," accessed May 8, 2023, hmh.org/library/research/genocide-of-indigenous-peoples-guide/; United States Census Bureau, "Native American Heritage Day: November 25, 2022," press release no. CB22-SFS.160, November 25, 2022, census.gov/newsroom/stories /native-american-heritage-day.html.

3. "What Happened on the Trail of Tears?," National Park Service, nps.gov /articles/000/what-happened-on-the-trail-of-tears.htm; Elizabeth Prine Pauls, "Trail of Tears," *Encyclopedia Britannica*, November 8, 2022, britannica.com/event /Trail-of-Tears.

4. "Results: Intra-American Slave Trade—Database," Slave Voyages, slavevoyages. org/voyages/IKRyteNH (the results show data for the vessels *White Lion* and *Treasurer*); "Results: Trans-Atlantic Slave Trade—Database," Slave Voyages, slavevoyages.org/voyages/laUYOcKV (the results show data for the vessel *Sao Joao Bautista*); Slave Voyages–affiliated academic Gregory E. O'Malley (associate professor of history at University of California, Santa Cruz) in discussion with author, September 16 to 21, 2021.

5. Henry Louis Gates Jr., "How Many Slaves Landed in the US?," *Root*, January 6, 2014, theroot.com/how-many-slaves-landed-in-the-us-1790873989; "Africans in America: The Middle Passage," PBS, pbs.org/wgbh/aia/part1/1p277.html; "Slavery, United States," Places in History, Library of Congress, loc.gov/rr/geogmap /placesinhistory/archive/2011/20110318_slavery.html; "Timelapse: Trans-Atlantic Slave Trade—Database," Slave Voyages, slavevoyages.org/voyage/database#timelapse; "Summary Statistics: Trans-Atlantic Slave Trade—Database," Slave Voyages, slavevoyages.org/voyage/database#statistics; "Summary Statistics: Intra-American Slave Trade—Database," Slave Voyages, slavevoyages.org/american/database#statistics;

Slave Voyages–affiliated academics George E. O'Malley (associate professor of history at University of California, Santa Cruz) and Alex Borucki (associate professor of history at University of California, Irvine) in discussion with author, August 26 to 30, 2021; Slave Voyages database numbers are subject to change over time as new research results in updates to data. As of August 30, 2021, transatlantic slaves to the United States were estimated at roughly 389,000 Africans, intra-American slaves to the United States were estimated at roughly 72,000 Africans, and professors O'Malley and Borucki estimated that roughly 463,000 enslaved people landed in what became the United States.

6. Brianna Theobald, "A 1970 Law Led to the Mass Sterilization of Native American Women. That History Still Matters," *Time*, November 28, 2019, time.com /5737080/native-american-sterilization-history/.

7. Federal Register, "Indian Entities Recognized by and Eligible to Receive Services from the United States Bureau of Indian Affairs," January 12, 2023, federalregister.gov/documents/2023/01/12/2023-00504/indian-entities-recognized -by-and-eligible-to-receive-services-from-the-united-states-bureau-of.

8. "Homestead Act," History Channel, September 13, 2022, history.com/topics /american-civil-war/homestead-act.

9. Philip Bump, "By 2040, Two-Thirds of Americans Will Be Represented by 30 Percent of the Senate," *Washington Post*, November 28, 2017, washingtonpost.com /news/politics/wp/2017/11/28/by-2040-two-thirds-of-americans-will-be-represented -by-30-percent-of-the-senate/.

10. Greg Timmons, "How Slavery Became the Economic Engine of the South," History Channel, September 2, 2020, history.com/news/slavery-profitable-southern -economy.

11. Justine Farrell et al., "Effects of Land Dispossession and Forced Migration on Indigenous Peoples in North America," *Science* 374, no. 6567 (October 29, 2021), science.org/doi/10.1126/science.abe4943.

12. "Homestead Act," History Channel.

13. Keri Leigh Merritt, "Land and the Roots of African-American Poverty," ed. Sam Haselby, *Aeon*, aeon.co/ideas/land-and-the-roots-of-african-american-poverty.

14. "75 Years of the GI Bill: How Transformative It's Been," United States Department of Defense, January 9, 2019, defense.gov/News/Feature-Stories/story /Article/1727086/75-years-of-the-gi-bill-how-transformative-its-been/.

15. "Adam Ruins Everything - The Disturbing History of the Suburbs," TruTV, October 4, 2017, youtube.com/watch?v=e68CoE70Mk8.

16. Erin Blakemore, "How the GI Bill's Promise Was Denied to a Million Black WWII Veterans," History Channel, June 21, 2019, history.com/news/gi-bill-black -wwii-veterans-benefits.

17. Hilary Herbold, "Never a Level Playing Field: Blacks and the GI Bill," *Journal of Blacks in Higher Education*, no. 6 (Winter, 1994–1995): 104, jstor.org/stable/2962479.

18. Jessica Semega and Melissa Kollar, *Income in the United States: 2021*, US Census Bureau, report no. P60-270, September 2022, census.gov/content/dam/Census /library/publications/2022/demo/p60-276.pdf.

19. William Darity Jr. et al., *What We Get Wrong about Closing the Racial Wealth Gap*, Samuel Dubois Cook Center on Social Equity, Duke University, April 2018, socialequity.duke.edu/portfolio-item/what-we-get-wrong-about-closing-the-racial-wealth-gap/; William A. Darity Jr., (Samuel DuBois Cook Distinguished Professor of Public Policy, Duke University) in discussion with author, June 8, 2021, January 20, 2023, and May 9 to 10, 2023; Natasha Hicks et al., *Still Running up the Down Escalator: How Narratives Shape Our Understanding of Racial Wealth Inequality*, Insight Center, Samuel Dubois Cook Center on Social Equity, Duke University, 2021, socialequity.duke.edu/wp-content/uploads/2021/09/INSIGHT_Still-Running-Up-Down-Escalators_vF.pdf; "Why the Racial Wealth Gap Persists," Takeaway, WYNC, May 15, 2018, wnycstudios.org/podcasts/takeaway/segments/why-racial-wealth-gap-doesnt-go-away.

20. Aaron Glantz and Emmanuel Martinez, "For People of Color, Banks Are Shutting the Door to Homeownership," Reveal, February 15, 2018, revealnews.org/article/for-people-of-color-banks-are-shutting-the-door-to-homeownership/.

21. Sam Thielman, "Black Americans Unfairly Targeted by Banks before Housing Crisis, Says ACLU," *Guardian*, June 23, 2015, theguardian.com/business/2015/jun/23/black-americans-housing-crisis-sub-prime-loan; Sarah Burd-Sharps and Rebecca Rasch, *Impact of the US Housing Crisis on the Racial Wealth Gap Across Generations*, Social Science Research Council, June 2015, aclu.org/files/field_document/discrimlend_final.pdf.

22. Glantz and Martinez, "For People of Color."

23. Reggie Shuford, "White Privilege Does Not Mean Your Life Has Not Been Hard. It Just Means It Has Not Been Hard Because You Are White," ACLU Pennsylvania, August 10, 2020, aclupa.org/en/news/white-privilege-does-not-mean-your-life-has-not-been-hard-it-just-means-it-has-not-been-hard.

RACE RULE #8

1. "Voting Laws Round Up: May 2021," Brennan Center for Justice, May 28, 2021, brennancenter.org/our-work/research-reports/voting-laws-roundup-may-2021.

2. "Voting Laws Round Up: February 2023," Brennan Center for Justice, February 22, 2023, brennancenter.org/our-work/research-reports/voting-laws-roundup-february-2023.

3. Michael J. Hanmer and Samuel B. Novey, *Who Lacked Photo ID in 2020?: An Exploration of the American National Election Studies*, March 13, 2023, voteriders.org/wp-content/uploads/2023/04/CDCE_VoteRiders_ANES2020Report_Spring2023.pdf.

4. Kevin Morris, "Voter Purge Rates Remain High, Analysis Finds," Brennan Center for Justice, August 21, 2019, brennancenter.org/our-work/analysis-opinion/voter-purge-rates-remain-high-analysis-finds.

5. Ashley Lopez, "In the U.S., Some 4.6 Million People Are Disenfranchised Due to a Felony Conviction," NPR, October 25, 2022, npr.org/2022/10/25/1130622918/felon-voting-state-laws-disenfranchisement-rates.

6. "Debunking the Voter Fraud Myth," Brennan Center for Justice, January 31, 2017, brennancenter.org/our-work/research-reports/debunking-voter-fraud-myth.

7. Wendy R. Weiser and Harold Ekeh, "The False Narrative of Vote-by-Mail Fraud," Brennan Center for Justice, April 10, 2020, brennancenter.org/our-work /analysis-opinion/false-narrative-vote-mail-fraud.

8. Weiser and Ekeh, "The False Narrative."

9. "Quick Facts: Iowa," United States Census Bureau, accessed May 7, 2023, census.gov/quickfacts/IA.

RACE RULE #9

1. Henry Louis Gates Jr., "How Many Slaves Landed in the U.S.?," *Root*, January 6, 2014, theroot.com/how-many-slaves-landed-in-the-us-1790873989; "Africans in America: The Middle Passage," PBS, pbs.org/wgbh/aia/part1/1p277.html; "Timelapse: Trans-Atlantic Slave Trade—Database," Slave Voyages, slavevoyages.org /voyage/database#timelapse.

2. "Slavery, United States," Places in History, Library of Congress, loc.gov/rr /geogmap/placesinhistory/archive/2011/20110318_slavery.html; "Summary Statistics: Trans-Atlantic Slave Trade—Database," Slave Voyages, slavevoyages.org/voyage /database#statistics; "Summary Statistics: Intra-American Slave Trade—Database," Slave Voyages, slavevoyages.org/american/database#statistics; Slave Voyages–affiliated academics George E. O'Malley (associate professor of history at University of California, Santa Cruz) and Alex Borucki (associate professor of history at University of California, Irvine) in discussion with author, August 26 to 30, 2021; Slave Voyages database numbers are subject to change over time as new research results in updates to data. As of August 30, 2021, transatlantic slaves to the United States were estimated at roughly 389,000 Africans, intra-American slaves to the United States were estimated at roughly 72,000 Africans, and professors O'Malley and Borucki estimated that roughly 463,000 enslaved people landed in what became the United States.

3. Laurel Wamsley, "Bill Maher Apologizes after Using N-word on His Show," NPR, June 3, 2017, https://www.npr.org/sections/thetwo-way/2017/06/03/531365550 /bill-maher-apologizes-after-using-n-wor-on-his-show.

4. "Ice Cube and Symone Sanders on White Privilege | Real Time with Bill Maher (HBO)," *Real Time with Bill Maher*, June 9, 2017, youtube.com/watch?v =gnwiYdFaRfk&t=147s.

5. Angela Helm, "Papa John Schattner Says He Was 'Pushed' to Use the N-Word That Ended His Career," The Root, https://www.theroot.com/papa-john-schnatter -says-e-waspushed-to-use-the-n-w-1827599519.

RACE RULE #10

1. BLM data are from a joint study by Princeton University and the Armed Conflict Location & Event Data Project. *Demonstrations and Political Violence in America: New Data for Summer 2020*, Armed Conflict Location and Event Data Project, September 3, 2020, acleddata.com/2020/09/03/demonstrations-political

-violence-in-america-new-data-for-summer-2020/.

2. *Demonstrations and Political Violence in America.*

3. *Demonstrations and Political Violence in America.*

RACE RULE #11

1. Meera Jagannathan, "Black People Are up to 6 Times More Likely to Be Killed by Police, Harvard Study Says," *Marketwatch*, June 28, 2020, marketwatch.com/story /black-people-are-up-to-6-times-more-likely-to-be-killed-by-police-harvard-study -says-2020-06-26.

2. Li Cohen, "Police in the U.S. Killed 164 Black People in the First 8 Months of 2020. These Are Their Names (Part I: January-April)," NBC News, September 10, 2020, cbsnews.com/pictures/black-people-killed-by-police-in-the-u-s-in-2020/; Mapping Police Violence, accessed March 31, 2023, mappingpoliceviolence.org/.

3. Gary Langer, "Confidence in Police Practices Drops to a New Low: Poll," ABCNews, February 3, 2023, abcnews.go.com/Politics/confidence-police-practices -drops-new-low-poll/story?id=96858308.

4. "Trust in America: Do Americans Trust the Police?," Pew Research Center, January 5, 2022, pewresearch.org/2022/01/05/trust-in-america-do-americans-trust -the-police/.

5. "Pat Robertson Slams Policing in America," *Morning Joe*, MSNBC, April 16, 2021, msnbc.com/morning-joe/watch/pat-robertson-slams-policing-in-america -110301253957.

RACE RULE #12

1. Christopher S. Chivvis and Sahil Lauji, "Diversity in the High Brass," Carnegie Endowment for International Peace, September 6, 2022, carnegieendowment.org /2022/09/06/diversity-in-high-brass-pub-87694.

RACE RULE #14

1. Nels Abbey, "Some White Artists, Like Elvis, Exploit Black Culture. So Celebrate Bobby Caldwell, Who Enriched It," *Guardian*, March 22, 2023, theguardian.com/commentisfree/2023/mar/22/white-artists-elvis-exploit-black -culture-celebrate-bobby-caldwell.

2. Arlin Cuncic, "What Is Cultural Appropriation?," *Verywell Mind*, November 8, 2022, verywellmind.com/what-is-cultural-appropriation-5070458.

3. Cuncic, "What Is Cultural Appropriation?"

4. Hannah Arendt, "Lying in Politics," in *Crises of the Republic* (Orlando, FL: Harcourt Brace, 1972), 7.

RACE RULE #15

1. Maui Smith, "Blackfishing and the Rise of the Culture-Appropriating White Girl," *Study Breaks*, April 15, 2020, studybreaks.com/thoughts/blackfishing-white-women/.

RACE RULE #18

1. "Mapping Police Violence," accessed March 31, 2023, mappingpoliceviolence
.org/.

2. Willem Roper, "Black Americans 2x More Likely Than Whites to Be Killed by
the Police," Statista, June 2, 2020, statista.com/chart/21872/map-of-police-violence
-against-black-americans/.

3. Isobel Lewis, "Kristen Bell Accused of Glorifying 'Colorblindness' in Children's
Book," *Independent*, June 12, 2020, independent.co.uk/arts-entertainment/books/news
/kristen-bell-colour-blind-childrens-book-racist-the-world-needs-more-purple
-people-a9563211.html.

RACE RULE #19

1. Tiffany Jana and Michael Baran, *Subtle Acts of Exclusion: How to Understand,
Identify, and Stop Microaggressions* (Oakland, CA: Berrett-Koehler, 2020).

2. Derald Wing Sue et al., "Racial Microaggressions in Everyday Life: Implications
for Clinical Practice," *American Psychologist* 62, no. 4 (May–June 2007): 271–286,
cpedv.org/sites/main/files/file-attachments/how_to_be_an_effective_ally-lessons
_learned_microaggressions.pdf.

3. Sue et al., "Racial Microaggressions in Everyday Life."

RACE RULE #23

1. The phrase "Encyclopedia Negrannica" was coined by actor Don Cheadle.
NBC News Now, X, June 2, 2020, https://twitter.com/NBCNewsNow/status
/1267969306014420996.

RACE RULE #25

1. Rakshitha Arni Ravishankar, "What's Wrong with Asking 'Where Are You
From?'," *Harvard Business Review*, October 22, 2020, hbr.org/2020/10/whats-wrong
-with-asking-where-are-you-from.

2. Ravishankar, "What's Wrong with Asking."

3. Ravishankar, "What's Wrong with Asking."

RACE RULE #26

1. Ijeoma Oluo, "Confronting Racism Is Not about the Needs and Feelings of
White People," *Guardian*, March 28, 2019, theguardian.com/commentisfree/2019
/mar/28/confronting-racism-is-not-about-the-needs-and-feelings-of-white-people.

2. The saying "Not everyone wants to take themselves on as a project" is attributed
to Julia Randall and Tamara Thompson.

3. Sheena Foster, "6 Phrases to Avoid Using in Conversations about Race," *Reader's
Digest*, March 25, 2022, rd.com/article/phrases-to-avoid-in-conversations-about-race/.

RACE RULE #27

1. "How to Apologize: Saying Sorry for a Mistake," Mind Tools, mindtools.com
/afhit60/how-to-apologize.

RACE RULE #28

1. "New Deloitte Survey Finds Organizations' Inclusion Efforts May Not Be
Addressing One of the Biggest Barriers—Everyday Bias," Deloitte, June 27, 2019,
www2.deloitte.com/us/en/pages/about-deloitte/articles/press-releases/new-deloitte
-survey-finds-organizations-inclusion-efforts-may-not-be-addressing-one-of-the
-biggest-barriers.html.

RACE RULE #29

1. Emma García, "Schools Are Still Segregated, and Black Children Are Paying
a Price," Economic Policy Institute, February 12, 2020, epi.org/publication/schools
-are-still-segregated-and-black-children-are-paying-a-price/.

2. Rebecca Klein, "School District 'Secession' Is Segregation by Another Name,"
HuffPost, September 4, 2019, huffpost.com/entry/school-district-secession_n
_5d6f03e5e4b0cdfe05774614.

3. Caitlin Young, "What Policymakers Need to Know about Racism in the Property
Tax System," Housing Matters, March 15, 2023, https://housingmatters.urban.org
/articles/what-policymakers-need-know-about-racism-property-tax-system.

4. Majora Carter, *Reclaiming Your Community: You Don't Have to Move Out of Your
Neighborhood to Live in a Better One* (Oakland, CA: Berrett-Koehler, 2022).

RACE RULE #30

1. This phrase was inspired by phraseology used by comedian Amanda Seales.

GLOSSARY OF TERMINOLOGY AND WORD INVENTIONS

1. "What Is Anti-Racism?," Boston University Community Center, bu.edu/csc
/edref-2/antiracism/.

2. "How to Explain Structural, Institutional and Systemic Racism," USC
Suzanne Dworak-Peck School of Social Work, University of Southern California,
October 26, 2021, msw.usc.edu/mswusc-blog/how-to-explain-structural-institutional
-and-systemic-racism/; "Systemic Racism Explained," KGW News, 2020, youtube.
com/watch?v=DBxfnXql0oo; "Being Antiracist," National Museum of African
American History and Culture, Smithsonian Institution, nmaahc.si.edu/learn
/talking-about-race/topics/being-antiracist; Paula A. Braverman et al., "Systemic
and Structural Racism: Definitions, Examples, Health Damages, and Approaches to
Dismantling," *Health Affairs* 41, no. 2 (February 2022), healthaffairs.org/doi/10.1377
/hlthaff.2021.01394.

Acknowledgments

When we give cheerfully and accept
gratefully, everyone is blessed.

—*Maya Angelou, poet and civil rights advocate*

Writing this book wasn't just a labor of love and sacrifice, and it didn't happen without a supportive team of cheerleaders, volunteers, and helpful foot soldiers who believe in me, my work, and my mission. I'm profoundly grateful for the wonderful people in my life who were excited to help shape this book and bring it into the world. I'm humbled by the outpouring of support from family, friends, clients, and colleagues who traded in personal time and humane workdays to champion a book on a heavy, emotionally draining topic like racism. I'm thankful to everyone who reviewed chapters and brainstormed concepts. I'm appreciative of those who offered encouragement and emotional support. I felt strengthened by those who said yes when I asked for help and generously strategized shining a light on *Race Rules*—knowing we were collaborating on important work serving a public interest.

First and foremost, I want to thank my mother, Amina Hassan. Countless times, you fell on the sword when I needed a last-minute pair of fresh eyes to review a chapter or do research. Repeatedly, you paused your own book writing to support mine. You embody what it means to invest in the success of your children through your actions and unconditional love. Thank you to my sister Halima Gilliam, cousins Rasheeda Garner and Kakuna Kerina, and niece Prosperity Jenkins for supporting my book. I couldn't have done it without you and the broader support of my large family.

To my literary agent, Jessica Papin at Dystel, Goderich & Bourret, thank you for believing in my writing. You never gave up in finding the right publisher and editor—especially since not everyone is well-suited for material on racism. Like with many books, finding a home for *Race Rules* wasn't without challenges, but it was so much easier knowing you were in my corner through thick and thin.

To my editor, Steve Piersanti, partnering with you in writing this book has been a wonderful journey. Not only do you have a great attitude, but this book could have never evolved to where it is without your mentorship, sage insight, and pushing me to expand on key concepts. I love how you rolled up your sleeves and provided space for my voice to shine through. It has been a joy working with you and the entire Berrett-Koehler family, especially Ashley Ingram, whose input and perspective on illustrations and brainstorming visual concepts was invaluable and a true collaboration that became friendship. I'm also grateful to Sarah Modlin, who provided helpful input on chapters, the book production team for making my book so refined, and the entire marketing group for working diligently to promote this book's success. Thank you, Jeevan Sivasubramaniam, for lining up a team of tremendous reviewers. I'm appreciative of my BK reviewers, Eileen Hammer, Sara Jane Hope, and Verónica Caridad Rabelo. You provided important feedback that guided my manuscript revisions. And thank you, Jennifer Brown, for setting the wheels in motion that brought me to Steve.

To my illustrator, Ilse Torres Harrison, I'm thrilled that our paths crossed. You are a skilled and talented artist. I appreciate your point of view and how you interpreted my chapters to bring them to life in visual form. Thank you for being a superb partner, bringing your great demeanor, vision, and flare to this project. I'm overjoyed with how exceptional you were in beautifully illustrating my book.

To my cohort of Wellesley women, you always answered the call when I threw out that Wellesley Batwoman signal, each day, breathing life into our motto *Non Ministrari sed Ministrare*. Thank you, Michelle Caruso-Cabrera, Siu Mei Cuthbertson, Elizabeth Derby, Janet Hill, Rana Hobbs, Claire Hubbard, Malika Jeffries-El, Elena Jones, Hillary Jordan, Sally Katz, Nadia Lacoste, Heather Long, Carol Liebman, Michelle Davis Petelinz, Betty Rauch, Yvette Ross, Maria Beltran Sandoval, Ellen Scordato, Laurie Stempler, Leslie Toepfer, Joy Tutela, Adriane Williams, Gail Winston, and Alice Yurke. Thank you, Siu Mei, for litmus testing material for a broader demographic. With very special thanks to Sally, Claire, Rana, and Leslie, who enthusiastically went above and beyond in supporting my success and reviewing the book's chapters. My gratitude includes Janet, who sadly left us too soon but never wavered in her mentorship and believing in me, this book, and opening doors, and my beloved "Nana" Nadia, who also passed away while I wrote this book and had unyielding faith in its mission. Nana, your enduring spirit lives on, exemplifying how two people from different races, cultures, countries, continents, and generations can form lifelong and genuine friendships overflowing with respect, love, and understanding. And thank you to the broader Wellesley community who've been supportive of *Race Rules*.

To my mentor Patricia David, whenever I needed help and a dose of perspective—from reviewing chapters and discussing diversity initiatives to advice on elevating the book's profile—you were ride or die from beginning to end. Thank you for being a consistent presence as I wrote this book.

To my Columbia crew, I'm grateful for your feedback, offering encouragement, and serving as a sounding board: Patty Ferguson-Bohnee, Michael Granne, and Ruth Moore. And thank you to my Harvard friends Douglas Freeman for brainstorming concepts and marketing strategies and Rebecca Flores, Stephanie Geosits, Saru Jayaraman, and Talat Shah along my journey to a publisher. I'm appreciative of my larger cohort of friends and contacts at both alma maters for offering support and access.

To my Berkeley High posse, thank you, Taura Taylor and Francesca Giorgi. Your support has been invaluable. Cecca, bringing your artist's perspective to illustrations was very helpful. Thank you both for reviewing my manuscript, especially Taura. You raised your hand and dove into the deep end to truly absorb every word, comma, and vocabulary invention to offer in-depth feedback and critique.

To my oldest friend—back from junior high days—Zoe Blaylock Giacalone. I'm grateful for how you offered feedback when *Race Rules* was in its early stages. Your input helped me structure this book as I shaped it to resonate with a white audience. And to Julia Randall and Tamara Thompson, who've known me since I was a kid in Berkeley making my presence known as my mother's child, thank you in offering prudent advice as I navigated the publishing industry and the book-writing process. You always showed up when I needed you and freely volunteered guidance, having my best interests at heart.

To Debra James, I'm grateful for your feedback on every chapter, sending interesting articles, and being supportive of *Race Rules*, even though you kicked me out of your book club since I lacked the time to do the reading. I'm glad my mother's book on civil rights attorney Loren Miller brought us together.

To William "Sandy" Darity, thank you for your research and scholarship on racial wealth gaps. I'm appreciative of your help when in search of data and studies from other academics. Thank you for routinely pointing me in the right direction and making introductions as I conducted researched for this book.

To Jami Floyd, I'm forever grateful for your time and efforts supporting this book's success with influencers and opening doors, even while writing your own important book on Justice Thurgood Marshall. I'm so appreciative that the White House Fellows program opened the door to our friendship. To Jodi Brockington, for leveraging your media and diversity contacts. A book's success hinges on people hearing about it. Thank you both for your support.

To Mary Rasenberger of the Authors Guild for your helpful advice as I navigated intellectual property rights and various legal questions, along with the entire staff of the Authors Guild in supporting writers. Also, I'm grateful to Joy Murphy at Universal Music in granting rights to Tupac's song and Justin Dowling of Blue Mountain Music in working with the Marley family to obtain permission for the Bob Marley lyric.

To Russell Galen, thank you for your continual advice whenever I reached out with a question and for helping me maneuver through finding an agent and the publishing industry. Your guidance was invaluable and led me to my agent.

Last but not least, Christianne Mora and Sabra Gandhi. Christianne, thank you for providing a warm, subtropical getaway with fabulous décor, great wine, and lots of laughs whenever I needed sunny days, a beach view, and palm trees as I wrote, not to mention enthusiastically taking my great headshots. Sabra, thank you for your friendship and open-door policy—whether in the mountains or sunny California. Both of you offered a supportive environment when I hit my limit entrenched in dark, mentally taxing topics like white supremacy and following the daily, deadly attacks on people of color. Both of you were instrumental with my self-care and ability to recharge on this journey to educate white people.

Thank you to everyone who helped and will support getting this book's message to more people, companies, institutions, governments, and countries. I'm grateful to anyone who reads this book, comes to the table with an open mind, and gifts *Race Rules* to someone who needs it. I appreciate anyone who believes each of us can make a difference along the road to disrupting racism, just by impacting one person and changing behaviors one choice at a time—especially if the one evolving is you. This book, anti-racism, and being a Racism Disruptor cannot and will not be successful without you.

Index

About the Author

Fatimah Gilliam grew up in Berkeley as a third-generation Californian in a socially conscious family with deep historical roots. She's a Black woman whose family's been in the United States for nearly four hundred years. Her family fought in every American war, including the American Revolution, War of 1812, and Civil War. Her large family stretches from coast to coast, throughout the South, and across the heartland in urban, suburban, and rural areas. She's traveled to over thirty-five states—including to promote universal access to voting. Collectively, these shape her understanding of her country.

Fatimah is keenly aware of her lineage and complicated relationship with America. She feels a profound obligation to push her nation toward democracy, racial and gender equality, and atonement for its past and present maltreatment of Americans of color.

Her family personally experiences racial injustice and has a longstanding history of advocating for change and supporting civil rights and racial equality. Her great-aunt and mentor, Vaino Hassan Spencer, was the first Black female judge and first on the Court of Appeal in California, serving on the bench for forty-six years. And her grandfather, Alfred Hassan, successfully challenged a Los Angeles restaurant for refusing to serve him in the 1940s. Her mother, Amina Hassan, is an award-winning public radio documentarian who produced stories highlighting race and gender issues and is a published author of the biography on civil rights attorney Loren Miller.

Fatimah's family has also felt the deadly consequences and collateral damage of institutional racism—like when her great-great uncle Jesse Ball Moore was executed by the US military without due process as a result of the Houston Riot of 1917 in what she classifies as a lynching, or when the Los

Angeles Police Department threatened to kill her theologian-poet father, Vincent Carver Gilliam, during a baseless traffic stop. Her centuries-old and ongoing relationship with this country informs her view of American society, race relations, and contemporary solutions toward progress. Her family's legacy—from slavery and discrimination to political activism and shaping jurisprudence—along with her personal journey affect how she sees the world and its global citizens.

Additionally, Fatimah personally understands aspects of the immigrant experience and the difficulty in assimilating into a new society. She lived in the Caribbean in Grenada as a child and experienced life as a foreigner—including living through a coup d'état, the US invasion, and being evacuated and repatriated by the US military. She's also lived, worked, and studied in South Africa and France, where she was an outsider once again. Speaking French and serviceable Spanish, Fatimah has traveled to over forty countries and almost every continent. Given her globe trekking and penchant for negotiating, one of her favorite hobbies is haggling in overseas street markets, experimenting through cross-cultural exchanges.

Fatimah began her career in New York City as a corporate attorney on Wall Street at Cleary Gottlieb Steen & Hamilton LLP, and later Manatt, Phelps & Phillips, LLP, worked for Citigroup overseeing campus diversity recruiting for all its US businesses, and oversaw corporate partnerships as the head of finance and fundraising for North America for the Nobel Peace Prize–winning United Nations World Food Programme. She founded her firm in 2013, The Azara Group, which provides diversity and inclusion, leadership development, negotiation, and strategy consulting services. Helping people and organizations "get what they want," she has advised Fortune 500 corporations, senior executives leading billion-dollar businesses, and industry thought leaders. Fatimah is a seasoned, sought-after speaker and both a diversity and negotiations expert.

Fatimah holds a law degree from Columbia Law School, a master in public policy from Harvard University's Kennedy School of Government, and a bachelor's from Wellesley College. She's active in her community, serves on several nonprofit boards, and is a volunteer attorney for Election Protection.

Having ties to both coasts, she considers herself a "Cali-Yorker." Her name Fatimah is phonetically pronounced "Fah-tuh-muh." Think "Fa La La" and you'll make her happy by getting the first syllable right.

This book is Fatimah's patriotic contribution to America's ongoing dialogue on race.

⬢ Berrett–Koehler
BK̄ Publishers

Berrett-Koehler is an independent publisher dedicated to an ambitious mission: *Connecting people and ideas to create a world that works for all.*

Our publications span many formats, including print, digital, audio, and video. We also offer online resources, training, and gatherings. And we will continue expanding our products and services to advance our mission.

We believe that the solutions to the world's problems will come from all of us, working at all levels: in our society, in our organizations, and in our own lives. Our publications and resources offer pathways to creating a more just, equitable, and sustainable society. They help people make their organizations more humane, democratic, diverse, and effective (and we don't think there's any contradiction there). And they guide people in creating positive change in their own lives and aligning their personal practices with their aspirations for a better world.

And we strive to practice what we preach through what we call "The BK Way." At the core of this approach is *stewardship,* a deep sense of responsibility to administer the company for the benefit of all of our stakeholder groups, including authors, customers, employees, investors, service providers, sales partners, and the communities and environment around us. Everything we do is built around stewardship and our other core values of *quality, partnership, inclusion,* and *sustainability.*

This is why Berrett-Koehler is the first book publishing company to be both a B Corporation (a rigorous certification) and a benefit corporation (a for-profit legal status), which together require us to adhere to the highest standards for corporate, social, and environmental performance. And it is why we have instituted many pioneering practices (which you can learn about at www.bkconnection.com), including the Berrett-Koehler Constitution, the Bill of Rights and Responsibilities for BK Authors, and our unique Author Days.

We are grateful to our readers, authors, and other friends who are supporting our mission. We ask you to share with us examples of how BK publications and resources are making a difference in your lives, organizations, and communities at www.bkconnection.com/impact.

Dear reader,

Thank you for picking up this book and welcome to the worldwide BK community! You're joining a special group of people who have come together to create positive change in their lives, organizations, and communities.

What's BK all about?

Our mission is to connect people and ideas to create a world that works for all.

Why? Our communities, organizations, and lives get bogged down by old paradigms of self-interest, exclusion, hierarchy, and privilege. But we believe that can change. That's why we seek the leading experts on these challenges—and share their actionable ideas with you.

A welcome gift

To help you get started, we'd like to offer you a **free copy** of one of our bestselling ebooks:

www.bkconnection.com/welcome

When you claim your **free ebook**, you'll also be subscribed to our blog.

Our freshest insights

Access the best new tools and ideas for leaders at all levels on our blog at ideas.bkconnection.com.

Sincerely,

Your friends at Berrett-Koehler